# LIVING
## — IN THE —
# 4TH DIMENSION
## VOLUME 2

### San Fransisco
Seminar/Tape series 1971

HERB FITCH

Editor: Bill Skiles

Copyright © 2021 by Bill Skiles.

ISBN   Softcover   978-1-956998-05-4

This is a work of fiction. Names, characters, places, and incidents either are products of the author's imagination or are used fictitiously. Any resemblance to actual events or locales or persons, living or dead, is entirely coincidental.

All rights reserved. No part of this book may be reproduced or transmitted in any form or by any means, electronic or mechanical, including photocopying, recording, or by any information storage and retrieval system without express written permission from the author, except in the case of brief quotations embodied in critical reviews and certain other non-commercial uses permitted by copyright law.

To order additional copies of this book, contact:
**Bookwhip**
1-855-339-3589
https://www.bookwhip.com

# CONTENTS

Foreword Volume II by Bill Skiles ................................................ v

Class 13. Living Outside Your Body ........................................... 1

Class 14. A Real And Permanent Body ..................................... 28

Class 15. I Am Not A Prodigal ................................................. 54

Class 16. Oil From Your Soul Center ........................................ 83

Class 17. Has Goliath Fooled You ........................................... 108

Class 18A. Three Measures Of Leaven ................................... 142

Class 18B. Cosmic Television ................................................. 156

Class 19. You Are Divine Life Now ........................................ 167

Class 20. Your Identity Already Walks On Water ................... 194

Class 21. Total Re-Identification ............................................ 222

Class 22. Here Is Now ........................................................... 250

Class 23. Divine Supply ......................................................... 275

Class 24. Christmas Everyday ................................................ 303

# FOREWORD

## VOLUME II
## BY BILL SKILES

When it finally dawns on you that you are going to have to lay down and step out of the personal sense of life, really stop from living by a human mind, planning, plotting, desiring, you will come to the end of your rope and hear an inner voice say to you: "Let go!"

Or as my first spiritual teacher said to me, "You will come to the edge of a cliff several thousand feet up from the ground and the voice will say, "Now walk." And you will walk and find that underneath are the Everlasting Arms."

Initiation comes at a time you think not. And it doesn't care if you have led a so called good human life or a bad human life; it does not care. It comes, it says walk or let go, and you do so or you return to the human life and wait for initiation to come around again in another lifetime.

But if you are ready, really ready to lay down your life for My sake, then these talks by Herb Fitch are the corroboration you have looked for and the instructions for dying daily.

"It is *'I'* be not afraid." Accept your Divine Sonship and abide in your very own Christhood. And it is your Father's pleasure, I assure you. Godspeed in your Journey from flesh to Soul.

Bill Skiles
Robbinsville, NC
04/27/21
Link: http://www.mysticalprinciples.com
(click the above link to go there.)

# CLASS 13

# LIVING OUTSIDE YOUR BODY

*Herb:* We read the words, "Before Abraham was, I am," and we know that the man, Jesus, was not before Abraham, and therefore "I am" takes a great significance. We also learned that "I am the way," and that increases the significance of I. But still lifting I, being raised to the level of that I which was before Abraham, even though it be the Way, is still a very dark way for most of us. You might even say for all of us. But there was such a group that knew the meaning of the Way, and they lived the Way, and they taught the Way, and they prepared the Way for the rest of us to follow.

When Philo speaks of the Essenes, he says the following: "The Essenes would not allow within their community at Qumran any maker of sorrows, any maker of spears or swords, nor any manufacturer of engines of war, nor any man occupied with a military avocation, or even with peaceful practices which might easily be converted into mischief." And so we find on earth, living right near the Roman Empire, a group of people numbering no more than 4,000 to 5,000 who would permit no one to live among them who was capable of any way becoming involved with things of war.

We can apply that to our thinking today to see the comparison, and so we find now a very unusual thing, a sect among the Hebrews which does not practice Judaism in the same way that the rest of the Hebrews do. The Sadducees, the Pharisees practiced their Judaism, but the Essenes lived a quiet life apart. And no matter what words we read about them, the words we hear generally are from historians, people who happened to live at that time or a little later, usually living outside of the group and judging by what they saw. And so they would say this was a quiet people, a very tranquil people, a people without servants. A people who had no need for riches, for to them riches were the contentment of the mind. There were no slaves among them. Every man was free. Every man was equal.

And so on, the historians would tell us wonderful things about these very unusual people. But more than what we read and even what we hear, they knew the meaning of the Way, the Way that I am, and being pledged to secrecy, they could not reveal the books they read. They were even pledged not to reveal the names of the angels that they spoke to. But you will find that a golden thread connected the Essenes to all of the past civilizations of the world. A thread that began with the beginning of the world, continued through the civilizations who taught spiritual living, right through the Essenes, preparing the way for the birth of Mary and Joseph, and through them, the final fulfillment of the Light.

Now, Josephus, a historian, says, "They despised wealth. None among them could be found richer than the other. It was their law that all who enter the sect must divide their property among the members of the society with the result that there's never seen among them either abject poverty nor great wealth. They all have, like brothers, one inheritance." Again, from the outside looking in, Josephus saw that they lived as One. He could not see that they were actually recognizing that One is all there is, that they were living in the great unity with the One spiritual essence of Being, and because they lived that way within, it appeared visibly, physically, tangibly that way outside.

Now Eusebius, another historian, quoted Philo, and he says, "So enviable is the Essene way of life that not only private citizens, but also mighty kings are filled with amazement and admiration at them and have honored the fraternity by lavishing praise and honor upon these respected and venerated men." And Josephus now comes back and says, "They never spoke about their human affairs before sunrise. The time before sunrise was devoted completely to the Silence or to speaking about the things of the Father. They stopped their work every day at 11 AM to purify their thought, bake their own bread. They said grace before and after by recognizing that God alone is the giver of Life. They allowed no noise, and the Silence that they entertained around them was somewhat strange to visitors. They satisfied their basic needs only."

Pliny, a contemporary of theirs, wrote, "This is a race remarkably different from all other men in the whole world. They live without women. They have renounced sexual love, and they live without money, and for companionship they have palm trees. So strange to say without any births among them, this race has lasted for thousands of years because so fruitful for them is the life weariness of others." And the meaning there, of course, was that others becoming disenchanted with their normal human lives would then ask for admission to the Essenes, and this is how the group kept growing and continuing in spite of no children. And finally, Pliny again: "These God-guided men are so free that they inspire their neighbors with a spirit of freedom. There aren't many of them, but that is not to be wondered at, for high nobility of that degree is always rare. These men have attained it by separating themselves from the common crowd to dedicate themselves to study the great truths of nature."

Now, there was much more to the Essenes than these random comments from contemporaries and later historians. The Essenes were like a mighty river into which flowed the tributaries of the world because before the Essenes actually became a brotherhood—a community, a series of colonies along the Nile and the Jordan extending into Egypt, into Alexandria, around Judea—there was a great spiritual inflow upon the earth. We find the great teachings of China, the great teachings of India, the great teachings of Chaldea, of Persia, of Egypt, and the long line of succession among the Israelites themselves. All of this flowed into the Essene community.

It received the highest teachings on the earth, absorbed them, and lived them. And in doing so, it became a channel through which West and East could ultimately meet, and the spiritualization of the Eastern activity of the Western activity could be joined with the activization of the spirituality of the Easterner, so that we could see a situation where the sun would rise in the east and set in the west, but it would be one sun. The Essenes, you see, were among the first world religions. Before Abraham was, I am, and this Christ that was before Abraham was the guiding principle of life among the Essenes. Universal Christ, not confined to geography, not confined to a race or a nation or a history, not confined to time or space. They were teaching the universality of God. And this was before the Master said, "The Kingdom of God is within you."

Now, they had a great secret, and until their great secret is your secret and my secret, we will discover that everything in the Bible to us represents a challenge that we cannot fulfill, and to find the secret of the Essenes, it would be well to look at these tributaries of spiritual wisdom that filtered into their community. So I'd like you to listen to a few things that were said by the Master egos, the great Masters of the sixth century before Jesus Christ. There was in that period from 650 BC to 350 BC at least five outstanding grand Masters on the earth: Lao Tzu, Confucius, Zoroaster, Buddha, and we'll see who else comes along, Pythagoras of Greece. Now mind you, this is 600 BC. The Essenes lived from approximately 200 BC to 300 AD, a 500-year period. And this is 400 years before the Essenes, 600 years before the birth of Jesus Christ.

And here's Lao Tzu. He is saying in the Upanishads, "I have heard that he who possesses the secret of life, when traveling abroad, will not flee from rhinoceros or tiger; when entering a hostile camp, he will not equip himself with sword or buckler. The rhinoceros finds in him no place to insert its horn; the tiger has nowhere to fasten its claw; the soldier has nowhere to thrust his blade. And why? Because he has no spot where death can enter." Lao Tzu is teaching that man is not living in his body, that he is divine Consciousness and must come to know himself as divine Consciousness so that death cannot enter, for death *can* enter the human body.

Then says Lao Tzu, "There is a thing inherent and natural which existed before heaven and earth. Motionless and fathomless, It stands alone and never changes; It [is] everywhere and [yet] never becomes exhausted. It may be regarded as the Mother of the universe. [And] I do not know its name." And so when we try to give the name "God," we are expressing the belief that we do know Its name. Joel gave it the name "the Infinite Invisible." And along the same line Lao Tzu continues, "[But] If I am forced to give It a name, I call it Tao, and I name it as supreme. [But] The Tao [that] can be expressed is not the [natural] Tao; the name [that] can be named is not the unchanging name."

And so he's teaching us never to try to control or manipulate the Infinite with the mind, but you must go beyond the mind, for you cannot name that which is infinite with a finite mind. Out of the body and out of the mind was his teaching 600 years before Jesus Christ. And he finally said, "Discarding the body is the great liberation." Now, this became part of the way of life of the Essenes, living outside of the human body, and today we have to learn what that involves.

They went about their day's affairs, letting the infinite Self run Itself without human interference. Each laid down his own personal sense of self. Each accepted the omnipresence of the invisible Essence of God. Each accepted himself to be the Substance of God and to know that that Substance is ever perfect. Each understood that Life exists before birth, in the interval between birth and death, and after death, and that Life is always the immaculate perfect Life of the Spirit. They even sought difficulties so that they could overcome them. They felt that wisdom is crystallized pain.

One belief they had was that unless one became a fit instrument for the indwelling Spirit, you were dead even though you walk the earth in a physical form, and so their complete life span was spent to make themselves an instrument for the Holy Ghost. They were without concept, without judgment, without condemnation. If there were criminals, they blessed them.

There were two groups of Essenes, the marrieds and the unmarrieds, and the unmarrieds took the vow of eternal virginity. They never married. They lived alone. They completely lived by the Spirit. The marrieds went into the communities and demonstrated by their purity and their way of life that they could attract to themselves those egos, who still unborn, were seeking a higher way of life. And by their divine Consciousness they attracted to themselves those unborn spirits seeking a way into mortality. This was the way they lived. In short, they tried all to live as later Mary was taught to live.

And so the Essenes became an unusual factor not only in their own apartness, but even when groups of Essenes would marry and go out into the communities, they brought with them this way of life concerning the fidelity to the indwelling Spirit, the knowledge of Substance as Essence of God. The knowledge that behind the visible changing world of the senses was a permanent Essence unchanging, immovable, ever immaculate, ever present. And this was the invisible Kingdom of God.

They walked in it consciously. All this seeped into them from the great ego, Lao Tzu. Confucius, of course, was not as high. Confucius was like Moses. His teaching concerned building a path of righteousness as a foundation, and so he taught the virtues. He taught trustworthiness. He taught humility. He taught zeal for study, eagerness to learn, so that you'll notice many Chinese are always very aware of the power of learning. The mark of Confucius is upon them. There were some students who were capable of higher learning, and he taught them about the Holy Spirit. Between the two, Lao Tzu and Confucius, we had the complete teaching of Moses and Jesus Christ, from law to Spirit. This became part of the Essene community.

We have Krishna way back in the twelfth century before Christ. Krishna was teaching one mind in the following manner. It stated, "As pure water poured into pure water remains the same . . ., [this is] the Self of [a] thinker who knows . . . ." Why, only last week we read about no concepts, and here it is 3,000 years after Master Krishna told us that pure water poured into pure water remains pure water. And so if divine Mind pours Itself into your mind with no concept, divine Mind will express through you as Grace.

"He who beholds all Being in the Self and the Self in all Being never turns away from it." Twelve hundred years before Jesus, "I and the Father are one" is said as one Self by Krishna. And this becomes the understanding among Essenes, the knowledge that although we see many forms, only one Self moves here. It is the divine Self, and we are all that one Self. And so the Essene is stepping out of the illusion of form into the acceptance of I am He who was before Abraham. I am that invisible Christ, the divine Man walking the earth.

Today it may seem new to us, but they lived it, and as they lived it, they were training those among them who were going to bring the Light of Christ to its fulfillment. For among them was the mother and father of Mary, Joachim, Hanna, and even Hanna's mother, Fostina. And they, being Essenes, were learning the principles of Lao Tzu, the principles of Confucius, the principles of Krishna. They were learning one Self. They were learning that I am the Light. They were learning that I am the Substance of which God is. And as a result, they having a child were able to produce Mary. And it is said that because of Mary's radiance, having been attracted to those who were living in the high Consciousness of the one Self, before she even appeared, her radiance was shining through her mother.

Of course, many stories are built about these great sages and seers. The only way you have any possibility of knowing the Truth is to receive them in your inner Self, for always before Jesus every great Master was immaculately conceived. Unusual events always attended their birth. They never had a human father. Always, God was the Father. And this became part of the tradition that later appeared as the birth of Jesus Christ. It was among these Essenes that Mary was trained, and although her parents died while she was still in her very early teens, she learned all of the virtues of the great teachings of the world which had filtered into this community. She learned secrets that the world does not even know today, and, of course, this was what attracted the Soul of Jesus. This is what attracted that ego which now became her child, and this Immaculate Conception was nothing more than the pure realization that all that comes from the Father is of the Father.

Years of purification of living in the Oneness of Spirit, of being a fit instrument for the Holy Ghost—all of this was necessary from the beginning of the world to the time of the birth of Jesus, through the great prophets, through the great teachings of civilization, through the Essenes to Mary and Joseph. This was the only child that Mary had that was able to show forth the perfection of Being. She had eight more. None of them showed forth the perfection of Jesus.

The first was the complete culmination of that which was to learn everything that had been taught through the Essenes to the parents and finally brought up to the pinnacle of understanding when he could stand and say, "I am the Way." The real birth was the change from the human appearance of body to the divine appearance of body, both being imperceptible to the human eye, so that you couldn't tell when the change occurred unless you were highly spiritually attuned. Jesus, in turn, learned to live outside of the body, so that at an early age he was practicing the principle of absent from the body, present with the Lord.

When he announced, "I am the Way," the human Jesus was no longer there. Only I, for it was I who announced, "I am the Way."

Now, we could go on and on tracing these past civilizations, and you would find many similarities in Gautama the Buddha, Pythagoras, all of the ancients, all culminating in the final pure Consciousness, which is called the rending of the veil by Jesus Christ, making it possible for everyone on this earth to receive initiation of the Spirit, for in the overcoming of the world mind, the Christ Jesus opened the Way for each one to enter beyond the veil.

Now, you have found a great frustration in trying to fulfill the commands of the Bible. It has told you to do many things, and although you have tried with devotion, there is always many a barrier standing there as if to say somewhere along the line the teaching didn't provide me with the method for doing this. But it did without your realizing it, because if you have come to the place where you realize that you cannot do what the Bible is telling you to do, you are in the right place.

It is only when you know that you cannot fulfill what the Bible is telling you to do that you're ready to fulfill it. That is when you say, "Now I'm ready to give up the one thing I haven't been willing to give up. I cannot fulfill the commandments of the Bible. I cannot know the Truth. I cannot walk in His Will. I cannot turn the other cheek. I try, but I cannot. I cannot enter the fourth dimension of Consciousness. I cannot love my neighbor. I cannot see the Christ. I do judge. I do condemn, and I have that great fear that I am not adequate to the task. I go up, and I go down." And then, finally, we learn to give up concepts. We read chapters on "Losing I-ness in I." And while we're striving to do it, we know we're not doing it.

And then we find among the Essenes the answer. *You* cannot do it. That's the secret. Of all of the commands in the Bible, *you* cannot fulfill them. Only God can. And the only way they'll be fulfilled is if you let God fulfill them in you, and that's why today is our turning. From today on, when you live in a body, you are denying the presence of God. You cannot live in a human body and say, "I worship God." The very fact that you're living in the sense of a human body is your denial of God.

We have had a 16-century detour from the Truth. When the state decided to start a religion called Christianity excluding the Essenes and excluding the Christ and giving us but a shell, and when the state appropriated the writings of the Essenes, the understanding of the Essenes, the teaching of the Essenes, and then emasculated it to suit their own convenience—understanding nothing about what the Essenes were doing or why they were doing it or how they were the great storehouse of ancient Wisdom come into fruition—that is when we all took the detour, and we had a religion that had words without meaning. We were in the letter of Truth without the Spirit.

From that moment on, man was unable to fulfill the Bible, even though he wanted to, because the great Truth that *only the Spirit of God can fulfill Itself* was lost when the state turned its back on the first world religion, the universal Christ teaching of the Essenes. As you go deeper into their life, you discover that it took three years to be trained, and at the end of those three years you were ready for the supreme test. That three-year apprenticeship led to the time when you were able to walk out of the body, and when you could live outside of the body, you were an Essene, not before.

They knew there were six heavens, meaning to them the six heavens are the levels of consciousness leading to living as the divine Self. To them the Bible was not what it is to the world today. They did not look at the Bible as a historical event or sequence of historical events. They understood the Spirit behind it. They saw it as allegory. They understood that Egypt was the human body. They understood that the march out of Egypt, which Moses led, was the leading of man out of his sense of body. They understood that the promised land or Jerusalem was the awareness of the one divine Consciousness as my Consciousness. So to them, Egypt meant human body. Jerusalem meant one infinite, divine Consciousness

They were marching from Egypt to the New Jerusalem, out of body into Divinity. And this was a broad panorama of what Moses was actually teaching. Much that we today take literally, to the Essenes was allegory. And we'll discover later that practically nothing in the Bible to them was a fact. Everything had a deeper, higher meaning. And the one thing they could never accept, even later, was the belief that God was born, coming down from heaven to earth and became the embryo in the womb of a virgin. They could never accept that.

They could never believe in a dying Deity who went through the ordeals of prenatal birth, adolescence, suffering, cruelty, and then the final torture on the cross—all so that men would see a resurrection of physical flesh and then believe that God's created world was all right. The whole preposterous idea was blasphemy to the Essenes. They did not believe in a physical resurrection or in a physical Christ. They knew Christ to be the Spirit. They knew the Spirit to be all, and they did not accept the Christianity that we have been sold. They were absorbed into the early Christian movement after the Ascension, and their work continues in more ways than the world is aware of today.

Their work is always behind the scenes. On the march, the flight from Egypt, they had helped Mary. When Jesus sent his disciples out, the 70 without script, little did they realize that they were helped by the Essenes. And always in your work, you will discover when invisible hands seem to be helping you, there is a spiritual Reality, an Essene of yesterday ever present to guide you, to teach you, to uplift you, to maintain you on the path, for these men not only learned to live outside the body, but they were in the twentieth century before you and I ever appeared here, for they walk in eternity. And with them, we are going to learn how to walk.

Now, your problem is not how to fulfill the commandments in the Bible, but how to learn that life in a human body is not the life of God. That is the counterfeit, and only when you are consciously *not* living in the body will you find that every commandment in the Bible is automatically fulfilled by the Spirit of God in you. This I Am which was before Abraham fulfills Itself in you when you have learned that I, the Christ, am not in a human body, but I, the Christ, am your Self. Now, when you face this, when you know that never again can your life in a human body be lived without the knowledge that you are violating divine Law, then you're at the place where you can say, "Do or die, I'm willing to pay the price."

I'm willing to pay that which is beyond price to turn from all that I have been in a human body, from all that the world has meant to me as a human being, from every concept of a mortal self in the flesh that will die, and to live now, developing my awareness that that which is the body is not me. It is a possession of the I that I am. Yes, I have dominion over that body, but I'm not in it. In fact, it is that which is given to me to have dominion over, so that I can know where my consciousness is. I can measure my divine Consciousness by the dominion that I have over that body, and I will have no dominion over it while I am under the belief that I am living within it.

When you face that, when you're determined that until you face it, studying The Infinite Way, the Christ Way, the Way of the Light, the Way of Truth is just words. And that there can be no real progress until it is faced and overcome. Then you're where you really must be. And you'll look at it and you'll say, "Why, this is insurmountable. How in the world can I live outside of a human body? What am I going to do with it? I can't leave it home every day. There's a chair down at the office I have to sit in, and the boss pays a salary to that body. If I'm not in it, who's going to take the money? Who drives the car, if not the person in this body? Who eats three meals a day, if not the person in the body?" And, oh, your mind will give you all kinds of reasons why you can't live outside of the body.

You don't know where to begin, but the Essenes found a place to begin. Their teachers found a place to begin, and everything you ever tackled in your life that was difficult had no place to begin, but you began somehow. You stumbled, you groped, you probed. But you began! You started pouring from that little cruse of oil. One way or another, you *did* something. James has a passage way back just before Revelation, before first John and first Peter, in which he explains the meaning of the Way. Well, the Way is for those who know, first of all, that you can't talk the Way. It has to be done. As Jesus, himself, had said, "By their deeds ye shall know them." So talking the Way was nice. It was the way of learning the Truth.

But living the Way is the deed part, the doer, the action.

Living outside the body is not talking about being outside the body. This is a conscious, continuous remembrance that the Spirit of God is not entombed. And when we come to a day called the day of Resurrection when He is risen, we're not going to face that day without the knowledge of its meaning: That the He which is risen is the I of my Being. That I am risen; I am not entombed. That resurrection means I realize that I do not live entombed in a physical form, condemned to decay. I am risen in Consciousness out of the belief that I am entombed.

No body of clay for me, no life within that body of clay, and therefore, who am I if I am not in that body of clay? If I am not in that mortal body, where am I? And you have no alternative. There's no in-between. You're either in the body or not. When you accept that you're not in it, that Christ is not confined to that body, you have the meaning of resurrection. Because if you're in the body and Christ isn't in the body, you're denying Christhood, aren't you? If you're in the body and Spirit isn't in the body, you're denying the spiritual Identity of your Being. And so the moment you are living in a body, whereas Christ is not living in a body, but Christ is risen, you are denying yourself to be the Child of God.

And so we have to face: Are we or are we not the child of God? If so, if I am, then I'm not in a body. And I am, and therefore, I am not in a body, and I must know where I am. Who am I? And I find that I am Consciousness without beginning or end because Christ has no beginning or end, and then I am Christ Consciousness without beginning or end. But Christ Consciousness is infinite, and you must accept that if you are not in the body, your name is Infinite Consciousness. Now you have who you are and who you are not, where you are and where you are not. You're not in the body anymore. The body is in your infinite Consciousness.

There's one thing I'd like to clear up. Let's keep this body a little while. Let's not toss it on the shelf and call it an illusion. We don't have to do that. The illusion is the belief that you live inside of it. You don't. The body is there for the moment. Even though you don't live inside of it, you now have a different Self to consider, your infinite Self. And now the problem is how to correlate this body with your infinite Self. It's like a big circle and a little circle. You've been living in the little circle. You want to move into the big circle, but you don't want to get rid of the little circle because you haven't yet made that transition from one to the other. So what you're going to do is synchronize the two, and you learn, instead of living inside this little circle, the body, you place your Consciousness in the larger circle, the Infinite, and you dwell there. "Abide in Me and let Me abide in you."

You abide in the Consciousness of the Infinite, releasing the consciousness of the body. You'll find, then, that every activity of the body will depend upon your Consciousness of your infinite Self first, and so when we say "going within," we really mean, then, going to your infinite Consciousness by releasing the consciousness of living in a body. Release it. Let go. Be an Essene. Prepare yourself for the indwelling Spirit to be released. Now you'll find that it's a matter of persistence, discipline, and dedication. Your

## Class 13: Living Outside Your Body

actual turning is to consciously know that I do not live in this form. This form lives within me, and I am infinite Consciousness.

Infinite Consciousness that I am has dominion over this form, and I dwell in that infinite Consciousness, resting, letting the Father fulfill the Father's commandments in me, letting the Father do all that I have been asked to do. He performeth. He perfecteth. He quickeneth. He goes before me. I rest in my infinite Consciousness. I and the Father are the infinite Consciousness. There are no longer two. And you do this for a few days, weeks, months, and you find the familiarity of it increases, and you have really found your cross, because this is picking up your cross.

As you dwell not in this form, but in your infinite Consciousness, it crosses out the belief that you live in form, and it crosses out the concepts that you have entertained while in the form, and the meaning of illusion becomes very clear then. The world around you was an illusion to the self that lived in this form. But when you're not in the form, your infinite Self takes a new view of the world around you, and that which had been illusion—meaning the concept you entertained while in this form—is clarified, and now you're looking at the creation, at the world as it is, instead of how it appeared to you in this form.

And you're looking, instead, now at the finished Kingdom without concept, and that which had been illusion is shattered, revealing the Reality that ever was there but could not be perceived by the changing human sense of self. And you are rising in Consciousness. Now, this isn't something anyone's going to do for you, and it's not something you're going to read in a book. It is the doing, which James was talking about, which brings you into the living realization of Christ, the daily doing. And this is your daily prayer without ceasing. This is where you establish your morning contact. Infinite Consciousness I am.

Now, we have to apply that, and this is where you can be inventive, if you wish. This is where you can take thought, if you wish. This is where you can open yourself to divine thought.

You'll discover that there are many, many things you learn about your infinite Consciousness that nobody's going to teach you, but they'll come to you from the Witness within. You might start out like this—and I know I can get you off in the right track, but I'm counting on you to let the infinite Witness within keep you on that track. You will realize that because you're not in the form, because you are infinite Consciousness, that you are everywhere, and so wherever this form goes, you already are.

The form is walking through you. Wherever the form goes, it is going to meet Itself. You begin to understand your everywhereness. You're out of the body. You are able to move consciously in areas that the body cannot move into. You're beginning to loosen up spiritually. You're beginning to find that it wasn't the hard work that you did that was important. What is more important is getting out of the way so that the spiritual Selfhood can reveal Itself everywhere as Its own harmony, Its own Life, Its own Law, Its own protection, Its own safety.

You're into the miracle of living, not confined by the consciousness that lived within the form. You're letting Grace *be* your sufficiency, and you find that your capacity to fulfill the Bible's wishes, to fulfill the will of the Father is being fulfilled without your doing it. That the Father is fulfilling His own Will in the absence of the human shadow. You're still in the form, you still move, and people see you as you were. But you're under new law because your new Consciousness is not in this body, but rather It embraces everybody on the earth. Now, this is how we turn, and this is the time to turn. From this moment on, we must learn consciously not to live in the body. You're going to feel inadequate at times, but be sure that if you do not make the starting point, the oil will not continue to pour from that little cruse.

Let your imagination run wild. There's no place in time that you're not. There's no place in space that you're not. There's no place that you ever can be in the future that you're not in already, because Infinite Consciousness is your name. You're in every tomorrow this minute, and the knowledge of that changes every tomorrow, making it bring forth the activity of the divine Image instead of the human. You're really breaking the fetters. You are letting all civilizations and their high teachings of Truth come to fruition in you. Now this is the beginning, which can and should take you into the Easter Consciousness of the Resurrection. I am the Resurrection. I am the Life. I and the Father are One.

And if you're looking for the way to do this, the way to accomplish this transition in Consciousness, remember: I am the Way. No one cometh to the Father except through Me. I, infinite Consciousness. I, the spiritual Kingdom within you. I, the fourth dimension called Christ. I, the identity as Christ, as the infinite Consciousness, I am the Way to fulfillment of every Bible promise. Absent from the body, we are present with the Infinite. And as long as we maintain the effort necessary to reject everything on this earth that wants to put an anchor on us and bring us back into the body, we will walk with the angels. Now on this we want to meditate before we take an intermission.

I cannot recognize two selves. Christ is not mortal. I cannot accept Christ and mortality in the same breath. I cannot be the Light and also be the human darkness. The only Self that I can recognize is the only Self there is, the Self of God. Nobody's ever going to bury that Self. Nobody's ever going to hurt it or harm it. No one is ever going to make it lacking or limited. No one is going to ever give it arthritis or a pain in any part of the body. The only Self there is is the Self of God, and I must claim that now. And I must be willing to accept the responsibility of turning from all that disclaims the Truth of my Being, for you know that no un-Truth can ever really happen. There is no possibility for un-Truth to happen.

I must learn that whatever is untrue has no way to happen because God is the only Self, and God is never untrue. Whatever is untrue is just another way of the world mind denying the All-ness of the Selfhood of God. But that is my Self. It is the Self of everyone I know. There is no other Self, and that Self never lives in a human body. It never has. It never will. That Self is immortal forever. It is the only Self there is, and regardless of what concepts men have been formed about that Self, they are still no more than concepts. I will not live in a concept. My day is to be one with the Reality of Being, rising above the belief in concept here, there, and everywhere. For that which is not the One Self is not here.

Consciously you walk in the one Self. That is the spiritual Kingdom of God within you. It is the I which was before Abraham. It is the only Life there is. Now I have infinite Consciousness, and I turn to It to let It guide that which is called the form. So whatever the form does, it will be because it is led by my infinite Self, my infinite Consciousness. Every action of the form is guided by the infinite Consciousness that I am. Always I turn to It before I begin whatever I'm doing. Always I turn to It, refreshing. Always I turn to It so that the Lord may build the house, until I no longer have to turn to It. It is I without opposite. It is here. It is functioning. It is the only Self I recognize. It is Christ living Itself.

They say it took six or seven years to become a Master under the Buddha. It took three years for the Essenes to accept one as a member of their community. We've been on this path many years, haven't we? Are we not ready to be accepted in the community of God as the one Self, the infinite Consciousness, so we're out of the small circle into the Circle of Eternity?

∞∞∞∞∞∞ END OF SIDE ONE ∞∞∞∞∞∞

Much has come about through a misinterpretation of one of the most important phrases in the Bible: "For God so loved the world, that he gave his only begotten Son, that whosoever believeth in him should not perish, but have everlasting life." And by taking that statement to apply to Jesus and not seeing the universal nature of it, we have taken billions of people and not advised them that this statement is about them. "God so loved the world, that he gave his only begotten Son," the Christ, as your Identity.

"Call no man your father upon the earth: for one is your father . . . ." God is the Father of Christ, and if God is your Father, who are you? And so the only begotten, meaning Christ, which is the I which goeth unto the Father, is your name. And it isn't something to attain. It isn't something to work to become. It is the acceptance that I, being the Christ, the only begotten of the Father, and God being my Father, for I have no father upon the earth, I can no longer identify as the mortal being I identified as before. So the secret of secrets is that I cannot live in a human body without saying to these statements, "They do not apply to me. I cannot agree and accept to call no man my father upon the earth, for only God is my Father. I'll stay in a human body." And the world has done that and suffered from it.

Now we see that from the far ends of the earth, Spirit has prepared the chain of command leading right to you. And so Spirit says, "I stand at the door and knock. From the beginning of the world to this moment, I stand at the door and knock. Get out of that body. Open the consciousness. Accept I, for I am the Way you've been seeking. I am the Way to the rebirth from generation to regeneration, and that regeneration is through I in the midst of you, which am mighty."

Oh, how beautiful the Bible becomes when we know who we are, and we discover every Word of the Spirit is the Word of my own Being, ever held before the false human consciousness that was rejecting it. Somewhere in Proverbs we're given the clue to this regeneration. It's in the twenty-seventh proverb, line thirteen. I wonder how I keep doing this. But that isn't it at all. It's the line about waiting on the Lord, and I can't give you the verse at the moment. Waiting on the Lord. And this is the Son, which you are, waiting upon the Father. And this is the regeneration.

As you accept being that Life which is not in body, as you accept being the spiritual Son not limited to form, time, space, lack, bad health, bad digestive system, bad this and bad that—none of this is you—as you accept this, you're accepting that spiritual Sonship, which is waiting on the Lord and which is fed by the Infinite. You find yourself to be Self-fulfilling. You find Grace is no longer something you read about. It's your daily experience. It's Self fulfilling Self.

You discover that I am the way to Grace, fulfilling Itself in you. In Hebrews—and this time I hope I have the right one—we have our friend Paul anticipating our hesitations, where we begin to say, "Well, tomorrow we'll get into that," and Paul tells us "No, let's get into it today." It may sound like a very strange step, but in Hebrews, chapter 10, Paul begins to tell us, "This is the covenant that I will make with them after those days, saith the Lord, I will put my laws into their hearts, and in their minds will I write them; and their sins and iniquities will I remember no more."

That's the end of karma, you see, breaking the law of karma. Their sins and iniquities will I remember no longer. There's no karma in the Spirit. It's only when you're living in the sense of physical self. Now, where remission of these is, there is no more offering for sin. "Having therefore, brethren, boldness to enter into the holiest by the blood of Jesus, By a new and living way,"—and that's what we've been talking about today: the new, the living way—"which he hath consecrated for us, through the veil, that is to say, his flesh."

So we have the flesh of the Christ, which is not the flesh of the mortal body. We have the spiritual flesh of Christ, and that has ever been the Reality of our Being right where we stand. Out of the body, listening to the inner Self, we watch the concepts change, and we can behold what we have been before the world was and what we are now.l I, too pure to behold iniquity, will reveal to you the nature of your own Being. This is the transition in consciousness, the renewing of the mind, which is the transforming agent for the transfiguration.

## Class 13: Living Outside Your Body

Now, it's not immodest, then, to be immortal. It's simply living in the Truth that God is your Father, and God is not the Father of any mortal being. We have no dying Deity. We have no dying Christ. We have no aging Christ. We have no sinning Christ. We have no unhealthy Christ. We have no lacking or limited Christ. All of these problems are the denial of Identity, and you know how subtly you deny Identity: "I have a problem." Well, does Spirit have a problem? "No, but I have." And, therefore, you're saying, "I am not Spirit." But Spirit is the Son of God. ". . . call no man your father upon the earth: for one is your Father, which is in heaven."

Spirit is your Father. Spirit is your Substance. Spirit has no problem, and therefore, you don't have to get rid of a problem. *You* haven't got one. That which you have called your body has one, and as long as you're in that body, you have a problem or 10. But *You* have no problem. Why don't you live in the You that You are and discover You have no problem? And while you're making the transition of living in this You that You are, You can face the problem and realize the problem exists only in the sense of body, which is not You. I am not in the body.

At the Palace of Fine Arts there is an exhibit, and it's called the Exploratorium. Now, in this exhibit it has the title, "Dedicated to Awareness," and if you go in on the right side, make that circle, halfway around the circle on the right side to the extreme right of it there'll be a little door with a sign: "Exploratorium." And it's open every day from one to five except Monday and Tuesday. Now, these exhibits are all, strangely enough, dedicated to the illusion of the senses. And one of the exhibits is the bust of a figure about eight inches tall, six inches, something like that. It seems to be copper-toned. You see the perfect bust of this man, maybe a Flemish or that period, and there's a sign that says, "Touch me."

Well, you reach to touch this metal bust, and to your surprise it's just air. You can't touch it. It's only an image. And then you figure out, "Well, how did this happen?" And you reach inside, and you find that there's a mirror inside, a convex mirror, a very large one, and all of this is enclosed in a box. And all you see is this perfect, three-dimensional image which you're sure is there, but it isn't, just blank air. And so up somewhere or down somewhere there is another bust which is shining into the mirror, and the mirror is catapulting an image out here. But there is probably another mirror, and that mirror shines into the mirror and creates the illusion of a mirror. And you don't see any of this because all of it's in the darkness. The illusion of mirror creates the illusion of the figure.

Well, this is all very primitive. The human sense of life, the cosmic mind does it in a more subtle way, but the result is the same with one exception. Here we not only have the image, but here in this human life we have the living senses with it. Now, if you were an image like that image, but also had the sense of touch, you'd never know the difference. You'd consider the physical image very real because you could touch it. And you see, this being such a primitive reproduction of the illusion of the senses, it's only when we put together a few more sense illusions with it that we build a perfect illusion called the human form, which has no birth in God.

It might pay some of you to get over there and look at some of the other exhibits. There are optical illusions in sense of smell, olfactory illusions, and some others that I don't recall. And then there are some movies about the laser light. It's from one to five, Wednesdays through Sunday, and if you do nothing else, when you go in, go to the left and across the wall—to the left and over to the right wall after you go to the left—and see this little bust and reach in to touch it, and then go to some of the exhibits right next to it to find out just why the illusions appear so real to you. And you'll be onto some of the tricks of the cosmic mind.

While we're on the subject of details like this, Joel's new book, *The Mystical I,* is coming out; be out about the 18th of May. If you're near a library, get it there. If you want us to order it for you, just leave your check and your name, and along about May

18th we'll have it, if it comes out on schedule. It'll be $4.85 plus tax plus 25 cents for mailing and all of that. Let's say $5.25 probably is the price of the book with the tax and add 25 cents for mailing. But remember, all the metaphysical libraries will have it, no doubt. For those of you who find it inconvenient, who are not near one, just tell us you want it, and we'll order it for you.

Next week, by the way, the study will be the next chapter in *The Contemplative Life*, and that is about the pre-Easter week, preparing for Easter, chapter four. But you are preparing for Easter in a different way than even reading a book, because we're now at a place where we're going to find that we're not too interested in books. They'll be nice to stimulate us. They'll be nice to give us a little start down the hill or up the hill or something like that. But ultimately the only book we want is the Book of Life, that inner book which must become unsealed as we live in the Truth of I. And that *The Mystical I* of Joel's new book will contain several of his last talks in London, just before the transition. I can't tell you anymore. I haven't read it.

When you begin to enjoy your new weapon for living the Life eternal—the conscious awareness that I am not entombed in anything that will die, that I am free Spirit; I'm everywhere; I'm in every century right now; there's no place where my Spirit is not—Then you're living your Life eternal, and even though it's only a preliminary to the *real* experience, it is the prenatal to this eternal Life. It is the new Womb for the new Man. And make no mistake about it. You must enter that new Womb to be reborn.

And so Paul tells us it is a new living Way. It is a Way provided by the Father. It is the Way of being reborn to the Spirit, of the Spirit, and by the Spirit. In the Spirit until Spirit, Christ Consciousness, Life eternal, Substance of God is the only Substance you recognize as a living Substance. Can there be a problem in the Substance of God? If you have such a problem, you are not that Substance in your consciousness, are you? And I have discovered, to my satisfaction, that as long as I'm willing to accept my Self to be that

Substance and have the patience, I can look at that problem and say, "You are not in my Substance, and that which is not in my Substance cannot continue to persecute me."

It needs a mind that accepts it to work in. It needs a human mind, a human consciousness. And because the Substance of God is the only Substance there is, every physical disability on this earth is nothing more than the bust of a man that you can reach out to touch, and you'll find it isn't there when you are in the consciousness of Substance. The cosmic illusion is unveiled. You don't have to get rid of it. That isn't the problem. Your only problem is to accept the Substance that you are and stand in It in your Consciousness, rejecting any other self. And then you'll find that there are no conditions in a Substance called God.

There's no poor today and wealthy tomorrow. There's no 104-degree temperature today and normal tomorrow. There's no changing condition in the Substance, and therefore the changing condition is telling you, you are wavering. You're not living in the Substance. You're not accepting the Substance. And, truly that's all you need do is accept the Substance as the only, the One, the infinite Substance, and that is where your body is. That *is* your body, and it is governed by the law of that Substance, which is the perfect law of Spirit. It is under the principle of perfection, and because that Substance is all, the principle of perfection is all that is here.

The imperfection is the belief that you are another substance. Don't you see, then, what separation means? The belief that you are another substance is separation from God, and two powers means that you do not believe you are the one Substance, and so you have powers of God in the one Substance that are perfect, but imperfect powers in the other substance which you accept to be there. And it isn't there. You've got false powers that only exist because you accept another substance that isn't there. You can live in the realization that the one Substance of God is the only

Substance that covers this earth. The Substance of God is the earth and the fullness thereof.

And all that denies it is a cosmic mind seeking entrance, and if you permit that cosmic mind to enter, you are denying identity. You can even get to look at that cosmic mind and say, "*You* have no existence. Nothing you can say or do or make me feel is true because the One Substance of God is all that is here, and the name of that Substance is I. It existed before Adam and Eve. It has always existed. It is invisible. It is present. It is God. It is now. It is forever. And as I dwell there, all the shadows are removed— the shadows of thought, the shadows of memories, the shadows of experience and sensation. The shadows that never were more than my concepts as I lived out of my true Substance, in a separate substance with separate powers in the world of dreams.

Come back. Do not be two. Do not be another self than I am. One. I and the Father, One. And I accept divine Substance, which is incorporeal. And we'll come way back to Lao Tzu, where there's no rhinoceros to put a horn in divine Substance. We'll build our little community of I am, the divine Substance, the Essence, which was the very Essence of being an Essene. And then the detour of 16 centuries caused by the watering down of the great Truth into a personalized deity sent to suffer on earth, and all of that nonsense is cast out from the belief of those who are enlightened to know the Truth that sets them free.

The substance of God is the only substance that ever was, is, and will be, and that is Christianity universal. That is the teaching of the universal Christ, which has ever been on this earth awaiting the recognition of those who wish to live as one with their Father. It has no race. It has no religion. It has no history or geography. It has no divisions. Son of Man has no place to lay his head, for we are the universal Spirit. This teaching will bear every test to which you care to put it, and it will reveal to you the Truth that your Spirit is invincible. To know I aright is to know God aright, for I and the Father are One. And to know I aright, then, is to live now as the Substance, to now enjoy your Life eternal.

By next week many of you will have found ways. Perhaps some of you will have been instructed by the Spirit in these ways to live with the conscious Awareness that that body you see of me is something over which I entertain dominion, like I do of my automobile. It is under my control. And the control I exercise over it is not by telling it what to do, but by resting in the knowledge that I am the divine Substance which lives Itself through my Silence, making me an instrument for that indwelling Spirit. And this divine Substance of my Being, being ever perfect, maintains that body Image in perfection, with no effort on my part other than obedience to the spontaneous spiritual impulse that never ceases to flow.

That is how your dominion is attained, by accepting its presence in the Spirit of your Being, knowing that perfection is self-perpetuating. Grace needs nobody to turn the key and make it run. It's running now, and you will find little tricks, little techniques, little ways to keep you in that knowledge. So you'll be working at the office, working in the home, doing something, and yet knowing I, the infinite Spirit, is my name. And I can almost stand aside and watch this body perform what it is ordained to do now perfectly without effort, without taking deep thought, without planning. Always it being responsive to that inner impulse which I, the infinite Spirit, am sending through—without effort on my part. You are lining up the infinite circle of Truth with that little circle of Truth which is your momentary Consciousness, and the two are functioning as One.

You are living in the higher order of your Self, and the lower self, the Egypt, will be guided by Jerusalem while you come out of her. This is a technique you'll have to develop within yourself to make you a doer and not a speaker, but you'll have friends in this work, and there will always be this inter-communion between us

## Class 13: Living Outside Your Body

in which we nudge each other along the way with little ideas that have come, or we move certain obstacles out of the way.

But it is your experience, and it is just that livingness of it which brings to you those of your own household, those necessary to your experience and to whom your experience is necessary, and builds for you your own individual Essene community. As you are living the Way, you will find those who must live that Way will find their way to your door. I in the midst of you am the Way, and no one cometh to the Father except through Me. Enjoy it because it is the most exciting thing you will ever know as it unfolds and unfolds into new mansions continuously.

First thing in the morning, as often as you can remember during the day, and watch how without any effort on your part beside that, It does the work. It performeth. That is the miracle of I. Perhaps our Easter will be the experience of Easter before it arrives. Certainly, we can come next week with that in mind, that I have been living not in the body, and I to some degree understand the meaning of the rising Christ.

I don't really want to say good-bye because I'd like to just dwell here and enjoy the warmth and love of Spirit. It has its own message, it's Peace. All the friction of the world goes away, and that great Peace descends. No human mind can ever invent such Peace.

[Silence]

Blessings and thank you.

# CLASS 14

# A REAL AND PERMANENT BODY

*Herb:* I want to address this first question to every woman who is present. I want you to imagine, for the moment, that you are a 13-year-old girl called Mary and that the angel Gabriel has come to you in Silence, advising you of this blessed event. Even your husband knows nothing about it. And now, through some miraculous circumstance without knowing your husband, as the Bible calls it, you give birth to this boy. You become a woman who in all of the centuries is uniquely different than every other woman on earth because you, without a man, have given birth to a boy. Now just what would that do to you as a person? How would you feel? What kind of a life would you live after that event?

And then ask yourself this: If such an event had occurred in your life, do you really believe you could ever be a physical woman again? Do you believe that you could have normal physical relations with a man again, considering you had just given birth to a child without a man? Could you possibly enter into normal marital relations and have children a normal way after that? Would you even consent to it? Would you not be away on a cloud somewhere living the glorious Life of knowing the Father in Oneness? Is it not ridiculous to assume that a woman went through such an experience and then gave birth to children the normal way, many children to be exact?

You know, sometimes the children of Mary are sort of swept under the rug. And we're told that Jesus had only cousins, not brothers and sisters. There will be a day when all of us, in the knowledge of the Truth of Being, will have access to a different kind of record. Some call it the Akashic Record. It's a sort of a cosmic tape recorder, and those who can read the cosmic tape recorder have much to say about the events in the life of the young Jesus, events that are completely eliminated from the mass consciousness because they're not recorded in the Bible.

And in these records, which are an expansion of the known facts to man, it is indicated that the first child that arrived to Mary after Jesus was the daughter, Miriam. And at that time Jesus was five, and do you know from the age of five for Jesus to his fifteenth birthday, Mary was having children one after another until he had five brothers and three sisters? And for your records, these are the names, and this is the sequence: There was Miriam, and then there was Joseph. Then there was James. Then there was Simon. Then came the second girl, Martha. Then after Martha came, oh, I think it was Jude and Amos. Finally the youngest daughter, the little child of the family, Ruth. Now these were the eight brothers and sisters of Jesus, and although most people would at least give Mary four or five children, the Akashic Records reveal eight.

Now then, the importance of these children is this. They indicate that, first of all, what we call the virgin birth was a spiritual way of designating a special kind of birth, and these children, then, became an integral part of the living experience of the young Jesus because, you see, at the age of 14 he had no father again. His father passed on, and the father of the family became Jesus at the age of 14. And all of this early history in which he had to learn—as you and I have had to learn—the patience, the forbearance, the tolerance; overcoming the afflictions of the world one by one, day by day; building within the strength, the understanding, and finally the awareness of Divinity. All of this was necessary to him as it has been to you and to me. And you cannot take the children and put them away and pretend there was one child, or even say, "This one came a special way, and the others came a different way."

We today are sophisticated enough not to *need*—not to *need* this strange kind of exaggeration that tries to give authenticity to Truth by inventing supernatural events. The events themselves as they were are quite supernatural enough without the imagination of man or the superstition of religion. Significantly, you must remember that John completely eliminates all reference not only to the virgin birth, but to the birth of Jesus at all.

Now, Jesus was an ordinary boy. He learned, of course, that the real Truth of his Being was not that Mary was his mother or Joseph his father, but rather that he was the expression of God. But let's look at his early life. We watch him grow up, and we find that in every respect he is a normal boy with one difference. He's rather sensitive to things that in some way deny the holiness of God.

At an early age he's taken to Jerusalem by his father, and he's amazed. He can't believe it. They won't let his mother in the temple. They segregate men and women, and he just cannot believe it. He's infuriated. Why in the world do they do that? That was one of the questions he was always asking his elders. Why do they separate mothers from the worshipers in the temple, so that women and men are not one?

And he asked many other embarrassing questions. He'd say, "What's behind the veil of the Holy of Holies?" To everyone else that was sacred. You couldn't talk about it, but he wanted to know what's there. And then he'd have another embarrassing question for his elders, "If God loves his children, why do we make all these sacrifices of blood and animals to win God's favor? Isn't that denying that he loves us? And if the temple is so sacred, why do we have all this trade and barter in the temple?" Question after question from a young boy, and the elders try to brush it off.

Now, there were many times in his childhood when he became aware that he was different. In fact, he became aware in his teens that he had a mission, and when at the age of 14 his father died, he was saved from something he didn't want to do. The plans had been for him to go to the rabbinical schools in Jerusalem, and he had been there. He had seen the hypocrisy. He had seen priests who are political appointees. He had seen all kinds of life that was a total denial of the presence of God, all under the name of religion. And at the age of 14 the last thing he wanted to do was to be guided into the channels of orthodoxy, learning all of the pious phrases without the Spirit behind them, and even though his father's death was a blow to the family, it prevented him from going to Jerusalem to study because he had now stay and be father to eight. The last child came just shortly after the death of Joseph.

In his fifteenth year, as he was teaching his brothers and sisters, they kept asking him how to pray. They wanted to learn certain prayers, formulas, you know, so that they could just memorize something and pray by memorization. And he was trying to teach them another way, a living way, and do you know he was only 15 when he gave them The Lord's Prayer? And its purpose was to teach them to pray spontaneously. God is here, and God is living, and to the living God who is here, your prayer is; "Thy will be done, not mine."

And all of us adults through the centuries who've tried to understand that prayer were trying to understand the prayer of a fifteen-year-old who was teaching it to eight little brothers and sisters. And not a memorized prayer, but a flexible prayer, a prayer that said, "Father, your will for me yesterday and your will for me today and your will for me tomorrow is ever to bring me into further understanding of You. To bring me closer to You. To to let me know who I am in relation to You. And I, having a finite human sense of mind, I release that finite sense of mind and let your infinite Mind guide me. Thy Will, Thy Kingdom, Thy Power."

And always the boy was now becoming aware of preexistence, not only of his ingrained Divinity, but of his Divinity before the form appeared. He was learning the secret that you and I probably have not really learned to the full. He was learning that he had always been alive. To the world, he was 15. To himself, he was an immortal Being. The mortal human selfhood had become conscious of its immortality, and by the time he was 20, he knew more about God than most of those who walked the earth, speaking the name of God in vain.

From the age of 20 to 30 he had an unusual problem. It was to stop the possibility that he would be famous. He didn't want his personal self famous, for it would be a competition to the message he was teaching. There were many in those 10 years who knew him to some degree, but did not know that he was the same one who had appeared somewhere else. For instance, there were those Hebrews in Alexandria who thought—even though he was quiet, staying at home, his fame spread to them—this man knew the Bible! This man knew something behind the Bible! And those who were closer to him had spread his fame in some way, even though he performed not a single miracle.

And so he was offered many positions. As a matter of fact, the Alexandrians said to him, "You know, Jerusalem is going to fall some day. We heard it prophesied. Why don't we set you up here in Alexandria? You can be their competitor for a while, but you will outdistance them, and you will take over when they are defunct." He thanked them very courteously, and that's how he did *not* become the head of religion out of Alexandria in Judaism.

And again, there was another offer from the Sadducees. He was given quite a number of offers, usually from wealthy bankers, people with good intentions, but people who thought they wanted to be near when the new regime came about. Just like his own disciples later felt that in the new regime, they would sit on his left and on his right while he sat on the throne of David. That throne of David, to him, was not where he planned to sit. He had already become conscious that he was not the Messiah to a little group.

## Class 14: A Real And Permanent Body

He knew about the Light of the world, and now his whole function was what you and I are learning to do—to be patient. He knew the meaning of long suffering. He knew the meaning of really surrendering to the Will. There was no temptation on the earth that could pull him out of simply day by day releasing himself to the inner Presence until there was a conscious Union, until there was a complete and total inner Crucifixion of all personal sense.

It's only when you become aware of his youthful trials that you can see him as Joel saw him, that his entire life was devoted to overcoming personal sense, personal limitation, personal needs, personal afflictions, even personal betrayal. Always the overcoming was accomplished in the knowledge that the Spirit of God stands right here performing its perfect work regardless of what the human mind sees or understands. He had learned not to deny the ever-present perfection of Divinity within his own Being, within those around him. He never denied the Omnipresence of God. He made no big public uproar about it, and so very few people knew him other than the son of the carpenter who died, the boy who took care of his mother's children so well, and he was quite good at it.

He was an excellent father. It was a fatherhood by proxy, and he was also good with money. He knew how to make ends meet. And he worked well. His work was highly regarded, but he knew his time was coming. Even though he kept saying to his mother, "My hour has not yet come," he knew it was coming, and so he prepared for that day. He said to Joseph, "It's going to be your turn now to take over. You're the eldest after me, and so now I'm putting the funds in your hands. They're not much. They're meager, but when I go away, I want you to know that I'll be sending some." And so for two or three years he prepared Joseph to run that house, and later Joseph prepared James.

And when he did leave in his twenties, he didn't go very far. He went to the city of Capernaum, met a boat builder, a man named Zebedee who had two sons, John and James. You know, the cabinet maker that Jesus had become now became a boat builder. He had a way of building boats that were more safe than any boat in that area. And so the father of John and James became quite wealthy through Jesus. They were partners, boat builders, and in that area most of the boats on the lakes were built by Zebedee, designed by Jesus. And this is how he earned his money, and this is the money he sent back to Joseph to take care of the family.

And often he would take a trip, and always on his trips he would be waiting for "his hour to come," the time when he could be visibly about his Father's business. And the time came. When the time came, there was a new Jesus walking the earth. He had been in the wilderness. He had been baptized by the Spirit. He walked in a celestial body, visible to men as a body called Jesus Christ. No one knew he walked in that celestial body. No one knew they, too, someday would walk in that celestial body. And now he had to show what would be considered unshowable, teach what was unteachable. He had more to face than any of us in this room.

He had the full ceremonial religion of Judaism with all its rituals, and he had the might and power of Rome. And in between the two, completely surrounded by ignorance of what he was doing and who he was and what he had learned and what he knew, he had to make manifest the power of God. He had to glorify the Father. He had to open the heart of the world to the fact that the Spirit of God not only indwells every mortal being on earth but is the living Essence and Reality of that which we call the mortal being.

It wasn't enough for Jesus to say, "The Spirit of God indwells you." He had to show that the Spirit of God *is* You. And so we come to a moment when he's on his hands and knees washing the feet of the disciples. He says, "You don't understand what I'm doing, but someday you will." Peter instantly shows he doesn't understand: "Oh, you can't wash *my* feet. I won't let an important

## Class 14: A Real And Permanent Body

one like you wash my feet." Now, what brings that to attention, of course, is that the ritual of the washing of the feet happens on Maundy Thursday, and we have discovered that throughout the ages this ritual has been repeated in all of the religions in some way.

The Pope saw fit to repeat it, as usual, and a very interesting parallel must be drawn, because after the Pope had washed the feet of 10 old men in a nursery home, he found a reason to comment on those priests who had defected the church, and without calling them "Judas," he referred to Judas. The implication was quite clear, that just as Jesus had his "Judas," Catholicism today has its defecting priests. That incident would have been maybe a bit insignificant, except for the fact that he had just washed the feet of these 10 old men. And the question is: When he washed the feet of the 10 old men, was he doing what Jesus did when he washed the feet of his disciples? Had the Pope understood?

And so we look at it, and we find that referring to the defectors as a Judas, as vile creatures who'd gone back on their oath, is a little different than Jesus turning to Judas and saying, "Here, take the sop and go about doing what you must do." One is nonresistance; the other is resistance. And wherever you see the difference between nonresistance and resistance, you're catching the spiritual message. Now, much of the ritual of churchdom today is along those lines. It does the outer things without the inner significance, without the inner realization.

And so just the same as people will lay hands on and think they're baptizing somebody with the Holy Spirit, they will wash the feet, and it really never penetrates to the core of what Jesus was doing. Having attained the awareness of Divinity as the Identity of every man, he was washing the feet of his disciples in recognition of their spiritual Identity: I see you not as mortal man, but as the immortal Self. I see you as the invisible Christ.

And he was going deeper. He was saying to them, symbolically, your feet I am washing—not your head, not your ears, not your face, not your hands—but your feet, because this is what you stand upon. This is the foundation of your physical self, and now I'm trying to change your foundation. I'm trying to make you aware not of your physical being, because certainly your feet don't need cleaning. I am making you aware of your invisible spiritual Selfhood, and I want you to learn to stand on *It*. I want you to stand on your inner Divinity.

And so in recognizing the inner Divinity of his disciples by the washing of the feet, he was telling the disciples, "Now go and do likewise. Wash the feet of your neighbor. Love thy neighbor. Recognize the Christ of your neighbor. Recognize that each one who stands before you is the invisible Christ." And that is washing their feet. You don't have to get a basin of water to do it. This is the outer symbolism. You wash the feet of the world every day with your knowledge of the universal Christ. Therefore, when you do that, when you recognize the universal Christ, you have caught the meaning of washing the feet.

Now, you cannot turn over here and wash the feet of these 10 and turn over there and condemn. The washing of the feet must be a universal, or you haven't caught it. And so we must compare the Pope's way of washing the feet with the Jesus way and see that they're not identical, and we must further see that this is a clue to the reason for the defection. The understanding of the indwelling Christ as the Identity of mankind has not permeated through the religious world into the consciousness of its practitioners. If a man knew himself to be the Christ, would the issue be whether I get married or not?

Do you see, then, that if Catholicism cannot convince its own priests of the validity of its teaching, that it cannot convince its own congregations? And this same washing of the feet is going to occur in other religions than Catholicism, and I doubt if it will occur with the same inner meaning of Jesus. I doubt that the President of the United States could understand washing the feet and send boys out to kill. I doubt that nations of the world could learn to wash the feet correctly and do what they do. I doubt that

## Class 14: A Real and Permanent Body

governments and religions and politicians and educators and the peoples of the world are completely unaware that Jesus was saying, "Thou art the Christ. As I am, thou art. As I have learned my Divinity, I advise you of your Divinity."

And I have to question this, too. If the priests who left the church because they're unaware of the message of Christ did not have it, what about those who remained? Did they not receive the same teaching as the ones who defected? What about the children who are learning from them? What are they learning? About the indwelling Christ or about man-made ideas? You see, when Jesus kneeled and washed the feet of the disciples, he was also washing the feet of every man on the earth. He was making it impossible for any religion on this earth to be an interpreter of the Word of God. He was personally dying to all personal human sense.

This was absolute humility saying, "Follow me." Your humility must be so great that you reach that high level of Consciousness which says, "I cannot interpret the Word of God. I cannot be a mediator between God and man." That humility was Maundy Thursday. You're watching the beginning, the preparation for Crucifixion, a Crucifixion that should have been acknowledged on Good Friday, and every other day, because the Crucifixion is the capacity to step out of the finite ties of a mind that is not the mind of God.

Who was that who kneeled before the disciples? Who said, "I am washing your feet?" Who is this I? Was this not the inner Christ saying, "I, the inner Christ am washing your feet. I, the inner Christ, am purifying you of the belief in a personal you. I, the inner Christ, am cleansing you of all personal sense. I, the inner Christ, am building my own temple within you, the temple of the Soul, the temple of the Father, where the will of the Father in you can be done."

The Crucifixion of personal sense on Good Friday was not just a day. It was, as Joel reveals to us, another spiritual principle. And again, that spiritual principle, that inner Crucifixion was the end product of a long line of inner Crucifixions within the man, Jesus, so that there was no longer a human being there. There was the pure Christ unadulterated by human sense, giving the pure Christ teaching that as long as there are two on the field, there is one too many. The real washing of the feet is when you take this to your Self in your innermost Silence and throw open the windows of the Soul and let the pure Light of the Father dissolve all mortal sense. This is the acceptance of Divinity—not Divinity *and* a human me—but Divinity, period. All of this, a prelude to Resurrection.

How could there be a resurrection unless the personal sense had been overcome?—Because resurrection is arising from the crucified tomb of personal sense into Self realization. We were looking not at a man teaching his disciples. We were looking at our own inner experience before it happened. We were looking at the experience through which we are now going, the preparation for the illumination through Christ realized. As we are crucifying personal sense, accepting Divinity here and now, we are taking the words literally: "To live, to move, to have your being in God."

And how can you do that? How can you live in God, move in God, have your Being in God and still say, "I have a problem"? Isn't that sort of a paradox? Can a problem be in God? How can you say, "I have a mortal body"? Can a mortal body be in God? How can you have a mortal life? And therefore, when we're told, "Live, move, have your being in God," we're not being told that the Spirit of God indwells your mortal body. We're being told that we *are* the Spirit of God. Live in that knowledge. Many people will say, "Oh, I know I'm the Spirit. I'm the Spirit. Of course, I've known that."

Yes, they know it, but they do not accept that they are the Love of God. They are the infinite Life of God. They are the Self of God which has no problem. They are the Self of God which never lacks supply. They are Self of God without beginning or end. They say, "Oh yes, I'm the Spirit, and I have a problem. I'm the Spirit, and this is wrong over here. I'm the Spirit, and I'm trying to become One with God." But the Spirit *is* God, and so you cannot say, "I am the Spirit." You might just as well say, "I'm an automobile" and think you are one because you said so. The Spirit isn't becoming anything.

When you are able to say, "I am the Spirit" because you are *Being* the Spirit, not becoming, then you're closer to Easter Day, Resurrection Day, because you have come out of the belief that you are that mortal self who has a lack or limitation. Mary always thought of her child as a child of promise, but the world has never quite put the finger on something very important about that child. It was a child of Divine Love, and that Love is Eternal Love, a child of Eternal Love. And that awareness grew in the boy Jesus, that he was a child of Eternal Love, so much so that he and his father had a discussion about it.

He was explaining his feeling about the love of God, and he compared it to the love of his father, and so he said to his father, "I know you love me, and I find that you are never really wrathful with me. Some things I do might disturb you, but I never raised you to the point of wrath. Why then should my Father in heaven, who loves me, be raised to the point of wrath? Does he love me less than you? I cannot believe that my Divine Father loves me less than my father on this earth." And Joseph had to say, "I see your point."

Jesus had done something. He had reached that place where he not only had faith in God, but he had faith in everything about God. He had faith in the Eternal Love of God as being his dispensation. When you and I say, "We have faith in God," it would be wise for us to check out whether or not our faith includes every quality of God, and you'll find that our faith is not a 100-percent faith. We think we can be separated from God, and that's not faith, because God has said he couldn't be separated from us. Any time we feel any imperfection is possible, that's not faith in God, because we are saying that we don't have faith in a perfect God. A perfect God does not permit imperfection.

Now, one of the fundamental blunders of all religious dogma is this: It teaches that the Spirit of God indwells a mortal man, and so you have mortal men going around saying, "The Spirit of God is in me." And if you ever confront one of these fellows with a problem like this, he really doesn't know what to say to you. "The Spirit of God is in you. How interesting. Where do you keep it?" "Well, it's—it's in me. It's part of my being." "All right. I understand your brother has trouble with cancer right now." "Yes, he's in the hospital. He has cancer." "Well, isn't the Spirit of God in him, too?" "Oh yes, It's there. It's in him." "Well, what is it doing while he has cancer?" "Oh, oh—well, I couldn't say." "How can the Spirit of God be in this mortal body that has cancer? Impossible. You mean the Spirit of God is standing there twiddling its thumbs while your brother suffers? Is that what you think of God?" And, of course, there's no answer to it.

The Spirit of God does not indwell a single mortal body on this earth. The realization of immortality is not that the Spirit of God indwells me. It doesn't indwell me at all. Paul may have said that 2,000 years ago to those who are on their way up learning. He was teaching them the grammar. He was teaching them basic arithmetic. He couldn't give them calculus in one day. And we don't have to be stuck with his relative teaching at that point.

You cannot be a mortal being, a body of clay that encases the immortal Spirit. How can immortal Spirit be in a mortal body? Well then, what about this thing? That's what this friend of mine said to me the other day, "I am the Spirit, but this carrier," he called it, a "carrier." He has every book of Joel's on his shelf, every book. Of course, he's never studied too hard. He can thumb through this Bible. He knows it well. He can recite passages you didn't know were in there, and he knows he's the Spirit. But he also believes that he's a "carrier" for the Spirit, and that "carrier" is having all kinds of trouble because there's duality.

Phrases like: Choose ye this day which ye shall serve, God or mammon—it means nothing to this man at that point. He can't see it. Now, when you put the boy Jesus in the womb of Mary and take away his human father and try to make him a virgin birth, then all of the work he has done from the age of one up to twenty and then up to thirty in losing personal sense, showing the way to Divinity realized, is erased from the Consciousness, from the teaching, and the whole point of his teaching is missed.

When you show him as he was: Growing up as you and I grow up. Learning to divest himself of every false concept. Crucifying the human mind which perceives iniquity that the Divine Mind can never see. Crucifying the belief in a mortal body that contains a spirit, but accepting that I and the Father are One. And then do not attribute that to one who is divinely conceived alone, separate and apart from other people.—But say instead, "This is the one who learned to do for all humanity what they must do and lived it."

And finally, the greatest discovery that was ever made by Jesus has not been made by the religions of the world. He discovered God, and how strange that they have never discovered that that's what he did discover. If he was the Son of God, that discovery would have been impossible. It would have been just—there it is—"Naturally, I'm God. God is my Father." But he discovered it, rising up out of human sense. Now, when you have accepted your Immortality, you cannot also accept your mortality. That's like saying the Spirit of God is in a mortal body. And as long as you try to live on both sides, the immortal and the mortal, you'll find you get hurt in both places. You can't split infinitives that well.

A woman had just learned that the Spirit of God was her Being. She had learned to some extent what she should do to overcome the belief in a personal self. All of this was making a great impression on her. And after she had it, she thought, she then said, "Now, about my husband. You know he's getting older, and we have this great acreage and these responsibilities, and he's not really quite able to do the things he used to. And he's kind of worried about it and I am, and I'm wondering what I can do to, you know, cope with the situation."

And I said, "Well, you can do one of two things. You can meet the situation humanly, or you can accept spiritual Identity for both of you. Now, I said, "Don't try to do both. Either you are the child of God and he is, or you accept that you're not the child of God, but if you try to be the child and act like a human, you're starting out in an impossible situation." Now, I said, "Suppose you decide that because he's getting older and all of that, as you see it, that you really do want to do something for him. You say he doesn't have the energy. Now, what can you do?"

And she thought about it, and she says, "There's really nothing I can do, is there?" There wasn't anything she could humanly do to give him energy. The only way she could really help that family was to be a witness for Christ within. She had to learn how to wash her feet and his, and while going about it, to wash the feet of the sheep on the ranch. The spiritual way is not an extra something that you do. It's not something you add to your human way. It's a departure, and you don't hold onto what you're departing from, and you don't turn back. The embryo that is born isn't still an embryo, and though we come now to a place where we're just infants, what about it? What's wrong with stumbling as an infant?

Haven't we learned that long suffering is part of the way? Of course, it's a suffering. How could we possibly walk on spiritual feet in one minute? And so we are prepared for what appears to be a struggle. What of it? At least in that struggle, nothing gets hurt. The only thing that gets hurt is your sense of impatience and frustration, but there's no hurt. In this new struggle as an infant in Spirit you are learning to do something that is breathtaking. You are learning how to let God be your Life. You are learning it's possible to let God be your Life.

You're not reading about a Resurrection in the Bible. You're not going to a ceremonial and watching somebody wash somebody's feet and going home and saying, "Gee, that was inspiring." You are the Resurrection! You are going through the experience of Resurrection from infancy and ultimately to full maturity in the

Spirit. And the Jesus Christ Way is totally different than even we know as we proceed along our spiritual sense of the Way, because suddenly we come face to face with a new level: "I have meat. I can give you living waters."

And you look, and you see you're a disciple, and there he has no meat whatsoever. What's he talking about? Or you're at the well and you look, and here's this man. He's dusty with the road. What kind of living waters can he give me? I've got the well, not him. And there he is without meat to see for anyone, without wine to see for anyone, without bread to see for anyone. And he says, "I can give you anything you want," but he has nothing. And that's the beautiful thing that Joel has pointed out. He has nothing, but he can give everything.

Why? Where is it? In his nothingness, in his elimination of personal sense, in the crucifixion of the man, in the removal of all humanhood, of all mortality, there stands the infinite, immortal Self, which has all. And the man with nothing who knows I of mine own self am nothing, who has crucified mortality, finds himself to be the Infinite Invisible expressing Its fullness. And this that little boy knew in his twenties. He knew this was his Way: Resurrection out of mortality, out of limitation, out of a brief lifespan. Out of all the lacks, the needs, the wishes, the hopes, the ambitions into the acceptance of Being. Not God to be discovered somewhere.

This is the story of Identity. Not God indwelling me, not the Spirit of God inside me, not seeking the Presence of God, but recognizing your Being *is* the Presence of God. Your Being is that Presence, and then you're in One. Then you're in union. Then you are casting no shadow, and then you are ready to see that every word, thought, and deed in the life of Jesus Christ was to bring you to the place where you and the Father are One and the same. That the Presence of God is your Being.

I am is just a word until you know I am the Presence. I am Spirit is just a word until you know that Spirit that you're saying you are is God Itself. And when you accept any imperfection in your life, any lie, any untruth, any error, any evil, you are denying your Identity. You are punishing yourself. You are being what you are not. You cannot have a problem and be the Identity that Jesus taught you are. Do you see, then, that you are rejecting Identity when you say: "I need, I lack, I want, this is wrong, that is wrong, I'm sick," or "I will die" or even that "I was born"?

Identity is your only name. Whatever you shall ask in My name, you shall receive. My name is Spirit. And when you are asking in the name of Spirit, you don't even ask. The acceptance of Identity is the asking. Resurrection is the realization of Identity. That one word is the key to the immortal Self. You cannot be that immortal Self unless you have put off the garment of belief in a mortal self. You cannot share the fruits of the Spirit with a neighbor unless you are that immortal Self. And you cannot be that immortal Self and accept problems in your life as a reality, nor can you accept problems in your life as a reality and say that you are the immortal Self at the same breath. Isn't there a lot, then, behind washing the feet?

Isn't this what our religion should be teaching about Identity instead of poor, crawling, mortal sinners? We say today, "He is risen." Where? Where has he risen? Look around you and see if he's risen. He hasn't risen in the consciousness of mankind where he should be rising. Mankind is still a density, but he is rising in our consciousness. That's where he's rising. That's where the Spirit of God ultimately reveals Itself as the Identity of every man, where the Consciousness rejects all temptation to believe that I am not that one Identity to which the Father said, "All that I have is thine."

You know he didn't give that All-ness to the mortal who dies. He gave it to that which is his own Self, the Christ of Himself, which is called His Spirit in you, and then you get rid of that "in you." His Spirit I am. And in his Spirit is the All-ness of God, and wherever I accept less than the All-ness of God as being present, I am denying Identity. I am denying His Presence. And now, if I

## Class 14: A Real And Permanent Body

wash my feet correctly and know who I am, and wash your feet correctly and know who you are, and wash the feet of the world and know who everyone is, isn't washing the feet the acceptance of the omnipresence of God?

Everywhere I am. Everywhere the Spirit of God is. Everywhere is the one Identity. You dwell with this, and you find that something lifts you above the limitations of a human intellect, and you come face to face with a wonderful paradox, which is very uplifting. If I have a mortal mind, how can it know anything except a mortal body, a mortal life, a mortal experience? Is God mortal? How can the mortal mind know the immortal Father? It cannot. It receiveth not the things of God.

And so I am lifted above this mortal mind. And now, finally, I reach a place where I for an instant glimpse the fact that the divine infinite Mind is the only Mind, and you live there a while. You experience Its what might be called rapture, the knowledge that I've been lifted above every human concept. I'm in the divine Mind, and it is my Mind.

∞∞∞∞∞∞ END OF SIDE ONE ∞∞∞∞∞∞

"He riseth from supper, and laid aside his garments; and took a towel, and girded himself. After that he poureth water into a basin, and began to wash the disciples' feet, and to wipe them with the towel wherewith he was girded. Then cometh he to Simon Peter: and Peter saith unto him, Lord, dost thou wash my feet? Jesus answered and said unto him, What I do thou knowest not now; but thou shalt know hereafter. Peter saith unto him, Thou shalt never wash my feet. Jesus answered him, If I wash thee not, thou hast no part with me."

Now re-translate that, seeing that I, the Christ, which appeared as Jesus, am saying to Peter, "If I wash thee not, thou hast no part [of] me." There must be a realization of the presence of Christ somewhere beginning in a person. The little cruse of oil has to start to pour. And though we are starting with the foot, this must take place. Maybe starting with the foot is a little inn where the Christ is born in Peter. But something must be done to bring him an awareness that I, Christ, stand here. And Peter, someday you won't be here. Only I will be here, and you will know that you and I are One and the same. "Simon Peter saith unto him, Lord, not my feet only, but also my hands and my head. Jesus saith to him, He that is washed needeth not save to wash his feet, but is clean every whit: and ye are clean, but not all."

As this recognition of Christ Self grows, so does the acceptance of the Christ Mind, and as you come into the awareness of the Christ Mind, superseding your former sense of a finite, limited mind, you must accept a Christ Body. You cannot have a Christ Mind and a human body. You cannot have an infinite Mind and a finite body. It's impossible. And so you come to that place where you can look out at the universe and say, "This is my Body." The universe is my Body, and not even the visible universe. Everything in this universe is imitating my Body.

I have an Infinite Body because I cannot have another. There is only the one infinite Mind, the one infinite Being, the one infinite Body, and there is no other. I do not have a piece of it, a fragment of it. I must begin to respect the integrity of my infinite Body. You will stop being concerned about five foot two when you become aware of your infinite Body, and you won't run into the problem of how can I improve my physical body? Because the minute that is the level of where you are aiming, you're denying Self again.

You cannot accept your immortal Self and not accept your immortal, infinite, universal Body. You don't have a personal body to take care of, and the miracle of having nothing and yet being able to give everything, as Jesus demonstrated, is the same with your Body. The miracle of accepting and living in the knowledge of your infinite Body is what takes care of what you have called your personal body.

## Class 14: A Real And Permanent Body

Now, you can read the Bible from cover to cover, and you can read every book of Joel's from cover to cover, and you're still going to have to do it yourself. You have to come into that secret place where you and you alone without mother, brother, father, or sister sit down and dwell in the knowledge that my Body has no beginning and no ending. My Body is everywhere. It is the Spirit of God without beginning and end, the Alpha and the Omega, and because It is the Spirit of God, my Body is a perfect Body. And the instant you decide that you do not have a perfect Body in some way, you are denying the Truth of your infinite Body, which is the perfect Body of God.

Again, that's the trap which enables you to deny Identity: "Oh, I've got an aching back." How strange, when you are the immortal Being. And all you're saying is, "I'm a mortal with an aching back." How can you expect the power of the immortal Spirit to help an aching back, when the immortal Spirit has no aching back?

When you have accepted God, then you accept God's intelligence. You accept God's perfection. And therefore, you accept that before any error could occur in this world, God had already eliminated the possibility of such an error to occur. Before any problem could be, God had eliminated the possibility of a problem. Before any imperfection could happen, God had eliminated that possibility. That is your faith in the perfection of God, not "I believe in God."—"I believe in the All-ness of God: the perfection of God, the totality of God without exception." And your faith, then, is a faith that every quality of God in its fullness is ever present and functioning to maintain a perfect, universal Self, which you are. As you put on the garment of Immortality, you put on the garment of an immortal, infinite Body.

When Jesus spoke of adultery, he spoke of that spiritual adultery which steps out of the immortal, infinite Body into a finite sense of body, and when you are not married to the Infinite, you are in spiritual adultery. Now, I have seen that when an individual dwells in contemplation on the infinite Body that I am, you'll find that regardless of what happens in the world anywhere, there will be in you an awareness that that cannot be true. The Body of the Father is immaculate. The Body of the Child and the Father are One. There is nothing but my immaculate Body everywhere. It is your function to maintain the integrity of that Body. If you do, you'll find the integrity of your human sense of body will be a perfect shadow of your infinite integrity.

Now, we who have not accepted an immortal, infinite Body will always be accepting our neighbors' afflictions with a twinge of sympathy. But you see, when you do that you're denying your infinite Body. You're saying, "Over there where my neighbor is there's an imperfection in body." But over there where your neighbor is is your infinite Body. And so you've got to overcome the personal sense which accepts the affliction, not only in your own sense of body, but in your sense of your neighbor's body. We haven't been called upon to do this in just these terms, but you'll find that unless you are doing this, you're at odds with your Self, affirming an infinite Mind and yet a finite body. The moment you left that finite mind, you left the finite body, and if there's any trace of belief in it as being your body, you're still in the finite mind.

Now, I think one of the great principles that Jesus taught here about supply, about having meat, about having bread, about having the wine, even though it was not visible, was that in the nothingness of a human sense of things, infinity pours. And it isn't so much going to get infinity. It's, rather, you tune into infinity by tuning out finity. You tune out this world to tune in the other. Tuning out this world is tuning in infinity, but you can't go to infinity and tune it in unless you're willing to tune this out. And as you dwell upon these things, you find that at the time of the birth of Jesus, it was Mary who had lost her sense of a finite body. She had been lifted out of the sense of a personal self, and this was the virgin birth. To live in, to move in and have your being in God means the complete relinquishing of everything that is finite and everything that you think with the human mind.

## Class 14: A Real And Permanent Body

Now, you must see that we are not ready for Resurrection until we have accepted the need for Crucifixion of all that is finite. You must see that there's a lot of spade work left to do. We can't say, "He is risen, or I am risen." We have to do the work that must be done. The eternal love of the Father is always where you are, and you cannot be separated from it. If we have faith in that love, then we are willing to get on our material hands and knees and on our spiritual hands and knees and spade away every mortal thought barrier, so that the love can shine through a transparent Self. And we will find that Grace really means that I, being nothing, have become transparent to the Holy Ghost. The Holy Ghost shining through my transparent Self is Grace, love, beauty, peace, harmony, and it matters not about the external war-torn world or inflationary or deflationary world.

I am nothing in this world. Not because I declare it, but because I live, I move, I have my Being, not in another god, but in Identity as the Spirit of God, which is infinite, unlocalized. And you begin to test yourself. You see how the declaration means nothing until you can answer the questions in the test. Are you in the twentieth century? Forget it then, because the Christ isn't limited to that twentieth century this minute. Your infinite body is in all that will be called "time" now. Are you in an airplane? Forget it, you're not. Your infinite body can never be squeezed into a 747.

Your infinite body can never be squeezed into a shape or a size or a time or a place. You must be conscious of your infinite Body. You must devote contemplation to the awareness of it and to the perfection of It and to the spiritual law that maintains Its perfection. And you will find all of this is the spade work that infiltrates your consciousness, as you do it, and lifts you 30-fold, 60-fold. And you must come, then, eventually to the 100-fold realization of Self. But never will you do it in the belief that you are in time, in a century, in a place, in a country, even in a hemisphere. You are the Son of Man, nowhere to put your head.

When Jesus saw the Book of Enoch, he was still a young man; he was in his teens. And there he saw it: The Son of Man, and he thought, "I've been wondering, what shall people know me as?" And that was his title that he adopted. The importance of it was to show that we must come out of mortality, out of manhood, and the Son of Man becomes the Son of God by the realization of Self. Not by an immaculate birth, but by a realization that I who had a mortal parent as a mother and a mortal parent as a father, I never was born that way at all. The form that came forth is the form that I do not accept. The Life which is there expressing as this image called form is the invisible Life that I do accept, and for that which was called my mother and that which was called my father, I do not accept their visible forms. That mental image called form, not being there, it could not give birth.

There is no more form for a Mary than there is for a Jesus or there is for a Tom, Dick, or Harry. There is only the one Divine Image. The illusion of birth is as much an illusion for Mary and Jesus as it is for you and your parents or you and your children. What is there is the invisible Consciousness of three people, three Souls: The invisible Consciousness of the mother, the invisible Consciousness of the father, and It is joined by the invisible Consciousness of the child to be. And the three produce a new form, an image, but you're looking at three Souls combining. Maybe you have discovered the Holy Trinity—three Souls combining to produce this new form—Soul of the unborn child, Soul of the mother, Soul of the father. And they are one Soul in Spirit. Two Souls welcoming you, and a child is born, and that's the immaculate conception.

Now, when we realize it, even though years have passed as far as human time goes, we are approaching the crucifixion of all that has intervened between that moment to this moment and erasing the concepts that we have mistakenly accepted. And as they are erased one by one, the Light of the Soul is coming through, resurrecting us to the Reality of Being. I and my Mother are One. I and my Father are One. In the Invisible we find our Oneness. And this being in the visible with a new law of the invisible functioning in our Consciousness is the exaltation of walking through the world, but not of it. Accepting that I am walking in God, moving in God, living in God. The invisible, infinite Self which I am. This physical form moves within my invisible, infinite form. Everywhere this visible, physical form goes, my infinite, invisible form is. This is the story of Jesus.

To give up the visible form, finally, is nothing more than the reflex action of having given it up in the invisible first. The crucifixion that we see is but the outer appearance of that which has transpired over the centuries, finally coming to take place in the visible, and so the principle of a Maundy Thursday of humility, of a good Friday of Crucifixion, of a rising called Easter.

So in the events of our lives, there are also these spiritual principles, and the spiritual principle of Crucifixion, or losing of personal sense, is that which finally eventuates in the dropping away of the physical form. It's all voluntary. And then the celestial Form[which we inhabit, which is the Infinite Self that we are accepting, is that which ascends. We come into the Ascension over material ties. Now all of this illumination takes place before the grave. The life of Jesus is only a crash course in what we must do before the grave.

And so when we look at his outer Crucifixion, when we read about his Resurrection and his Ascension, we are reading about me today, here, now—what I must be doing to put on the garment of Immortality here and now on the earth. Compressed into three years, visibly, was a teaching of what my life must consist of in order for me to experience that Grace which has meat the world knows not of, which has bread and wine, which has Life without end. And all of this must be accepted without adulteration, without second-selfing. Without a self that wants to leave the priesthood to get married, which is unaware of its Christ Self as the only Self. Without a second self, a second mind, a second life. The key word will always be, "Have I denied My Identity?"

When you find you're not denying Identity, you might as well start saying goodbye to your friends. You won't be here very long. Whoever reaches the point where he is not identifying as anything but the infinite Self *in every way* is the Christ realized. The purple robe is waiting, the philosopher's stone, the celestial body. The infinite, eternal Life here and now. We still haven't reached the end of a between Resurrection and Ascension, but we will.

I want to leave you today with that word "Identity," which shatters the belief that the Spirit of God indwells me, which shatters the belief that I am Spirit *and* physicality, which shatters belief that I am seeking the presence of God. Identity means the presence of God is the only Being standing here, and all that is not that Presence is not here, but appears to be. The only Presence here is My Being. The only Presence where you are is My Being. The only Presence where anyone is is My Being, and the name of My Being is the only name that I can answer to, truthfully, without committing spiritual adultery.

When you do that, when you deny My Being as the only Being, you have divided his garment. To you God is not all, God is not One, God is not the only, and you are still in the shadow of turning. Contemplation, meditation, not communion here on an altar out there, but communion in the heart, within the Being, until *Being* is your name, not becoming. Identity. Spirit, complete. The total Self with nothing missing, ever. This is the path to Resurrection.

Therefore, the answer to how do we live, move, and have our being in God? The answer is we accept that Identity, which is the presence of God, to be the only Identity of all who walk the earth. We are sowing to Identity, not to the flesh. You will not do it with a busy intellect. When you stop to think about these things with that intellect, even if you reach the pinnacle of acceptance, you still have to commit it to your Consciousness.

The mind will not be able to hold Truth. It will never hold Truth. The best the mind can do is to be a clear crystal of still water without thought, without concept, without movement, waiting on the Lord. And then you'll find that great moment of equilibrium between everything that moves in this Universe. You will be resting as a clear transparency for the Word of Being. Then you will have meat the world knows not of. You will have wine and water. You will be that which is expressing eternal Love.

I think we have all been blessed with the priceless opportunity to accept the Life of God as our own. And to share this understanding with those in the world who are drawn to us by that measure through which we can demonstrate the Presence as the living Self of all is one of the most unexplainable joys there is. You have experienced it whenever you have been able to be useful to someone who was floundering, who was reaching out and could touch the Light of your Being, and you know what It is.

This minimal Light that we all have felt up to now is as nothing compared to the fullness that surrounds us, unknown to the limited sense of self. The moment that limited sense of self is crucified even for an instant, the floodlights are like a blinding experience of Damascus. You realize what Infinity is, not as a word, but as an experience, and you know the miracle of Infinity stands right outside the limited human consciousness, ever knocking.

If we could accept Identity now, we would all be accepting the same Identity, the infinite Self. We would all be accepting the same Body, the infinite Body, and then we would all be joint heirs in Christ, not because the Bible said so, but because we know that what it said is so.

[Silence]

So I thank all my immortal Friends for being here today. Blessings and love.
Thank you.

# CLASS 15

# I AM NOT A PRODIGAL

*Herb:* You will notice that throughout the Bible there is either man under the dominion of the forces of the world or one who comes out of the forces of the world and takes dominion over them. To bring it into our contemporary life, we might say that we either will be controlled by our environment, or it will control us. We know, of course, that in the main we are controlled by our environment. And so I was led to a very strange parable in the Bible. The strangeness of it was that it was so familiar to all of us, a parable that we all feel we understand, so much so that we take it for granted and go right by. And so I more or less said, "Father, but I understand that parable, the Prodigal Son. Why, everybody knows about that. We can't go back to McGuffey's Reader." And yet for some reason the Prodigal Son kept popping up, holding me there. And so we took a look at it.

There it was, the same old parable, but there were new eyes looking at it, and I think you'll agree that we have here in the Prodigal Son a story about ourselves, which up to this moment we have not fully seen through the eyes of Christ. Really, it shouldn't be called the parable of the Prodigal Son, for we learn that it is impossible for the Father to have a prodigal son. And then the word "parable" becomes quite meaningful. To the unlettered in the deeper teaching, this is about a spendthrift. He simply squanders his father's money, comes home, and asks for forgiveness, gets it, and once more he's in the household. And then metaphysically we say, "Oh well, that's for those who don't see the deeper meaning. I do." And we say, "Why, the prodigal son is the one who wanders away from the will of the Father, the one who lives in mortality, the human." And that's true enough.

And then, going deeper into esotericism, we find that the esoteric Truth of the parable takes us away from the standard cliches. We have two brothers, not one, and even the second brother has a complaint to register. What about him? Who is he? What's he doing there? What's his purpose in the parable? And now we look at it very carefully. We see a father has two sons, and something stops you and says, "Wait a minute. Wait a minute. You're reading it as a human being: A father has two sons. Who is writing this parable? Who is speaking it?" And comes the great awakening: Why, these are the words of I. I within me is my Teacher. I is speaking. I is telling me a story. Why? Because I is trying to awaken me. I is trying to tell me that this so-called me has gone through many incarnations as a prodigal, many human embodiments as a prodigal, away from I.

I is telling me that the human race is a prodigal, and then I begin to see the meaning of the two brothers in a very different light. The father has two [sons]. The first book of Genesis is the first brother, the perfect spiritual Self, and the younger brother who follows, but not quite, and comes into incarnation, the second book of Genesis. And so we are really being told about the Reality and the unreality. We are being told about the way in which man comes into a second sense of self. Some call it the lower nature and the higher nature, but as you dwell with it, you'll find that it's a story about cause and effect, and that none of the Prodigal Son, not one whit of the story, takes place outside of your own Self. All of it is your inner experience as a person finds himself, turns within himself, and returns to his own Self.

So we find this younger brother turning to the father, and that is the journey of the ego into the flesh. To the father, we say,

"Give me my inheritance. I'm leaving home." And so way back at the beginning of the world, your incarnation, your birth is the beginning of the prodigal experience. The moment of appearing in flesh is the moment when the prodigal begins. Mortality is the inception of the prodigal son. And now mortality wanders away from immortality, and we have the divided consciousness, the sense of self which must struggle to earn its own living. The sense of self which must feed itself. The sense of self which is unaware of the ever available, present inner Self.

And so now we find a clearer definition. The older son, who remains at home, is the inner Self, and the outer self is the human sense of self which wanders off into the far country, taking its life substance with it. Now, we are told that he squanders his substance, and this, then, takes us into the understanding of separation from Self. Now we are wandering off in the flesh, in the human sense of things, in the human sense of what to do and when to do it. We are the mortal, separated from the immortal Being, which we are, only by the hypnosis of the senses, and now we are divided, separated, unaware of Identity. And we find that, somehow, the world doesn't satisfy us. More and more we lose our Substance. We get further and further away from the Reality of our Being, and finally the husks of matter, of material living, show us that we have followed a mirage.

There is a place where we lose all satisfaction in what the world can give us. We see through the tinsel. We understand that even though we may crave a deeper sense of life, that the complete, total human race can evolve no higher than it is. There is a place where human evolution can go no further, and this is it. That is when the prodigal realizes that back home the hired servants are eating better than he. He is so completely at a loss to sustain himself that he now needs external help. He finds a citizen there and asks for help. In the midst of the Garden of Eden we walk needing help, unaware where we are, who we are, for we are prodigals from our own Self, and then we're put to feeding the swine. We must live in the outer self with outer selves because we have not yet come to the realization of an inner Self with which we must be One'd. We're not even half a self, and so we want to come home.

The realization of wanting to come home is the turning. It is the beginning of another process called involution. We evolve out, incarnate. We involve in, back to the home of virgin Spirit, back to that place we had inadvertently left at the moment of incarnation in our very first human birth. The complete and total journey of the flesh has now reached the point where we are ready to find Self, and as we come home, although we are far away, the Father greets us. And this is the story about the Omnipresence of the Father wherever you are. The inner Self is always present, never absent from the outer self. And the instant there is a realization of turning to the inner Self, there's no place to go: "Here I am." And the son returns, and he is greeted with open arms. He's given the robe. He's given the ring. He's even given a new pair of shoes, and we find these shoes are no longer the shoes of the senses, which he was told to go out without before. The shoes of the senses have been discarded. Now the shoes of the Soul—the senses of the Soul—have replaced the senses of the brain.

Material man, mortal man is home again, but here's this elder brother, and he's quite resentful. "What about me? I didn't squander my money. I didn't go out in riotous living." The father says, "Son, all that I have is thine. Thou art ever with me." And we find something very interesting in this statement, the blending of the inner and the outer. As the prodigal in the outer, unwedded to the inner, whatever we do is unordained. It is form without content, without Substance. The elder brother is the Substance.

If you look all through the East, you'll see many who sit cross-legged living in the self-indulgence of the inner Self. How glorious to be lost in the caves. Then they can get up and walk away with rheumatism, arthritis, all kinds of physical ailments because they are the elder brother resentful of the younger brother. They don't want any part of the outer world any more than the outer brother, the younger brother, wanted any part of the inner world.

And so the father says, "You must be content not only with your level of Self as Spirit; you must manifest." Just as the outer brother was a prodigal, so is the inner, for you must spiritually manifest the Divine Image. The Content, the Substance of the inner brother, must be wedded to the form of the outer brother. The outer and the inner must become one, so that the form on the outer receives Substance from the inner, so that the Substance on the inner takes form in the outer. And then we have the wedding of Substance and form. We have the anointing. We have the mystical marriage, which in the book of Revelation is the marriage of the bride and the lamb.

And we look at ourselves again, and we find that we have not wedded the inner, and therefore, the outer forms of our lives are without Substance. And at times we have wanted to retire within the inner, never letting our deeds shine forth, but hiding our Light, self-indulgent to the point of saying, "Look how spiritual I am," but not going forth to show the fruitage of it.

And so now, the inner is the cause. The outer is the effect. But as a prodigal, as one living only in the consciousness of matter, the outer effects have no Substance. They are not sustained, and we find we must go to other citizens for help, and we find ourselves feeding the swine. When, through the acceptance of the inner, we let the inner Self give Substance to the forms, then Divinity within us is manifested in our lives.

There can be no Substance without manifestation. There can be no cause without effect. Our function is to combine Divine cause with Divine effect so that cause and effect are truly the marriage of the two brothers as one and so that the Father no longer has two sons in us, but one. Cause and effect are one'd, and that One you accept as your name. I am that One.

We can measure our progress along the straight path of initiation by whether or not we are still a prodigal, whether or not we have surrendered this outer material consciousness to the elder brother within, for the marriage of these two is the preparation for Christing. Until the outer turns and says, "Let me serve the inner," as the prodigal does in this parable, the inner cannot function as the living will of God expressing in us. And so we say, "How do I know if I am still a prodigal?" By their fruits you shall know if you're still a prodigal or not.

Once the prodigal has returned, something in you is manifesting His Will. Something in you is manifesting the Divine Image. Returned out of the mortal consciousness, we no longer accept ourselves to be mortal being. Returned, we no longer accept ourselves to be living in a human sense of self or in a human sense of body. Returned, we no longer have a human sense of love or a human sense of life. Returned, we have no beginning. We have no ending. We have no opposites. We have no pros and cons. We have no shadows of thought. We are willing to abide in total trust without a concept to guide us. Returned, we find that we are the center of a spiritual Universe.

It's as if you were in a plane as a pilot and all around you is this big body of metal, and it's either going to go up or not, depending on you. The equipment is there. The instrument panel is there. There are switches and knobs and buttons and lights, but they're not going to move themselves. There's a relationship between them and you, and it's up to you to move that plane up. Everyone on board depends on you.

Now, we're in the same position as that pilot. Our plane is a little different. It's invisible, and it's not finite. The plane around you is your Universe, and you're in the center of it, and you've got to pilot that Universe. And you say, "I can't do it." And the Father says, "I will do it." If you're going to try to do it, you're the prodigal. You're not wedded to your inner Self. I in the midst of you, I'm the pilot. And so you learn to reach back deep inside. You reach beyond your mind. You reach back into your Universe way, way back until you have no concept about yourself.

You reach back into infinity, and until you have found that you are not aware of yourself, you are not back where you belong. Your invisible plane is not going to take off because there is no human mind that can work the panel of instruments for this plane, only I, the Father within. If you want your universe to be a spiritual experience in God, you must be wedded to the elder brother within. And so we're not in this form at the moment. We're reaching back until we're out of it. We're not in this human sense of mind. We're reaching back until we're out of it, until there's a feeling that there's no person present. There's no human thinker present.

I reach back. All that is present is a spiritual Universe. That spiritual Universe is your Identity. That is your infinite Self. That's when you'll know you're not a prodigal. And now in your infinite Self, you are living only by Divine Revelation. You are fed completely by the Infinite, sustained, maintained, and every quality of the Infinite is right where you are. This is how you know whether or not you're still in a parable or you will come out into Self. And then by your fruits, by the inner expression becoming manifest in the outer, you can see how far the ego has progressed out of the sense of flesh into the realization that I, Spirit, stand before the world.

I, Spirit, have never indwelled a mortal being. I, Spirit, do not need a human being as an instrument for my work. I, Spirit, do not function through human beings. I, Spirit, do not function in a prodigal. The prodigal is that sense of self which has never existed. Only I am present, only the Father. If you stay out there as a human trying to come back home, you're still under a state of hypnosis. The Spirit of God has never left God. The Son of God has never left home. There never was a prodigal. There was a self that we accepted which never was there, and as long as that self has a trace, or even a lingering memory, you're still under the hypnosis of a second sense of self and living in separation. I never was a prodigal. I and the Father have always been One, and we stand there, letting the living Spirit of our own Being clear our vision. Clear away all the cobwebs until there's no prodigal or human or mortal trying to be. There is simply Being Itself.

You become aware of the radiant Invisible all around as your Being. I *am* the radiant Invisible. I am Self. I am One. There never were two in my Father's household. The illusion of division is removed. You have really subtracted that which is not, and in doing so, you have multiplied the Lord. You multiply by subtraction. As you remove the veil of illusion, you multiply. And now the moment you lose this Identity, you go back into prodigality. You return to the illusion of mortality and separation and open yourself to the good and the evil.

The outer sense of self, which lives in the world, is divorced from the inner sense of Self, which lives in the Father. And in this inner divorce, we find the cause of much of the outer divorce that takes place in this world. An individual, separated within, will discover that outside separation occurs. One day he gets up and leaves or she gets up and leaves, and they wonder why. And if you look inside, you'll find that inside themselves they are separated, and the inner separation externalizes as the outer separation. Always, when there is a One inside, you find that Oneness is forever.

You can tell when you have been One'd within. Then you are complete, and you understand the meaning of the Master's words to the disciples, "We shall make my mother male." We find that the elder son is the male. The younger son is the female. These are the two aspects of an individual, the masculine and the feminine. As you come into matter, you're in the feminine, the negative. And always, there is this urge of the negative to find the positive, of the feminine to find the masculine. There is this great driving urge, like gravity, of the two to become one. But the unawareness of what that *is*, makes us two become one in many different ways than the purpose behind the outer activity of physical oneness.

It is the urge to unite within yourself the male and the female, the positive and the negative, the cause and the effect. The two that must become one are within our own Being, and when this is done we are fulfilled. You can never do it in two human beings. Each must unite the masculine and the feminine within that one individual. The positive and the negative must become one. The elder brother and the younger brother must become one within you, within me, within her, within him. Then we are whole Being. Then we can see that one, like Jesus, who has become One, no longer seeks outside of his person for another one.

We find Eve coming out of Adam's rib. This is the symbolic way of telling us that the one has now, in the human sense of things, become two. This is the division of the elder brother and the younger brother. And Eve must go back into Adam's rib and become one within each of us. You find that in a passage which I didn't explain in the Revelations. When Jesus returns as the Christ, meeting his disciples in the heavens, it is said that he is girded about the loins and the paps with a golden girdle. And this is the statement that he has become both male and female, One'd.

It is this necessity for wholeness of the male and female element of each individual which causes many of the unusual circumstances we see in our outer world. The unawareness of it makes us condemn. The unawareness of it makes us not even know that it must happen within ourself, that the two—the inner and the outer, the positive and the negative, the cause and the effect, the higher and the lower, the invisible and the visible, the infinite and the finite—ultimately in us become One, and we are married to the Lamb. Then I am, and yet before all this occurred, I am. Before Abraham was, I am. But finally, the acceptance, the realization, the dissolution of the false personality which does not know that I am. And Mary is made male, meaning whole, complete, one within oneself; not depending on an outer, second self.

When two outer selves become complete within themselves, you do not find divorce for the simple reason that they are already united in the Spirit. Always in our outer self, which is never complete, mingling with other outer selves which are not complete, we find everything out of focus. Our environment then controls us. We have no weapons against it except human ones. We're meeting everything on the level of effect. We're not living in the cause. And so we're in the forms that have no content, shell among shell. This is the level of exoteric religion. The complete human experience is the unawareness of this mystical marriage. These are fragments of ourselves trying to find fulfillment where it cannot be discovered.

Now then, your dependence ceases to be on someone else, because no other person can unite the fullness of your Being for you. It may seem so, but that is when we discover what the prodigal discovered, that he had followed a mirage. He had wasted his Substance by turning away from it unknowingly. Living, then, in cause is the mystical Way. Now, united to the inner, wedded to the inner Self, we find that is the method whereby the will of the Father functions in us, and then the Father, through our inner Self, manifests in what we call the outer self, showing forth not the human image as others see it, but showing forth that Divine Image as exemplified by he who was called Christ Jesus.

The Divine Image shows forth, and though it may be wheat, and though others may appear the same, they are the tares, and you cannot tell the difference between the wheat and the tares. One is shining forth the Divine Image, the other the human image, and they look alike until the judgment, until harvest time, until you discover the Divine Image never stops at the grave.

We are learning how to be that Divine Image by the inner wedding, the Oneness which identifies as Spirit, and instead of a prodigal trying to find the inner Self, we have probably come now to the place where we are the inner Self calling in the prodigal. And I would like you to make that turning today, so that we are not the human trying to become immortal. We are the Immortal convincing the mortal he has no real existence. You will discover this method is the way you are true to Self. The other method is the mirage. The mortal can never become immortal. The mortal can never find Reality.

Reality is a now. Immortality is a now. We do not stand in the unreal trying to find the Real. We stand in the Real rejecting the unreality. And so your work is I, Spirit. And now how do I live that way? How do I function, think, work, show forth my complete experience as the Divine Spirit? How do I walk in Him? To say that I'm going to walk in this world and find heaven is ridiculous. It cannot be done. You cannot identify as Spirit and walk in the world. Spirit lives in heaven, and until you're willing to live in heaven, you cannot identify as Spirit. If you are Spirit, heaven is your home, and heaven is where you are. And, therefore, you must accept that all that is in heaven is perfect. All that is in heaven is under spiritual law. All that is in heaven is the actual God Life living Itself.

If you are not in that God Life experiencing Self, then you are the prodigal. If you are in that God Life experiencing Self, then everything pertaining to the prodigal cannot be true and cannot be accepted. I, Spirit, must now move and have my Being in the Spirit of Being everywhere. You cannot have a mortal neighbor and call yourself Spirit. You cannot have any problems in your Life and call yourself Spirit. You cannot have a physical form and call yourself Spirit, nor can you have a physical form and be free of the karma of physical form. Either the ego has finally left the concept of flesh and has journeyed through incarnations to the point where you see the illusion of that ego, or you still live in it, and for you the parable of the prodigal is not McGuffey's Reader. It's still a fact of mortal existence. You're either out of it or in it.

This world opens up at a place and makes you visible as a physical self. The world calls it your birth. It isn't. It's the invisible world made visible where you stand. Around you is the garment of a universe, and that is your self, but that is your mortal self. The mortal universe around your mortal flesh is your mortal self, and as you come out of that belief, accepting your spiritual Self, then around you is the spiritual Universe, and *that* is your Self—all of it. No part of It is not You, and your fidelity to that spiritual Universe is the opposite of being a prodigal.

And that's how you finally take your plane up into the air. All those instrument panels of thought are no more. Spirit lives Itself where there is no prodigal. Spirit lives Itself where there is no second self. You are reaching so far back into Self that all there is is Self to live Itself, and you are learning to trust the Infinite Invisible to be Its own perfect Self everywhere that you are concerned.

The plane goes up in the air without you touching any of the material instruments around you. Spirit has dominion over air, over land, over sea. Why? Spirit is the cause, and the cause is the only power. And you learn to live in spiritual Identity, which is cause, and you never have to be concerned about effect. You never have to feed the swine. You never have to go to an external being to give you sustenance. Spirit lives Itself in your spiritual Identification. Your plane is your Universe. It is always flying well. It is always moving through Itself. You are always letting It control Itself. You are no longer in and under the dominion of your environment, for your environment is God's Self.

The parable of The Prodigal has another meaning. It is not only a parable to teach the literal mind of man as well as those who are ready to go higher. There are sides of the parable that teach the outer of you and the inner of you, and the side that teaches the inner of you is teaching the elder son within you, teaching the elder son within you that it must show forth the deeds of Spirit in order to be a worthy son. It is teaching the elder son within you fidelity, sincerity, trusting the omnipresent perfection of the Father in spite of what may appear out there.

There are not two prodigals, one within and one without. There is only One realized Son, and the male and the female of you are now combined in this into one Being. The form no longer fools you by its appearance. We now have God the Father, and God the Son, and the Holy Ghost. Joel gives us a perfect way to understand that. He says take the figure one, the number one, and see that first behind the visible number one there is an Invisible; that's God the Father. And now see the visible number one, and that's God the Son. And now see that that visible number One, God the Son, is maintained by the Father's invisible activity, which is the Holy Ghost.

Between the Son and the Father is the Holy Ghost maintaining the Son, and we who accept I am Spirit, we learn that the Holy Ghost is maintaining my appearance as Spirit. I seek no outer. I and the Father are One through the Holy Ghost. And, therefore, I *am* the Holy Ghost. I *am* the Father. Thou seest Me, thou seest the Father. I am no longer a prodigal wandering in the far country of mortality wasting my Divine Substance by ignorance of It, by infidelity to It, by depending on outer circumstances, by letting the environment control me. I *am* my environment. And the dominion given in Genesis is realized, accepted, and lived in, only because I, Spirit, is accepted with total fidelity. This is the preparation for transition.

Our complete experience on the earth in this earth period is to attain this Oneness of Consciousness. We are really here to establish what might be called the fifth Kingdom, to move into the sixth, where only the will of the Father is done, as a preliminary to the total Christing and the living in eternal Life. When the Master said this is a straight path, he meant that straight—God the Father, the Holy Ghost, and the Son, One—and wherever you are seen visibly, you must be all three in One appearing.

As you reach back further into loss of human selfhood, you find the everlasting arms. You find a new level of Truth, a new order of Life. You find a Life that is little suspected by the human mind. You find how small human life really is. You find how magnificent is the Infinite Invisible awaiting our experience. God ceases to be a noun. The words "love" and "life" cease to be nouns. We move into the new order of experience. We are no longer metaphysicians.

We live the God experience. We live Life. We find the meaning of a living God, and the word "God" exchanges Itself into something else. It is no longer a word. It is no longer a mental concept, a mortal idea. God begins to be Life living Itself fully, joyously, rejoicingly, exultantly because It is without opposite. It is the realm of pure perfection in all things. Eternity becomes Reality. Infinity becomes the playground. We move into a different place, a different time, a different space. We're out of the illusion life. We're into Reality.

Now, that experience tasted, lived in, opens us up to the meaning of the real bread of Life. We see why we have come so far. The new Heaven and the new Earth is an experience that you enter long before you make your transition. It becomes a now Reality. The Soul of you yearns to move only in It. And the more you are able to live out of this inner, elder brother instead of the outer self, the more you know your eternal Life has passed the stage of words and hopes and plans—that you're really living It. It is your Being now. It is your living experience day by day. You find that Reality has a new ring to it. You find the meaning of "Put up thy sword." You find there's nothing to defend against except an illusion. These are some of the things that tell you the prodigal is dead and crucified.

[Silence]

We set, then, a goal to live in the cause of things rather than in the effects, and this becomes quite a discipline, quite a challenge to live in Cause because that's the only way to control environment. Cause is invisible, spiritual Substance, so whatever comes to you must be seen through to its original Substance. There must be a conscious awareness that the Substance is always present, functioning, being Itself, maintaining its perfect Substance right there as invisible, perfect manifestation. And though the appearance may be different and is, the Cause is there, and the

Cause being perfect, its form must be perfect. And by living in this knowledge of the presence of Cause, you're living in the knowledge of the presence of perfect manifestation. You're weaving your garment of one piece, your wedding garment.

The moment you move out of Cause, you're in karmic law. Spiritual Cause, and this keeps you right on your toes, spiritually alert, watching. Your lamps are always trimmed this way. You'll find that you're taking control over your environment. It externalizes to the level of your awareness of spiritual Cause. Scripture has reached us to the point that we are put in the understanding that when we are defending ourselves against anything, we are living in the effect, whereas when we are living in the cause, that effect needs no defense anymore. You can do it with your eyes shut or open.

Living in Spirit means living in Cause and beholding the added things which follow. You move into a room, aware of spiritual Cause being present. Everything you see outside, you approach from the level of spiritual Cause. Everything that you take into yourself, you take in from the level of spiritual Cause, so that the traffic going out of you is Spirit; the traffic coming into you is Spirit. You're living in the conscious awareness of Spirit as the only Presence. Only God is there, and only God is here, and so there's nothing to be improved or corrected, except to be revealed. You do not tame the tempest. You reveal *I* present.

Now, the reason we're getting to the point of living in *I am that Spirit* is it's the only way that you're not in duality. It's the only way you're not in effect. It's the only way you're not in karma, the only way you're not a second self. You're going to have to practice that in this coming half until instead of healing anybody, instead of improving anybody, instead of improving any situation that you have, you are standing in the high ground of spiritual Identity knowing that is Cause, infinite Cause, which can only cause infinite, perfect effect. And there's nothing more for you to do but trustingly, patiently abide in that knowledge, and then you're in the one without opposite, and you will not experience the opposite.

What is not in your consciousness will not externalize, and if opposites are in your outer world, they will be dissolved when your consciousness has risen above the consciousness of the opposites to I, Spirit. It gets narrower and narrower and narrower to the point of *nothing* before it widens out and becomes the mustard tree with branches in which the birds, the divine thoughts, the divine impulses come to bring you Divine Bread. The little seed grows.

Let's pause a moment before we proceed.

∞∞∞∞∞∞∞ END OF SIDE ONE ∞∞∞∞∞∞∞

I in the midst of you am He who spoke through what the world called Jesus. It is always I, and when I speak through you, then I speak words of authority that you can trust. If the words that you hear are not the words of I in the midst of you, there is no authority, and you will be following false prophets. And so it's important now in this parable, as we review it, to see that it is the Word of I in the midst of you to both the elder brother within you and the younger brother who has gone out into a world of flesh.

A certain man had two sons. These two components are introduced to you at the beginning of the parable, your inner and your outer, and the outer must become aware that there is an inner. The younger of them, meaning the outer, said to the Father, "Father, give me the portion of goods that falleth to me." And he divided them unto his living. The division, the belief that you have a portion of anything, is shown here to be untrue. You cannot have a portion. The moment you want a portion, you are the younger brother. The moment you are willing to settle for less than the infinite Substance of God, you are the younger brother. This is the human mind forming its finite judgments that certain things belong to me. This is the beginning of the prodigal experience.

Now let us, therefore, know that if we are to erase the errors that are made evident to us here by I within ourselves, I in you is saying, "Do not divide my garment. All that I have is thine. You cannot have less than all. I cannot divide my Self. You cannot have a portion of My Love, a portion of My Truth. You cannot have a portion of Identity. You cannot walk the earth as a fragment. Your name is Identity, Spirit." The All-ness of God can never be less than infinite where you appear. Never can you make infinite God finite by saying, "I have a portion that belongs to me." You are going into second selfhood. I am that Infinite Spirit, and the moment I am willing to be less, I've fallen into the trap of humanhood. I'm no longer a disciple of the Christ.

This is the first mistake, then, the division of the mind, which says, "I'm going out into something finite." It is the rejection of infinite Reality. "And not many days after the younger son gathered all together, and took his journey into a far country,"—And that is where we are, the sense of humanhood. The complete human race, then, is this prodigal living in a sense of humanhood. God, being Spirit, being All, all that is not that Spirit is the prodigal. All that believes itself to be something other than the Spirit of God is the prodigal, living in a far country. There are about 86 of these far countries scattered around the hemispheres.—"and there wasted his substance with riotous living." We've all done that. We know all about it, and in our ignorance of the infinite Self that we all are, we continue to do that. Wherever we have a finite belief, we are wasting our Substance. "And when he had spent all, there arose a mighty famine in that land; and he began to be in want." Now this famine, then, is our spiritual barrenness. Suddenly it's revealed. We're barren spiritually. That's why there's a famine. And so we can look all over the world where there is a physical famine, and what is our answer? Prodigal existence, unawareness of Self, barren within, and therefore, barren without. And so the Bible tells us, "[I've] never seen a righteous [man] . . . begging bread." When you're spiritually righteous, that is your bread, and the absence of food or the appearance of famine is the absence of spiritual content.

It cannot make itself visible because it isn't accepted as being present. There's no Consciousness to manifest it. There is no famine in Heaven. There is no famine in Spirit, and therefore, a famine is unreal, though it is real to a prodigal, a prodigal from Spirit. You cannot be a prodigal *from* Spirit if you *are* Spirit. And therefore, the acceptance of spiritual Identity is the end of the prodigal, and the shadow of turning is over.

"And he went and joined himself to a citizen of that country;"— This is the need now for external help. No longer fed from within, we have to be fed from without—"and he sent him into his fields to feed swine." So often you read in Joel's books that in the material world we have to toil for a living, and we often scratch our heads and say, "Toil for a living. Well, what else would you do?" And he's giving us the great secret of Grace. Spirit doesn't toil for a living. The flowers do not spin, but they are fed. The birds do not store in barns, but they have. All of this part of the inner teaching that when you have accepted Substance to be You, there's nothing to store. It's forever flowing.

That word "Substance" becomes more important than the added forms. With the Substance, you'll have the forms. Having only the forms, you will not have the Substance. You'll have the oranges without the tree. Substance is the tree. In the material sense of life, we waste our Substance. And so we re-Identify here all the way through, eliminating all the prodigal ideas of living in form, living in matter, living on *my* wits. I must not remain unplugged from spiritual Identity. That's where you plug in.

I, Spirit is where you keep standing in the face of every appearance and let Substance reveal Itself. Let Substance not improve the cripple, but reveal the perfection of Being where cripple appears. Let Substance not sell the house, but reveal that there is no buyer or seller other than I, Substance. Let Substance show that there is no son who has taken up narcotics. There is only I, Substance. Let Substance show there's no divorce in this family. There is only I, Substance. *Always*, in the acceptance of Substance,

Substance will reveal Itself in its infinite perfection wherever a material need appears.

I, Substance, Spirit, not just here, not just there. I, Infinite Substance is not a prodigal. We hammer that into ourselves until every prodigal, every errant thought, every concept, every human sense of belief is revealed as a shadow, and the sunshine of I, Substance reveals there are no shadows present. Always *I*, Substance is the way you put up your sword.

"And he would fain have filled his belly with the husks that the swine did eat:"—So great was his famine; so empty was the world. But who are we speaking about, a prodigal in the Bible? We're speaking about my mortal life. What is it going to get for us? You know what it gets: a mirage of success, a mirage of this and a mirage of that without Substance. Why? Because it's perishable. Mortally, you can succeed at nothing that is *imperishable*. Mortally, your complete attainments are perishable, and that is the husk. It looks so great until you grab it and hold it and find it's gone. The illusion of mortality without Substance becomes a husk, and we are completely famished within because we're without our Substance.

And so this is about me, my mortal self and how foolish it's been, how blind. How willing to accept the unreal while the invisible Reality of Being is saying, "Come, be my Infinite Son. Live in that which is imperishable. Live in that which is eternal now, here." "And when he came to himself,"—That's when the mortal in you is recognized as the mortal in you, and you see through the myth of mortality, the illusion of a mind that is not your own, doing its thinking through you as you, making you believe that you're doing the thinking. You find how cosmic mortal mind through you is thinking, and all these thoughts that have been coming through were not your own, were not even your thought. You were not thinking at all.

You are merely receiving the thoughts of the world mind and saying, "I think. I think I hurt. I think I lack. I think I want. I think I need." And these things weren't true at all. There was a ventriloquist within you saying, "I think, I need, I want." And that ventriloquist was the world mind, posing as the individual mind and fooling every one of us. The Mind of God is too pure to behold the iniquities that the ventriloquist beholds. And so the double-minded man is uncovered here. He comes to Himself. Himself is the one Mind, the Divine Mind, the knowledge of Reality. Suddenly it's clear, "I've been off in a far country called mortality." But there is no such place.

God is immortal, and God is all. I've been wandering in a dream of nothingness, calling it real. Oh, it had so many pleasurable things in it and so many sad things, and neither the good nor the bad were real. All that was present all the time was the perfect Reality of God, and just think if I had stood still to enjoy that perfect Reality how I would have really enjoyed the Truth of Being, the fullness of Being. I would have known the imperishable. But it's not too late. I still can know the imperishable because that is why I'm on the earth: To discover the difference between Heaven and earth, between Reality and concept. To see that earth has no Reality. It is nothing but a mortal concept about the presence of Heaven.

Heaven Is. Earth is the concept we entertain about the Isness of Heaven, and they're both in the same place. He is coming to Himself. Something within himself is turning around. He is beginning to know and glimpse there is a Reality that is unseen by the senses of the prodigal. All of this is taking place in each of us to the degree that we have felt the Light. At this point, he is feeling the Light. He is beginning to know that Spirit is his name.

I'd like to suggest an assignment, which I think can be very useful. It begins with I, *Spirit*, and then you write down, not what you're thinking, but what Spirit tells you to write down. You just take a sheet of paper and a pen, and you sit there and you say, "I, *Spirit*," and then you turn within to that Spirit and say, "Spirit, now tell me about Yourself. Tell me what I am." And then Spirit says, "I am not mortal," or Spirit says, "I am the Holy Son of Israel." Spirit says, "I never know pain. I never know sickness. I know nothing about mortality." And you write these down as Spirit talks to you, and you're not in a hurry.

It might take you 20, 30 minutes, and then it might take you 20, 30 minutes again at another time. And you might do it for an hour or two or three until Spirit tells you what I am, and you find that Spirit, which is telling you what I am, is telling you what You are, for "Spirit" is your name, and "I am" is your name, and that is who You are. The very things you are writing as told you by Spirit is what You are, and to that You must learn to be true. "I can never know sickness." Well then, that's the Truth of your Being. Now who is going to know the sickness? Only a false sense of You. *I* can never know sickness.

And you'll find you have found your Teacher. Your Self is your Teacher, and your Self teaches the outer prodigal how to come home. And then you see sickness, but now there's a new You there which says, "Uh-uh. I can never know sickness." Where did it go? And why did it go? You're amazed to find that the Mind which refuses sickness dissolves it. And until you've had that experience, you can't believe it. Why, it was just there a minute ago, but it isn't now. And we see the double mind, the prodigal mind which sees it and experiences it, and the real Mind which doesn't see it and doesn't experience it. And you'll find they're right both in the same place, one a shadow of the other.

You live in one or the other, and as you keep entrenching yourself in letting Spirit teach you from within, and then accepting those words as the very Substance of Being, this is the oil you work with. You're living by Revelation. You're living by the elder brother within, and he's being wedded to the outer brother. It's happening. You're coming to your Self. You're turning. "And when he came to himself, he said, How many hired servants of my father's have bread enough and to spare, and I perish with hunger!" The word "servant" is coming in here. The brother has hired servants, and he's beginning to want to be a servant. I am beginning as a prodigal to want to serve. I want to serve someone. I want to serve the Spirit.

It's no longer a me running out to serve me, but to serve the Spirit. And so you find service, the willingness to serve whatever Identity tells you to do, is the sign of a turning. You are yielding the human ego, the human desire for possession, for attention, for achievement. You're learning that if I want as a human to do this, and he wants as a human to do that, and the other wants to do, there's going to be conflicts. But now the elder brother and the younger brother are going to become in one purpose. There will not be the conflict within ourselves, the two orders of life, the inner knowing the Father and the outer not knowing the Father. The separation is being annealed, and so I'm willing to serve the Inner. And this willingness to serve the Inner brings you on the way home.

All through the teaching, you'll find the Master telling if you love me, serve my sheep, feed my sheep, love my sheep: "[If you love me], feed my sheep." Serve your fellow man. How? By walking among your fellow man as a spiritual Being and recognizing your fellow man as a spiritual Being, and recognizing that that spiritual Being that he is, and this that I am, is my one spiritual Self. The service is spreading the Light of Being in Consciousness. The prodigal doesn't do that. He's out for himself, his little finite ego.

The turning is the knowledge that I am going to shed my Light, let it shine, walk among the sinners, walk among the publicans, walk among the winebibbers, walk among the outcasts. Let the Pharisees rile at you. Your function is to be the Light, see the Light, speak the Light. Not to see evil, not to speak evil, not to hear evil. But let your Light so shine that those who are prodigal in their consciousness receive of the Light within their own Being through your recognition of It. So we're turning. We're learning the meaning of spiritual service, which means that I, the outer self, serve my inner Self. That's the beginning of service. Before I can serve my neighbor, I have to learn to let my outer serve my Inner, for my Inner goes to the Father, and the Will comes through the Inner to the outer. The obedience to let the outer serve the Inner is your turning.

[Now] "I will arise and go to my father,"—Now you're ready. The Inner is ready to serve as the focus of your Being because the outer is yielding to It. So you go to your Father now. You see, the Inner goes to the Father. Until the outer will serve the Inner, it cannot arise and go to the Father. You're finding the divine sequence of Being.—"and [I] will say unto him, Father, I have sinned against heaven, and before thee, And am no more worthy to be called thy son: make me as one of thy hired servants."

This is surrender of self, isn't it? Willingness to be obedient unto the Father alone. There's a spiritual Sonship accepted as I am the Spirit of God, having no will of my own, but letting the Spirit Itself live me. This is the acceptance of Identity with trust and with confidence that all that the Father doeth is perfect, regardless of every visible circumstance. All mental concept is being laid aside. No second guessing, no doubts, no uncertainty. It's a total trust in the perfection of the Omnipresence of God. "And he arose, and came to his Father. But when he was yet a great way off, his Father saw him, and had compassion, and ran, and fell on his neck, and kissed him." "When he was yet a great way off"—and so you see, right where you are as you turn, as you accept, behold, there is the Father. I can never leave you. Thou art ever with me. The moment the outer turns, the Inner is there. The Inner never went anywhere. The Self has never gone away. You're always the Self. Only the stray personality thinks that the Self is somewhere else, but it's always there. You are always the Self. In the moment the stray personality finds that and arises, it finds Self right there, and forgiveness is instantaneous.

The Self does not condemn your outer personality. The Self is God, too pure to behold iniquity. The Self is the Father within. And so there is always an instantaneous forgiveness when you are ready to let the stray personality surrender, wherever you are. You don't have to find a nearby church. You don't have to find your Bible. You don't have to wait till the right time or place. Wherever you are, whenever the stray personality says, "I surrender, and I'm willing to serve the Spirit," that is when the Father embraces you, kisses you, falls on your neck and says, "Welcome home." That is when the prodigal is no more.

And this goes on until the elder brother complains. We must learn from that, that when the Father says, "Son, thou art ever with me, and all that I have is thine," that even the complaining elder brother, that Inner Self of you is not sufficient. It must now go through into the manifest world and make Itself visible by deeds. It must marry the outer brother. They must be one, so that Inner and outer are the one expression of the Divine Father, like the inner and the outer of the tumbler in Joel's story of the tumbler. Is it glass on the outer any different than on the inner? He was teaching us that the brothers must be married. The two, the outer and Inner self, must be one Self. This is the preparation. This One Self is the mystical marriage, that wedding. And this prepares you to sit on the right hand of the throne of the Father.

Now, all spiritual law functions in that One. There is no Grace until that One has been attained. There's a place here in Ephesians where Paul has some of this. Ephesians two, twelfth verse goes on like this: "Then at that time ye were without Christ, being aliens from the commonwealth of Israel, and strangers from the covenants of promise, having no hope, and without God in the world:". You see, the prodigal doesn't have God in the world. He says, "I love God, I worship God," but he's turning away from God within himself, which is his Identity. And so his deeds are without the divine experience, divine safety, divine protection, divine manifestation, and while he's professing God with his mouth, his very life is saying that he is separate from God. You can go through all kinds of religious experience worshipping God, and if you have not accepted I, the Spirit of my Being, *is* God, there's no God in the world. It seems rather sad, doesn't it, that we can have such real dedication on the part of so many millions, and yet God is not in the world because God is not in the prodigal, who is not in spiritual Identity.

And God is not in the prodigal for one simple reason. The prodigal is an image in the mind. There is no such being, never having been created by the Father. "But now in Christ Jesus, ye who sometimes were far off [like the prodigal, far off] are made nigh by the blood of Christ." The acceptance of spiritual Identity is the blood of Christ. "For he is our peace, who hath made both one"—the Inner and the outer, One. This is the Christing. And when the both are made One, we are told that you feel closer to God than you do to your own mother. You feel an ineffable peace, a rest, a warmth. You know that the Infinite is your home. You know your name. You know your infinite Self. You know your eternal Life. You realize there is only the Father, and the Father and I are One.

Now, the very experience that is recounted in the Prodigal Son becomes your living experience. It ceases to be a parable. You can feel that wayward self within being wedded to the true Self, dissolved out of its own false sense of existence, and you find that the parable was not a parable at all. It was nothing more than the narrative of an inner experience that each of us is going through, as Paul shows us here, when the two become one. "[And] Having abolished in his flesh the enmity, [which is the conflict between inner and outer] even the law of commandments contained in ordinances; for to make in himself of twain [one, to make of two One] one new man, so making peace;"—and this is what we're going through, making of twain one new Man to find that peace which passeth human understanding. Paul had well experienced the prodigal experience.

In many ways the deeper you are able to read these parables into your consciousness, the more you'll discover that they are really outer verbal expressions of deep inner experience. You can talk about leaven and three degrees of it, but you have to go through mind, body and Soul before that becomes experience. You can talk about wheat and tares as a parable, but you can go through the experience of the tares of human experience being replaced by the pure wheat of divine illumination. You'll find every parable is cut right out of your Being to lead you right back into Self, until you have had the full experience of that parable, and then, having lived through it, for you it is no longer parable. It is the pathway of a disciple.

Now when you take your lesson to heart, I, Spirit, you are removing the twain, the two, and you are making the outer listen to the Inner and then say, "Let me be your hired servant." You are taking the outer out of the husks of the material way of life and trusting the Inner to yield to it the full, glorious purpose of God in every movement. You'll be surprised with the things that you'll write down, and when you write them down, remember these are the commandments given to you by your own Soul. They're not little pieces of paper with words. They are the living oil of the Soul. If you accept it in that Spirit, they will lead you, and if you're not ready for that, you'll find the words will not come. The words will only come from the within to one who invites them by reverent Silence. I come where I am invited by your love, by your peace, by your Inner trust. I come where there is one who says, "I am poor in Spirit. Make me pure at heart." I come to the child of God who is faithful, obedient, true. There *I* dwell.

And when that is your Way, there I am. And so we prepare the Way for I to direct us. And in this communion between the Inner and outer, union is attained, union through communion. The Infinite becomes your living home, and you draw from It the complete fullness of Its storehouse with no need of an outer citizen. But rather, you are like Paul, supporting all of the seven churches. You are giving of your Light to those around you in spiritual recognition, and that Light is coming from the Inner of you to the outer. You have turned. You have repented. This is regeneration. This is transformation. This is the building of the invisible Body of the Soul. Truly, that is the Body which you must come to realize, and there is no other way than the way of discipleship to the Inner-ness of your own Being.

Now, the Father thought that the study of The Prodigal Son, at our level, would be important to us. You'll find that its importance goes beyond your capacity to make it a Way. You'll find that it is something that you can use when others come to you. It seems to be a universal language that everybody knows. It is a point of meeting, a common knowledge that we can share. But you can take those who come to you with their knowledge of it and lift them gently to understand more of the prodigal, more of the purpose behind it. To show them that the parable is a parable in many, many ways, and that many levels of the parable are teaching many levels of themselves.

This way you are given the weapons to educate spiritually those who are trying to move out of materialism, out of mentalism into the discipleship, and the Father gives us this unprovocative way of entering into their household. It doesn't frighten anyone. It's something they're familiar with. And as you point it out to them, you'll discover the subtle way in which the Spirit extends its influence over the mind of man. To all persons the parables will have different meanings, and two years from now you will go back to this very same parable and discover things you never even knew, just because new eyes will look out at them.

The younger son is being eliminated from this earth. The second book of Genesis is being swallowed up by the first, and in your Consciousness and mine, as this happens, we are eating of the Flesh of the Christ. I, Spirit am Infinite. I, Spirit, am not finite. I, Spirit, am perfect. I, Spirit, am not imperfect. Do you love Me? "Feed my sheep." Feed them My Truth with your heart, not your mind. The more you have of the inner Spirit, the more compassionate you will find yourself. There will be the remembrance of the days when *you* needed compassion. These are the measuring sticks to tell you whether or not you are moving closer to the experience of your Divine Selfhood or still lingering in the remnants of humanhood.

Another way to find where you really are is to take all of the parables in the Bible about Heaven: "The Kingdom of Heaven is like unto. . . ." Well, if it's like unto this, are you going through that experience or not? Because if you're not, you're not in the Kingdom of Heaven. And so we find that I really have gone before this mortal self, for I did say, "The Kingdom of Heaven is like unto. . . ." I have placed before you a feast of Truth. All you need do is come, sit at the table to sup. I have told you what the Kingdom of Heaven is like unto. It is in your Bible. It is placed there by I, and if you want to know what it's like to be sure that your Inner experience is true, you'll find it out here in every parable that I in the midst of you have placed before you.

So we might look at more of those: "The Kingdom of Heaven is like unto. . . ." The whole chapter of Matthew 13 is full of them. We can use them as measuring sticks to see if I am in that level where the Kingdom of Heaven is my experience, and our Bible is beginning to be food and Substance, living experience instead of words in a book. We are in the living experience of the Truth of Being, and everything that we read must be digested into experience.

Your God is your Being, and your God is a living God. To experience God is to live in the Kingdom of Heaven here and now, consciously. I, Spirit, can only live in the Kingdom of Heaven. Where else can I, Spirit, live? And when the Inner tells you that, you know where you are, and you know that you must be true to that in every possible way. I, Spirit, move in the Kingdom of Heaven. Yes, those appear to be winebibbers to other people and outcasts to others, but I, Spirit, recognize I, Spirit. There are no winebibbers in Heaven. There are no outcasts in Heaven. *This* is Heaven. Everywhere is Heaven. And what is not in Heaven is not here. It is an appearance. Whatever is not in the Kingdom of Heaven is not here.

If your name is I, Spirit, to this you must be true. This is part of our assignment. To be true to I, Spirit, omnipresent is to accept Heaven here, now, and judge not by any appearance. We must make this an experience and not a word teaching. The little child is turning, and the little child will grow, and the little child will return from Egypt. But while we are little children, let us be willing to be children in Heaven, not on earth, for we have been through the earth experience.

It is now time for the involution, the experience as children in Heaven on earth, always knowing the Father is not afar off, but here where I stand is my Father. The still small Voice that Elija heard, that you hear, that I hear is ever present as the guide, the armor, the living Word, the food, the Substance of Being. I, the still small Voice, I am your Substance, and I go before you. Follow Me.

When you have finished your assignment, you'll discover you're writing with invisible ink, with spiritual ink. You're receiving the blood of Christ, and you're putting it on paper, and this is a living ordinance of God. Treasure it. It is the Infinite teaching, that which is learning It is Infinite, the Way to Christ.

Thanks very much. I want to tell you what a privilege it really is to share these discoveries of truth together. There's no words to describe it. Thanks very much.

# CLASS 16

# OIL FROM YOUR SOUL CENTER

*Herb:* Good afternoon, everybody.

We're striving now in this work for something slightly different than a knowledge of Truth. Everything we're doing now is geared to the experience of the presence of God, which is the source of all Truth that we can ever know. Now, if you have been slow in your progress, if you find that you're still in a state of worry at times or fear or bad health, if there are problems, be sure this is normal. There's no one so unusual that he or she is without them, and all of us become impatient. This is all very normal.

But now, Spirit plays a trick on us. It says, "Yes, you've gone through many things in your pathway to Truth, and they were necessary." And you even come to a place where you think you know Truth, and then Spirit says to us, "The only reason you had to get to the place where you think you know Truth is so you could just begin to glimpse what God already knows. There is nothing you have learned on the way, not one single stitch, that God does not already know." And therefore, as you begin to feel that entrance into the third degree, you discover that you're now told to know no truth whatsoever. God already knows It. What's the point of you duplicating God?

Are you a different self than God? Are you unwilling to rest back and say, "Father, do you know?" And so the real dying to self begins at a point where you can say to yourself, "I have nothing. I am nothing." And this will not come to an individual who has not been touched by the Presence in some way so that the individual feels the vision, the courage, the ultimate possibility is only there when the Spirit of God Itself is accepted as the Presence, the Life, and the Identity of your own Being. You cannot want to know Truth with your mind and still accept spiritual Identity, for one belies the other.

Now, in our way to discovering our own inadequacies, one of our major problems has been that we have relied upon human wisdom. There was always my finger in the pie, and in so doing we had used the mind not as an instrument to receive the Father, but as a thinking, creative, even worrying mind; a mind that was going to find solutions. And we discover that trap, that mind which wants to find solutions is not your mind.

Now every one of us who comes to the point where we're willing to give up our mental knowledge of truth receives what may be called an anointing. That anointing is shown to us in the Bible in many unusual ways, and it contains in itself probably one of the greatest secrets of illumination. You see it in a scene where a woman, not identified in Matthew, a sinner, comes and pours this oil over the Master from an alabaster vase. And you see it again in John where this next pouring of oil from an alabaster vase is from a different woman perhaps; one who now is identified as Mary.

We find Judas objecting because this is expensive oil, but the Master says, "No, the poor you always have with you, but I will not always be with you." We find in this a secret teaching, a teaching that perhaps goes way back to Zechariah in the Old Testament. In fact, it's interwoven throughout the Old Testament wherever you find the name of oil spoken insome subtle way, like an olive tree, the olive tree symbolizing olive oil, and oil symbolizing this secret.

We're going to look at Zechariah. We see that he, ordained by the Spirit, is aware that within the invisible lies the Self, which is

## Class 16: Oil From Your Soul Center

the Self of all men, and to convey this to us, he uses the symbols which later appeared in Revelation:

". . . the angel [who] talked with me came again, and waked me, as a man that is wakened out of his sleep . . ."

This is Zechariah, fourth chapter. The complete fourth chapter is the secret of the Oil. ". . . [he] said unto me, What seest thou? And I said, I have looked, and behold a candlestick all *of* gold, with a bowl upon the top of it, and his seven lamps thereon, and seven pipes to the seven lamps, which *are* upon the top thereof:

And two olive trees by it, one upon the right *side* of the bowl, and the other upon the left *side* thereof. So I answered and spake to the angel that talked with me, saying, What *are* these, my lord? Then the angel that talked with me answered and said unto me: Knowest thou not what these be? And I said, No, my lord.

Then he answered and spake unto me, saying, "This is the word of the Lord unto Zerubbabel," saying, "Not by might, nor by power, but by my spirit, saith the LORD of hosts."

Not might, not power, but by My Spirit. But what? What not by might? What not by power? What by my Spirit? And a further clue:

"And I answered again, and said unto him, What *be these* two olive branches which through the two golden pipes empty the golden *oil* out of themselves? And he answered me and said, Knowest thou not what these *be?* And I said, No, my lord. Then said he, These *are* the two anointed ones, that stand by the Lord of the whole earth."

". . . the two anointed ones that stand by the Lord of the whole earth."

And therein is our clue to what we are striving to do. Our subject is oil, the symbol of something else. Wherever you have found a problem, you have lacked that oil. Wherever some inner substance has come to dissolve the problem, it has been that oil. But hit or miss, getting it by random, by accident, has to be substituted now by knowing where the oil is, what it is, and how you open the Soul center to let it flow.

We see a flower. We know the oil of the flower becomes our perfumes, and we know one little tincture of it is powerful. Just think of a tincture of divine oil and what a tincture of divine oil received in consciousness does to release an individual from every pressing problem. Then go a step further and see that the oil, being spiritual Substance, is here presented as one of the deepest mystical secrets.

The oil is the spiritual Substance which forms the body of the Soul. All progress in the path to absolute illumination is for the purpose of attaining that spiritual Body, which is independent of the material world. And because this attainment is the destiny of every individual, regardless of the level of consciousness they entertain at the moment, only the highest initiates are even aware that divine Oil becomes their spiritual Body, their incorporeal Self attained and realized and lived in.

And so, in our first and second degrees we were more concerned with other things. In our first degree all we wanted to do is be a good human being. And after we got that far, we began to take the mind and open it up, letting it become an instrument for the Father, an instrument for the divine Mind. And always in these progressions, we discovered that we were being made more comfortable, happier, more harmonious with all those around us, and we were learning pet phrases, which we thought we could hide behind at times as a sort of an armor against the world. We could smile while other people suffered and say, "If they only knew the truth that I know. If I could only tell them." But now, now in your third degree, you come to a place where the Spirit demands more of you.

Whereas before you wanted to build your humanhood and you enjoyed the experience of opening the mind to the invisible, now you are told all that must go. That the Oil of the incorporeal body, that Oil which forms the Substance of your eternal body, can never flow into a human being. To be awake to Christ and dead to self becomes the way in which the Soul center opens to express the divine Oil, which takes us into the transitional experience.

And so our two olive branches, our two olive trees, which are the two witnesses of the Father on earth, become the sentinels which we must pass through in order to receive the Oil. And dying to self in order to become alive to Omnipresence becomes the single-minded dedication of all of our time and thought. Our whole heart and our whole Soul is bent in the direction of releasing that divine Oil, which makes the divine Body our living experience.

Now let's look at this woman who comes to anoint the Master. We find her in several places. We find her in Matthew in the twenty-sixth chapter.

"And it came to pass, when Jesus had finished all these sayings he said unto his disciples, Ye know that after two days is *the feast of* the passover and the Son of man is betrayed to be crucified.

Then assembled together the chief priests, and the scribes, and the elders of the people, unto the palace of the high priest, who was called Caiaphas, And consulted that they might take Jesus by subtilty and kill *him*. But they said, [no] Not on the feast *day,* lest there be an uproar among the people."

Now, he knew in two days there would be a passover and he would be betrayed to be crucified. We know now what they didn't know then, that he already had attained the Soul Body, and that's why he could speak so evenly about crucifixion.

"Now when Jesus was in Bethany, in the house of Simon the leper, There came unto him a woman having an alabaster box of very precious ointment, and poured it on his head, as he sat at *meat.*"

Now, alabaster, the whiteness, the box is actually the vase, and it's a symbol of the Soul. And so pouring this ointment over the Master, she was saying to him and to us, she was expressing outwardly her inner Consciousness. She was telling him she had come into the experience of the incorporeal Body of the Soul. Inasmuch as the woman in other parts is described as a sinner, we may assume this was the adulterous Mary, Mary of Magdala, for the moment.

"But when his disciples saw *it*, they had indignation, saying, To what purpose *is* this waste?"

His disciples said, "To what purpose is this waste?" They had no knowledge of the meaning of the alabaster vase and the oil she was pouring. But you see, she couldn't help herself. That which is your Consciousness must externalize, and having attained the inner Body, she showed it forth as the pouring of oil upon him. He, though, was the Christ. She was revealing that the Christ of her Being was pouring Oil within her; that she had gone through the first, second, and third degrees that we are going through. She had died to personal self. She was no longer a human being. She was not mortal. She walked in what appeared to be a form, but she was not in time and space.

Her life was lived external to her body. She knew the meaning of omnipresent Spirit. The disciples did not. They said, "Why all the waste? That cost 300 pence. We could be giving that money to the poor." You see, the disciples were not the highest in ordainment at that time. Lazarus was higher.

"For this ointment might have been sold for much, and given to the poor." When Jesus understood *it*, he said unto them, Why trouble ye the woman? for she hath wrought a good work upon me. For ye have the poor always with you; but me, ye have not always. For in that she hath poured this ointment on my body, she did *it* for my burial."

Having attained the Soul Body, she understood that he was in the Soul Body. She was aware he would walk through death. All of this secret conversation, unknown to the readers of the Bible, who merely see a woman pouring oil.

"Verily I say unto you, Wheresoever this Gospel shall be preached in the whole world, *there* shall also this, that this woman hath done, be told for a memorial of her."

Mary of Magdala was the second highest initiate, right under Mary, the mother of Jesus.

Now, the understanding of this changes when we go to the Gospel of John. This is the outer event. John, ever the symbolist, the esotericist, takes us even deeper. And you wonder if they are speaking about the identical incidents, because here it said, you know that passover will be in two days, and then we come to John in the twelfth chapter, and when we find it said this way:

"Then Jesus six days before the passover came to Bethany, where Lazarus was which had been dead, whom he raised from the dead." If you've wondered about Lazarus, what happened to him—well, here he is again. "There they made him a supper; and Martha served: but Lazarus was one of them that sat at the table with him." We have Jesus, the invisible Christ appearing as Jesus, and now we have the invisible Christ appearing as Lazarus, both having supper with Martha and Mary. "Then took Mary a pound of ointment of spikenard, very costly, and anointed the feet of Jesus, and wiped his feet with her hair: and the house was filled with the odor of the ointment. Then saith one of his disciples, Judas Iscariot, Simon's *son*, which should betray him, Why was not this ointment sold for three hundred pence, and given to the poor?"

Now we have the odor, the fragrance of the ointment introduced, and this is because in the Soul Body we are told there is a different fragrance. Some of you have noticed in deep meditation that you're aware of fragrance. You may be aware of your own body of the Soul.

Now, Mary, the sister of Lazarus, is identified as having the body of the Soul. We find here, through John's very significant purpose, an interesting revelation, not only about this body, but about the resurrection of Lazarus. You recall that he had been buried four days. And the purpose, or at least one of the purposes was to show that after three days the Soul does not leave the body. In other words, the body and the Soul are not conjoined. The Soul is completely independent of the body at all times.

But now we see that Lazarus represents something. This was not only the resurrection of the man called Lazarus. Lazarus was dead for four days, meaning he was d-e-a-d, dead, totally dead. And the point here that John wishes us to know is that you cannot awaken to Christ until you are totally dead to self. The four days represent the total human deadness of Lazarus, and unless we are prepared not to hold out a remnant of humanhood, that Soul Body which walks out of the tomb of mortality is not formed. And, strangely, that's only part of it, and that's why Mary had to pour the oil.

You see, Mary and Lazarus constitute the inner and the outer, the male and the female, the higher and the lower. And in each of us, Mary and Lazarus must be redeemed. The positive and the negative, the higher and the lower, the inner and the outer must be redeemed. Lazarus represents the elder son who stayed home. Mary represents the younger son who wasted his Substance going out into the far country. And they both represent the inner Self of Jesus, showing that the male and the female elements had been redeemed into Oneness. The Soul Body was completed, and at this point, where Mary, the sister of Lazarus, reveals that she, too, has become aware of and is living in her Soul Body, indicated by the fragrance of it and the oil. This is the preparation, of course, for the triumphal entry into Jerusalem, for it is the marriage of these two, which is the mystical marriage.

Now we're in a place where the human mind is of no value. There's nothing it can do for you. It has to surrender. You reach that place where this human mind, which would observe, which would sort out the facts and catalog them, which would make inferences, has no capacity to entertain the living Christ. It's as if in your mind, at the moment, you have certain knowledge. Now, if your mind were also able to have the knowledge that is, let's say, in the mind of a scientist, you would have your mind's knowledge and his mind's knowledge, and you would have the knowledge of both minds, but his mind doesn't contain all knowledge.

And so if you took another individual's mind and had the three minds, you would have a wider basis of knowledge. And you could go on and on like that, but you reach the place where all of the addition of human minds still cannot give you spiritual awareness. And you have to come to the place, above the mind, where this mind is looking up at the Divine Mind and saying, "This is as far as I can go. I have to turn to you. I have to relax my mental attitudes, my mental probing."

I have to come to that place now where I do absolutely nothing, simply look up to the face of the Father and wait, because my mind does not have the capacity to experience Omnipresence. You simply can't encompass Omnipresence with the human mind, and even though you know the meaning of the word, can define it, can talk about it, and probably make a good case about understanding it, you'll find that you have not accepted Omnipresence.

The human mind cannot accept Omnipresence, and to give you an idea of why not, let's say you go into a cave, and it's dark. And now what you're doing in the cave constitutes the all-ness of your human selfhood. You're only concerned about what you're doing there. You're not concerned about anything else. Now when you go into your physical senses, it's the same way. You're only concerned about what's happening within your physical senses. That's your cave. Your mind is your cave. You're only concerned about what's happening in your mind.

And when you with that mind try to reach beyond your mind, there's no place to reach, and you find that you have been relying on your own human wisdom to find out things. And as a consequence, to you Omnipresence means one thing. To someone else's mind, it means another, and every human mind will tell you a different meaning of Omnipresence. But no human mind will tell you that You are Omnipresence, that your Identity is Omnipresence, and that the acceptance of Omnipresence can never be made with a human mind.

In fact, the acceptance can only be made when the human mind, which knows not the meaning of Omnipresence, has been rolled away. For when you have accepted Omnipresence, you're in a very startling Universe. The things you understand would be quite shocking to the individual you were before Omnipresence was your understanding. You would discover, perhaps, that Omnipresence takes you right from this instant here straight through your complete human past, mineral past, vegetable past, animal past, through every material past, through every incarnation straight to the doorway of God without interruption. Right from God to this instant is Omnipresence, and that is You: the one, continuous, uninterrupted Life of Spirit.

And if you look back on that one, uninterrupted line of spiritual Life, it has no form in a corporeal world, and so the acceptance of Omnipresence eliminates all that you have called your human past in all incarnations. It eliminates mother, father, brother, sister. It eliminates all your human attainments. It eliminates all your human possessions. It also eliminates all your human fears, doubts, and worries. Omnipresence says, "Spirit is. Spirit I Am." And Spirit being All, there is no other Self. The mother who birthed me was my Self. How could there be a second self there to birth me? If I am Spirit and mother was Spirit and one Self is Spirit, was there a mother? Was there a son, or was there not just one Self being Self, appearing outwardly as two?

And then you're coming into your third degree of accepting Omnipresence as your Self, realizing that Omnipresence will do nothing of Itself unless It's recognized. Just as if a pencil were not going to get up and write: You'd have to pick it up and know it's a pencil and that it can write. You then begin to recognize Omnipresence accepted. Live in it, rejecting all else that is not Omnipresence, and you find the Oil is pouring. The Oil is forming that invisible Body. The transmutation from physical sense to spiritual awareness is coming through as a new Body, a Body that Mary, here, was showing the Master she had, for you have found the two olive trees, Spirit, and its companion, Truth.

The two, Divine Truth and Divine Spirit, made One in you produce the Oil. The Oil produces the Body of the Soul. The Body of the Soul is recognized as the one infinite body. And in your third degree, you rest in the quiet, conscious realization that the Body of the Soul is the only Body I am. It knows no pain. It knows no lack. It knows no limitation. It knows no need. And therefore, when I express a lack, a need, a limitation, I am rejecting my Body. I am rejecting Omnipresence, even though my mind had known the Word and had been able to pronounce It and speak about It. Omnipresence eliminates all that is not the Spirit of God as Reality.

In your third degree, Omnipresence is the law of your Being, the nature of your Being, and the activity of your Being, and therefore, you are not living, then, in a physical form. Your Life doesn't consist of the activity of that physical form. You have an external existence to the Body made possible only because the Soul Center opening up yields the Oil, which becomes your spiritual discernment, your spiritual Consciousness, your capacity to trust the Invisible.

Now, the reason the Bible tells us about Mary doing this and Lazarus is for the faint-hearted who say, "Oh, Jesus did it, but of course he did it. Who else is Jesus?" The more you study the Bible, the more you discover that many people did it, and that we are doing it, but not with, as Joel puts it, "our spare time and our spare change." No, he says, only when all of you is dedicated to that which is greater than your human self. The anointing, the Oil carries with it the ordainment; carries with it the Will, the power, the self-fulfillment.

And we find now we're becoming aware of our invisible bodies. We're learning to rest back, accepting not only is the outer body the temporary fleeting image, but there is, *is* an inner Body of Light that is real. We know it will not come forth without our recognition of It. We begin to rest in It consciously, letting the government of the Father do Its own work. In the third degree, your patience is deepened. You're willing to go through long periods of seemingly outer inactivity. You're letting that divine Seed take root. You know that all of the frantic outer activity has nothing to do with a root of the Seed, and just like a seed in the ground, you're letting It take root in the invisible Infinite. You do it consciously, quietly.

You meditate, not with a purpose of attaining something or receiving something, but just to know quietly, as I do this, the root of my Christhood is becoming deeper and more firmly entrenched into my consciousness. I simply rest in that knowledge, knowing this is how my confidence in Omnipresence is strengthened. You merely rest, knowing that this is the way for the Soul center to open to lead you to a mystical realm above human consciousness. Not to receive something, but to be opened to that inner Vision. To be taken out of all the psychic realms, the emotional realms, the mental realms. We are fasting from personality, fasting from the mind that wants to know, fasting from everything that will not give us that precious Oil, the Oil that ordains us, the Oil of the divine Son.

In this way we are preparing the way for the ultimate initiation. Quietly resting, seeking nothing, but feeling the knitting within of Being Itself. Accepting the Spirit of God as your invisible Body and letting the divine Mind act upon that Spirit to animate It, motivate It, guide It, direct It, feed It, sustain It, clothe It. Completely trusting that invisible Body to be maintained by the invisible Father. Not seeking even outer signs. Resting in the work. That is the I of your Being. And the me out here with its worries, its problems, its doubts, its needs, its limitations—this me is revealed to you as a false side of yourself, without meaning, without existence. And the more you are aware of this invisible

Soul Self, the more you know that any clinging to the outer man is a denial of the inner Self.

Once you reject the inner Self by being concerned about the outer self, you are denying the All-ness of God. You are a prodigal from Omnipresence. You are outside of your own Identity. And now all we're concerned about is being true to our Self. Every worry is faced with the knowledge that I can only be worrying about a me that doesn't exist because my name is Omnipresence.

My name is Spirit. I go back to the Father, all the way. I go all the way ahead to the Father, all the way up and down and around to the Father. Wherever the Father is, I am with Him.

Spirit is my name. The only Body I have is made of pure Spirit. There is no other substance. And as your inner integrity deepens, increases, it multiplies the Oil. It multiplies the final moment when the Robe, that inner garment of the Soul, is bestowed upon you, signifying your Soul Body is now ready for you to live in, independent of all karmic law. You've earned your spurs. You can walk with Mary, with Lazarus, with all those who have gone through the crucifixion of self to the inner Resurrection to the Ascension over material law. You're ready to make your triumphal entry into Selfhood.

The reason patience is stressed is because in the earlier degrees there were signs following, signs following. Always there were signs. In the inner realm, there are no more signs following. There is only the acceptance and the realization that that very Presence that you were seeking is your name. You no longer are seeking the presence of God. That Presence You are. It is the fact of your Being, and that is what is meant by moving, living, having your Being in God. You move as the Presence, you live as the Presence, you have your Being as the Presence, and you deny not the Presence, because it is Omnipresent.

What if you do not hold this 24 hours a day? If you hold it for three minutes a day, the Oil pours, and that Oil increases your capacity to hold this Consciousness again and again and again.

And so the key word today is: Omnipresence is meaningless unless I consciously recognize Omnipresence, not as a word, but as God *active*, not passive. And now watch this: God is active. If you're not doing what God is doing, what are you doing—if God is All? What can you possibly do that has any meaning, if it's not what God is doing?

And so the activity of God functioning as your Soul Body is the only way in which you can be doing what God is doing. And that is why you must find that great capacity to release all that is not your invisible Soul Body to live in It, because It alone is acting in the Will of God. It is the living expression of God where you stand. The activity of God in your Soul Body is what Jesus was talking about when he said: "The Father worketh, and I work hitherto. Thou seest me, thou seest the Father."

He had come out of the dual sense of life, out of the fleshly sense of life into the Soul Body, which is the activity of God, as we will do. Then I and the Father are one activity. The Mind of the Father becomes the activity of my Soul Body, and what I do is because the Father is doing it. And so you find God is living God's Life as your Soul Body. ". . . I live; yet not I, . . . Christ liveth [my life]." This is the Soul Body activity, and until you are in the conscious awareness of that Body through the realization and the conscious practice that Spirit is all, Spirit is your name, Spirit is Omnipresent, and therefore, Omnipresence is your name, you will still be finding fractions and patches and flaws in your life, whereas these fractions, patches, and flaws are not your life at all.

Your Life is Omnipresence. Spirit, everywhere Being Itself, is your Life. And the experience of going all the way back in time, through time, through space, and then out of time and out of space to the throne of God; to establish in Consciousness the continuity of your Life, and then to not leave that conscious Continuity, gives you a foundation which enables you not to deny who you are and not to be concerned about where you are in the physical form or what you are doing in the physical form. Because all that can be happening is the activity invisible of Omnipresence. Your conscious knowledge of that brings that invisible activity into visible manifestation as the fruits of Spirit.

If you are not wherever God is, you are not Omnipresent Spirit. If you are not Omnipresent Spirit, what are you? Grass. Nothing! And so we don't wait to discover that we're grass, that we're nothing. We accept that now this human selfhood is laid aside in the third degree. And in order to find that Resurrection experience of Lazarus, which is rebirth, I go through what may be called the Ascension without Crucifixion while in the form—while appearing mortal, while living in a mortal existence, the transmutation of Consciousness, the conscious awareness that the Oil flows when I accept Spirit as my Identity. When I pursue that Identity to see that It is everywhere, It is Omnipresent, It is I—then I learn to rest in that and behold a power of my Omnipresent Self, behold how self-supporting Omnipresence is.

Only in our fidelity to omnipresent Self as your Self, my Self, his Self, and there being no other Self—only then are we totally dying as was demonstrated through the so-called death and resurrection of Lazarus. This is an inner activity of your Self. It was this dying and rebirth which all had been completed before Jesus began his ministry. What we saw were only the outer physical crucifixion, the outer physical resurrection.

You can tell when you're in that third degree when you have confidence in your own Being. You're not too easily shaken now by the world around you or the apparent disasters or things that threaten from time to time. You don't wake up with a dread of today or even the anxiety of what will today bring. You're waking up in Omnipresence. You're going to sleep in Omnipresence, and it is the omnipresent Self that puts that physical form to sleep and wakes it up again.

It is the omnipresent Self that maintains its perfect spiritual integrity 24 hours a day without any human help, and it is that omnipresent Self, which you begin to know is your eternal Life without beginning or end, never born, never dying. And now you have left mother, father, brother, and sister, for they are your Self. If there is another on this earth who is not your invisible Self, you have lost Omnipresence. Wherever you go, your invisible Self is all that is there. You are the one Self of a one Universe. And there was a time on this earth where the only Self here that was realized was in Christ Jesus. There was no one else on the earth but his Self.

And every character in the Bible represents another facet of your human sense of self, facets that have to slowly be dissolved: the Herods and the Caiaphases, even the Jameses and the Johns. All must be slowly dissolved until all that stands in your Universe is Christ, the living expression of God the Father, and it doesn't matter what form you see. That's what you're accepting because it is your invisible Self—one, undivided, invisible, spiritual Self everywhere. This is Omnipresence, and as you live in it, you'll find that your Self, in any part of what we call this world will never be harmful to your Self where your body stands. Your Self in any part of this world will gladly give its last dollar or its last ounce of breath to your Self here. Your Self everywhere will be in harmony with your Self where you stand. Nobody is external to your Self.

When you have one Self, you have eliminated all human differences and all human divisions and all human discords. Because in your acceptance of them, you are denying the one invisible Self that You are, that They are, making your inner division which translates into an outer division or discord. Omnipresence I am because I and the Father are One. Now, this is given to us by the Bible as the way to the release of divine Oil to build that transitional body which walks through the fire untouched, comes out of the tomb of mortality, and ascends above every material limitation in the present, in the now, in the here. And then all of the ecclesiastical promises about a heavenly hereafter no longer are the trap laid for the gullible. We learn God is active here and now, and that activity is the activity of my Life *now*.

## Class 16: Oil From Your Soul Center

The last veils of fear and doubt should fall away. You should be able to look at all of the activities around you with a detachment. They may seem to endanger your possessions, your physical self, your future, but that is the belief of one who is separated from the real Self of Being, who has not yet found that Soul center, but is living apart from it, and so accepts other powers than the Omnipotence of the Spirit.

∞∞∞∞∞ END OF SIDE ONE ∞∞∞∞∞

There is an important sequence here. We find Jesus stepping out of the Jordan, baptized by a man, suffering it to be so now, then the dove, the baptism of the Spirit. We know now that the descent of the Ghost signaled that the human sense of body had completely been overcome. Now there stood a man who was no longer a man of earth. In his Consciousness there existed only the Omnipresent Self, the One. To human eyes it was the same body they had seen, but it was not. It was the body of the Soul, indestructible. I'm quite sure he needed no food. He lived on Light. He was Light. He moved as Light, and he'd announced that I am the Light.

The mission of Jesus Christ could not begin until the Soul body had been formed, completed, realized, and lived in, and this is the birth of the Christ. This is the moment of being begotten of the Father, and only then did Christ walk the earth without human interference from a man named Jesus. Only then could Christ move through the earth giving the teaching, for now there was One, not two. The Christ Body and the Christ Mind lived and walked, and this was identified by human sense as Jesus. And there were still remnants of humanhood, and therefore, the wilderness experience had to follow. And after the wilderness experience, which was the Ascension—the complete overcoming of material law—there had to be the three temptations to show what Ascension means. Ascension meant that all personal self had been destroyed.

There was no desire to wear a halo. No desire to be identified as the One who came from God. No desire to own anything, not even the kingdoms of this world in all their power and glory. No desire to possess. And no lack, no limitation, no need unfulfilled. I, Spirit, am Self-supporting, complete. Nothing external to Self was needed, Self being the *infinite* Self. This acceptance became the realized Christ now walking forth to demonstrate to mankind the Identity that stands behind every form that walks the earth, saying, "When you reach back into your Self, you'll find I, and I am the Way. When you reach back into your Self, I will pour the Oil. I will release you from all measures of iniquity that appear to your limited human consciousness. I stand where you are. All that I have is thine, and I will never leave you."

This is who was now walking the earth called "Jesus," but it is I, the infinite Invisible. Because the man, Jesus, has died to the Lazarus within him, to the Mary within him, to the Herod within him, to the Pilate within him, even to the Judas within him. The man, Jesus, is no more. And it was only because all this had happened to purify that consciousness completely of humanhood, of finitude, of a denial of omnipresent Self as the One and Only.

Now he could step forward, and now the Spirit could speak words of Truth that can be depended upon, words that you never have to examine suspiciously and say, "I wonder if this is true." You can do that with people, but with the words of Spirit, you say, "Thank you." This is more true than anything ever divined by a human mind. This I can depend on. This is Life Itself talking, and this Spirit steps forth and gives us the reason why it can now walk the earth doing the miracles. And the world sees Jesus saying this, but it is the omnipresent One behind all of us saying, "I."

"The Spirit of the Lord *is* upon me, because he hath anointed me to preach the gospel to the poor;"—And those poor are us. Those who are poor because they have not let the Oil flow. Those who are poor because they have not accepted Identity. Those who are poor because they are still clinging to a human concept of possession, who do not know that Spirit possesses nothing, for Spirit is all.

"The Spirit of the Lord . . . hath anointed me to preach the gospel to the poor; he hath sent me to heal the brokenhearted,"—In other words, as I within you is received, that which was the broken heart is shown not even to be the heart itself. There is no separation in Spirit to be broken up about. The broken heart is the denial of Omnipresence. When we say, "I have lost my husband. I have lost my wife. I have lost my child," we are denying Omnipresence. We do not realize that the Self, which is my child, the Self which is myself, are One and the same, never separated, no matter what the human picture may show. Never separated, and that is how you heal the broken-hearted. The realization of the true Self reveals the absence of the possibility of separation in Omnipresence.

". . . to preach deliverance to the captives,"—those who live in the caves of their own mind, prisoners entombed—and "recovering of sight to the blind,"—those who are blind to Christ—"to set at liberty them that are bruised, To preach the acceptable year of the Lord." Someone said this before the man Jesus said it, for the Christ in Jesus was the same Christ in Isaiah, who had said it before. That same Christ in Isaiah, in Jesus, in you, in me, in Joel, in whoever has accepted Omnipresent Spirit to be the only Self, finds the Christ giving you that precious Oil to share.

Oh, how we want to accept that I am Omnipresent Spirit, but it's harder for a rich man to get through the eye of a needle than a camel because even though we're willing to accept I am Omnipresent Spirit, the habits of years are not discarded by a phrase. Is there pain in Spirit? Is their property in Spirit? Are there problems in Spirit? Is there a physical form in Spirit? Are there human conditions in Spirit? How can you have these things and accept Omnipresent Spirit as your Name? Can you possess 10 cents and be Omnipresent Spirit? The very fact of Omnipresent Spirit is the denial of the existence of matter. There cannot be Omnipresent Spirit "and." Omnipresent means there is no other. Only Spirit is.

And therefore, what about our possessions that we worked so hard for? We learned that we are merely given the use of them, and we say, "Thank you." I am their custodian momentarily. They are not my permanent property. How can that be if my name is Spirit? That which passes in front of me for my use is recognized as the activity of the world consciousness, and only to the extent that I transmute world consciousness by the acceptance of spiritual Consciousness do I find that those things that appear as mine are working in coordinated harmony with the fullness of my Being. Then they begin to have a relevancy to what I am doing.

Then the activity of the Spirit, translating into these appearances called possessions, all works in one direction. No one can take your spiritual possessions. They can only take your mental, physical possessions. Your spiritual possessions are nailed down inside your Consciousness. You don't have to protect them. Spirit is constantly pressing them forth in such abundance that it's hard to keep up with it. And so you must learn how to practice in your meditation periods the knowledge that I have nothing, I own nothing, and I am nothing. As long as you think you have, you own, and you are something, you are saying you are not pure, perfect, omnipresent Spirit.

Oh, the human mind begins to fear that if I think I have nothing, it'll disappear. Somebody will take it away. What if somebody comes to rob it? I won't try to protect it. All of these fears pass through the one who is not in the third degree, not even glimpsing the third degree. You might get to the place where you want to make all kinds of foolish tests, and say, "Well, I'll just pile all my things in the car, and I won't lock it." You're just falling into the tempter, who's trying to make you jump off the roof to show that somebody will catch you. You are Spirit, and there is no other. And there's no need to prove anything. There's no one to prove it to, and if you want to prove it to your human selfhood, you're making a mistake.

And so we do not lose our sense of responsibility. If anything, we have a higher sense of responsibility because we can see through the material appearance to the spiritual Reality. And whatever Spirit places in your hands to be used is a treasure. But it's used in the manner in which Spirit placed it in your hands to be used, so that the activity of whatever that appears to be is released to the Spirit, which placed it before you. We are not setting up the mental road blocks as to how things should be.

I have found that when there is a continuous effort to meditate on "I own nothing," that there comes to you a great release, and the release takes an unusual form in that you become more aware of your spiritual Identity. It was only the physical sense of self which clung to the idea of owning. And in giving up the sense of possession, you find that what you are giving up mentally is almost zero compared to what you discover you do have. You give up the transient sense of things, and you become the proud possessor of the infinite.

All of the Infinite can function through the one who has given up the sense of owning. The minute you try to put a label on the Infinite or carve a piece of It for yourself, you lose it. It has an innate awareness of whether or not you are letting It flow unmolested, uninterfered with. And then it comes to you as a great dispensation that all that the Father hath is yours. And when you are clinging to material possessions as your possessions, that is the denial that all that the Father hath is yours. In our human sense of clinging, we are rejecting the fullness that is available. You find everything is upside down.

Another thing we have to learn to meditate upon is that "I am nothing," and this I we are speaking of is the human self who goes to work, the human self who has friends, the human self who mingles with people. "I am nothing." Why? Because right here where this me appears, only the Spirit is, and when that sense of a me is gone, the Spirit that is realized here appears as a me in harmony with my environment. But it is only the Jesus appearing where the Christ is. It is the Mary appearing where the Christ is, the Lazarus appearing where the Christ is.

One day the you is Mary resenting the fact that Jesus wasn't present when needed, and the next day the you is Mary boasting, happily showing forth the Soul Body. Look how quickly that transition took place within three years. When he sent forth the disciples two by two, it is said that they not only healed, they anointed the victims with oil. What does that mean? They opened the spiritual Consciousness of those people to their Identity. James says in one of his epistles, "Is something wrong? Do you have a problem? Well, find the oil, find the oil." Opening up your spiritual Consciousness to the acceptance of Identity, you've found the Oil.

Now, all of the tricks of the human mind will keep preventing you from accepting Omnipresence. You'll have a birthday in the Omnipresence of Spirit, and then you'll have a death day in the Omnipresence of Spirit. You'll have human holidays. You'll have all kinds of human events while talking about the Omnipresence of Spirit, and you'll have all kinds of adverse conditions in these human events, but they aren't there. The Omnipresence of Spirit is there and ever has been there. And that Spirit is not in your physical form, and so you cannot be living in that Spirit and in your physical form. You do not even possess a physical body once you have accepted Omnipresent Spirit. You have a Soul Body, which appears to human sense as a physical body.

And that Soul Body is the only one you acknowledge in all your ways as perfection Itself, for it is your eternal Body. And it must be lived in, experienced, to become your permanent realized Body. When you were given the assignment last week to write down to yourself "I am Spirit" and then let Spirit tell you what you are, I'm sure some of you received some inner knowledge. And maybe some of you received a sort of an inner demand, a spiritual impulse which said to you something that is yours alone to tell no man. Now, this must be realized that whenever you receive this inner demand from Spirit, every inner revelation you receive *is* a demand.

Every true spiritual vision is a demand. Remember, spiritual vision—not psychic, not emotional, not mental—and those spiritual visions always bring with them an understanding of what they are, even if that understanding is merely that this vision was to tell you that I am present, with no other meaning intended. But every inner revelation is a demand, and that means that unless you live up to the level of that demand, you are saying to the Spirit, "Don't come back." Because your Teacher is saying, "This is where I want you to be now. I am teaching you, for example, that you are the Omnipresent Spirit. Before Abraham was, you are the Omnipresent Spirit."

In the year three billion, you will be the Omnipresent Spirit, and you are that now, and if this becomes your inner revelation, that is a demand for you to rest in the Word until you can say, "I know it, I have it, I feel it, I accept it. I will live it." And until you do this, you'll be waiting a long time between inner revelations. Your inner Teacher says, "This is the level I've established for you, and you cannot change the sequence. You can't mentally run ahead and try to direct traffic. This is what I have ordained for you." And it is as you follow these inner ordainments to the level that they are requesting, demanding, that you one day will find the Voice speaking that the Spirit of the Lord has ordained me, anointed me, for the anointing is the ordainment.

Way back years ago we used to come out of a lecture and say, "That was great," and then come back next week and hear some more. Now we don't do it anymore. All the talk is is a means of together sharing the spiritual impulse and letting that spiritual impulse establish its invisible activity as our own Being all through the week—living in the God experience—in the spiritual experience above the calculating mind, above the self-preserving mind, above every human consideration.

And you'll know when you have no human considerations and you're just up there experiencing that the Oil is flowing. You're being anointed, and that anointing is the preparation for the entire fulfillment of the purpose of this lifespan, the realization of Self as God Self. With our human minds, we are not capable of this realization. Only through the Soul Center, and only through living throughout the day, alone, in that Soul Center while in the midst of the world is that precious ointment flowing.

Next week our chapter will be the fifth in *The Contemplative Life*. Always, I'm depending on you to supply that inner vision, to see that behind the words is always the intent to lift you into omnipresent spiritual Identity. And between then and now you should be working on the inner acceptance that Spirit, which you are, never has a problem. And the acceptance of the problem, then, is the denial of your spiritual Self. That Spirit never has a division, and the acceptance of a competitor or a husband or a wife or an enemy or a friend, without the realization that "This is my invisible Spirit," is making a false division in your Consciousness.

And that Spirit does not end at the horizon or at the end of a year. It has no ending anywhere, and therefore, you have no ending anywhere. And no matter what may appear in the world, it is but the outer garment of the mind camouflaging that where it appears to be, only You, your Spirit is. To accept your infinite spiritual Self is the only way you will ever live in your infinite spiritual Body. This is what we must be working on. It does not come through Grace. It comes through effort, and then through Grace. It comes through application.

It comes through conscious knowing repeatedly. It comes through conscious experience.

And then when you have opened out a way, when you are receptive through the continuous application of Truth in consciousness, then through Grace you will feel your infinite spiritual Body as a living experience. And no one will be able to deny it to you by word or deed. They won't have wars in your infinite spiritual Body. They won't have pestilences or poverty or famine. Your invisible Consciousness will be maintaining a perfect incorporeal Body everywhere, and you will know it. This is part of our third degree.

Let's all do our homework, telling no man. For now the things we would tell any man would be foolishness, indeed. Chapter five, *The Contemplative Life,* and whatever else the Spirit has in Mind.

Thanks very much.

# CLASS 17

# HAS GOLIATH FOOLED YOU

*Herb:* The story today is the fifth chapter of The Contemplative Life and whatever it brings out in us, and I think next week we'll go right ahead into the sixth chapter of The Contemplative Life. I'm really anxious to get through with it so we can move into Joel's next book, The Mystical I, all prepared for it.

When we have finished this book we will have what may be called the foundation of the transcendental Consciousness. We should be at a place where we can without flinching an eyelid be aware of the nothingness of all error without taking thought about it. This book should be for us a preparation for that Consciousness which needs take no thought about the problems of the world and of the body without having to sit down and intellectualize about it. There is such a Consciousness. At times you find you're in it; at other times you have to rise up from the valley.

A friend of mine said the other day sometimes he feels that he's walking up the down escalator. And we all know that unless we are continuously moving up, up, up, the moment we stop, the consciousness of the world takes us right down back where we started, and sometimes even further back. But there is a top. It's the landing, the momentary mountaintop, and on that top, there's Goliath out there, but he doesn't stand a chance. It's an unfair fight. Poor Goliath could never win because you stand in a different Consciousness in which Goliath to you is actually nothing. Not a giant, not a bully, not an insurmountable thing in front of you, taunting you, telling you you can't get by. But your Goliath has been conquered, and you're ready for new things.

Now, according to the morning paper, Mr. William Randolph Hearst, Jr., has provided us with a little sidelight to today's lesson. He is expressing the fear that Russia is getting there quicker in the arms race than we are. He is seeing his Goliath, and he is pointing out to us that we must fear and outrace that Goliath. And if anyone were to say to Mr. Hearst or those who share his opinion that they have no faith in the Bible, they would throw up their arms and say, "What are you talking about? We're God-fearing men." "But what about what God says in the Bible? Do you accept it?" "Oh, yes." "Well, what about David and Goliath, and what about your story this morning?"

Let's look at the story, and then let's look at David and Goliath and see the difference in the mind of man, typified by the Hearst story, and the Mind of Spirit, typified by the words speaking through Samuel to us about a man who's in a vision [that] enables him to walk through an insurmountable object without taking arms. Mr. Hearst says, "Today, the U.S. bomber force is less than 600. Our sub-launched missiles have numbered 650 for 4 years, and our land-based missiles have totaled 1,054 for 4 years. And during the same time, the Soviet bomber force has remained about constant, but their sub-missile force has grown to almost 400 launchers and is expected to overtake ours in 2 or 3 years. And meanwhile, a Soviet land-based Inter-Continental force has risen to over 1,440 operational launches. More on the way. And so while the Soviets are gaining and will soon exceed us in missile weaponry at sea, we have already fallen distinctly behind on land."

Now, that's a very imposing series of statistics, and I'm sure it'll make the Pentagon do something very quickly. But of course, you realize that the Pentagon reads the Bible, too, and believes in it. And therefore, we must see that people can read this Bible and believe in it while their actions are completely opposed to what they believe. According to this, the David and Goliath story should have been written another way, perhaps. David should have looked out and said, "Oh, look at that giant and look at that armor and look at the weapons. Now let's see, how can I go out and fight him? What we need to do is get together and build better weapons. We have to outpower him or perhaps outsmart him, or we need a great general to outflank him. We must do something physically or mentally." That would be the Bible version if it meant us to outpower Russia or outpower other nations.

But the Bible version says, "Not by might, [not] by power, . . . by my spirit . . ." And really, the greatest observation you will ever find on the David and Goliath story is in the fifth chapter of *The Contemplative Life*, because without a lot of fanfare, without a lot of psychology, Joel has given us not only the secret of David and Goliath, but the secret of the transcendental Consciousness that *we can live in*. We're going to trace that, because in order to understand his secret and the secret of Samuel and the secret of David and the secret of Christ Jesus, it isn't enough to see that a little fellow went out with a slingshot and that we can do the same. We must see what went [on] inside the consciousness of David. What is the inner David doing while the outer David is overcoming this insurmountable object?

And very nicely, once we start to look at what the inner David is doing, the scripture tells us precisely that. Practically every line tells you what's going on in David's consciousness, and it's a perfect blueprint for us of the path to what David eventually becomes. He becomes a king. Goliath is just one stepping stone on the way. As you move past Goliath, there are going to be other Goliaths. Let's not pretend that the moment he got past Goliath, everything was roses. He got through four or five wives, too. He got through many things on the way, all part of his spiritual path. He lost one whom he loved very dearly; he lost Jonathan. And you will notice that he even lost his own followers. But always, this invisible path of Spirit gives us the outer signs; and if we're looking, we recognize them and we make them part of our continuing developing awareness of Truth.

We find right out that David was tending the sheep. We know that Christ Jesus later said, "I am the good shepherd. My sheep hear my voice." We know that he said to Peter, "If you love me, feed my sheep." David was feeding the sheep, tending the sheep. Now, this is a sign, then, a symbol to us that he is in the preparatory stage of initiation. He is one of eight sons. He's the eighth, and he is the youngest. He is in a far country. He's not in his own kingdom at the moment.

The king of this country is Saul, the king of Israel, and now we have Israel pitted against the Philistines; and shall we say, then, that mind and body are having a little war? But Saul looks with some degree of favor upon David, and so something is happening that will make David the champion on the side of Israel, on the side of mind coming into a higher sense called Soul. And on the other side, their champion—the champion of physical force of the body of man, of the base nature of man—is the incarnate evil called Goliath. Two champions: One representing body. One representing that emergent awareness of Soul, coming above the level of mind.

Now, before we go any further, you're able to see that Goliath represents the old man of yesterday. David represents the new. Actually, there are many facets to Goliath, and they change as you change. At one point Goliath will represent to you the accumulated karma of your entire life, all standing out in front of you saying, "You can't go any further." At another stage, Goliath will only represent a momentary problem. But one thing that Goliath does represent, always, is this: Goliath is not an external obstacle. Goliath is not an external condition blocking your path. Goliath represents the complete fullness of your own false sense of self.

This Goliath that we encounter in scripture is your second self. David is your emergent real Self becoming Self-aware, lifting you out of the false belief in a second self; and every problem, every pain, every ache, every evil; every form of darkness, lack and limitation; every belief in anything finite is included in this Goliath, this present sense of self. And when you look out at a problem, we learn you're not looking *out* at a problem. You're looking at the Goliath of the false sense of self which says, "Here's the problem, and here's what it's going to do to you if you don't watch out."

The problem is never external to your being. It is always the Goliath of your false sense of self standing in front of you, looking down at you saying, "Here's what we have to face today." Goliath is not your enemy out there. Goliath is mortal mind in you, making this vast image of an impregnable armor which says, "You cannot defeat me." You may be recovering from an accident and your mind can't figure out how in the world this condition, which has settled into a seemingly permanent condition, can ever be overcome; and so you study spiritually and you study and you study. You're walking up that down escalator and getting nowhere.

Sometimes it seems, "I've got it." Other times you're back at the bottom looking up. Goliath still says, "But it did happen. The bone's set this way. You can't do anything about that now. It's done. It's finished." And your Goliath there is the belief that it happened. Because if it happened, when it happened God wasn't there, and that situation has never happened. In other words, Goliath is your hypnosis in the material events of the past as an accepted reality. Yes, there is a way to overcome the hypnosis of the past as well as the present and the future. And all of that is Goliath, the braggart standing over us putting fear into our hearts and telling our minds, "You can't figure out this one."

All of this is said when we are told about the size, the stature, the scowl, the armor; the loud, ominous voice. And all of this is contrasted by a quiet little fellow who was feeding the sheep. Just a young fellow with a ruddy countenance; a child, you might say. But somehow he doesn't hear the braggart as others do because living in the inner Self, feeding the sheep, resting in the Consciousness of God's presence, he develops the capacity to see with the eyes of God. To see no evil, to hear no evil, to speak no evil. Goliath. It's almost hard to focus upon this fellow, Goliath. Did God make such a creature? Did God make anything destructive? Did God create a problem? Goliath. Who can this be? A nothingness, not created by the Father.

But who is David? Is David a nothingness, too? Yes, he *is* a nothingness. He's as much a nothingness as Goliath. There's no David there. There's no Goliath there. And only David is aware of that. "I am the Light," said the Master Jesus. And now David is realizing himself to be the Light of God because having fed the sheep, the Consciousness has developed to the point where Light, Spirit, Substance, Essence is the Identity of David and the Identity of Goliath. All that is present in the pure Consciousness is the true Identity of Spirit.

There are not two forms and nothing more. There are two body images standing in the one invisible Light, and who is the majority but the one who knows this? Now David, being an initiate of Truth, and Goliath, representing that force in him which stands in his way to the kingship or Christhood, is really waging an inner conflict which has nothing to do with other people or other events. This is the change of consciousness within David made visible. This is spiritual Consciousness manifesting outwardly as outer events, but you're going to discover as we go along a little further that the language of the Soul is what we're looking at.

We're looking at these symbols appearing as body images and body conditions and world conditions that are put forth by Consciousness as it is accepted or rejected. And all that we are witnessing now is the acceptance within David that the Kingdom of God is within himself, that his Spirit is Omnipresent Spirit, that his Omnipresent Spirit stands where Goliath appears to be. He cannot deny Omnipresence and accept the intimidation of Goliath at the same time.

Once he has accepted Goliath as a reality, a force of destruction, he is saying, "Omnipresence is a lie. Spirit is a lie. Spirit is not here. The power of Spirit is not here." And as a human being, this is precisely what he would do. But having been tending the sheep, having had that spiritual beginning within himself and that rising knowledge of the inner Christ, all the strength, all the power of the Kingdom in his Consciousness must manifest in some way as the non-power of Goliath. And the great vision that came through Joel about this is the secret of your work. It is something that is not explained by any of the religions of the world because until no power is accepted, you cannot explain David and Goliath except in the usual cliches.

No power here means just this: God, being the only Presence anywhere, only the perfect power of God is functioning. And when you are trying with the mind to cope with that thought, you find you're unable to support it for a long time. You can memorize it, and you can try to jot it on a card so that tomorrow you remember it. You can try to hammer it into yourself with a recitation, but it isn't enough. Non-power has to be a state of Consciousness, attainable, in which you are able to know that because God is everywhere, there is no power needed in any circumstance on this earth.

Now, that may manifest as a boy with a slingshot casting a stone on the forehead of a giant, and you'll say, "Well, he did *something*. He didn't exert no power. He did *something*." Yes, only because if he did absolutely nothing, it would not be as it is in actual human living. You would have no way of understanding what was happening. In human living, you would be putting on the armor and going out to face this giant. In human living, you would face your adversary, and you would usually use the identical tactics of your adversary. You'd want to match him, brain for brain, brawn for brawn, strategy for strategy. That's not the spiritual way. The spiritual way is first within yourself, and within himself David knew no power was needed to overcome this adversary. No power needed. No armor, no sword.

The slingshot and the five stones become symbols to teach us. In fact, if he had gone out with a sword and armor, you wouldn't have heard this story again. He'd have been annihilated if he met his adversary with the tactics of the adversary. If you meet the liar with a lie, the cheat with a cheat, the force with a force, you're just locking horns. You're recognizing it as a reality. And here this vast, monumental figure compared to the little boy is shown to be nothing but a mirage. An externalized belief—the sum total of all human fear, externalized into one mammoth figure with no substance, no content, no power—unless he has an adversary who believes he has power.

And when you translate this to every problem in your life, you find you are really saying that every problem in your life is without substance, without power; is nothing but your externalized belief made visible as condition, thing, person, adversary who needs to be faced only by the little David in you with a slingshot—meaning inner vision. For that which finally makes the giant succumb is the stone of Truth. One little stone of Truth, and the giant is slain. This is the eternal warfare between all of the material grotesque problems of the world and your one little stone of spiritual Truth. And what is that spiritual Truth which makes it possible for you to stand in the Consciousness of no power? Only Spirit exists. There is only Spirit.

I *am* the Light. You *are* the Light. These forms of a world mind are not Substance. These are shadows in the Light. And the consciousness of Light as your name, your Substance, your Being; the awareness of the omnipresence of the Light worked with; and that's feeding your sheep, living with It. And every time a thought runs out of line, you bring that thought back into the fold with your rod of Truth. So that every little sheep—every little thought that moves outside into fear, hate, rejection, resentment, material thinking is a lost sheep; and you gently bring it back into the fold.

You are feeding the sheep of your mind until all that is in there is the Truth that Spirit is. Spirit is. Spirit is.

Does Spirit have pain? No. Does Spirit have any problem? No. Does Spirit suffer? Does Spirit have a heart attack? Is Spirit blind? Is Spirit deaf? Does Spirit die? Does Spirit have anything that we encounter in the world as a problem? Is Spirit all? And every little sheep that says, "There's something besides Spirit" has to be brought back into the fold in your consciousness until all your sheep are in the fold, until Spirit is your Consciousness.

Now, where is Goliath? Just one of the little sheep. Just one of the little sheep who got too big because he wasn't watched. And now we look at Goliath. He's not quite as big anymore. He has shrunken some. Spirit is. And he's been telling you how powerful he is. He's been denying that Spirit is the only power. He's been telling you what he's going to do to you if you ever dare to come out on the battlefield with him. But Spirit is all that is here.

Spiritual Identity is yours, and that spiritual Identity is omnipresent. There are no opposites in Spirit. There are no Goliaths in Spirit. There are no Russias in Spirit. But you'll never know this until you know there's no David in Spirit either. As long as there's a David, there's a Goliath. As long as there's a personal me, there's a Goliath. But when I am Spirit, Goliath was just shot, murdered, killed, annihilated. He never existed. The absence of personal sense in me is the end of Goliath, because that's who Goliath was. My personal sense is Goliath, but I know I am Spirit. The slingshot has found its mark. Truth has conquered Goliath. All the problems were in Goliath.

When I know I am Spirit, the problems contingent upon the existence of a personal self are no longer there. You cannot find a problem in Spirit. And when you have accepted Spirit as the All, as the Self, as the Self without beginning or end in time or space, as the Self everywhere now, you're in the Consciousness that needs no power. We have to illustrate that for you. The dog bites the boy.

The mother is worried. The shot is given to the boy for rabies. There's a 14-day period before you really know. So you wait.

Goliath says, "The boy can have rabies." Mother says, "We have to watch out. The boy can have rabies." Medicine says, "The boy can have rabies." There's a power called "rabies" where there is no awareness that Spirit is All. Now then, this comes to *your* attention, and you are aware that Spirit is All. Goliath is standing before you. Maybe to you it's not much of a Goliath anymore, but it is to that mother. And behind it all is rabies, the threat, the possibility. Why, even the other day a boy in the paper passed on from rabies, and so she's worried.

Now, none of us should have that worry because if you are feeding your sheep, if you are living in the Consciousness of Truth that Spirit is All, you will be in the Consciousness which can say— really can say and know without any great effort, but instinctively and automatically: "There is no dog. There is no boy. There is only Spirit. There can be no rabies." And in that Consciousness, you have fulfilled the first two points of your healing Consciousness: the knowledge of the non-reality of the Goliath called matter, the non-reality of the Goliath called condition in matter. That is impersonalizing and nothingizing just by being in the Consciousness that Spirit is All. You automatically do not go into a long wind-up, a long harangue, and a long series of quotations.

It comes to you and you simply know Spirit being All, there is no material selfhood and no material condition, and there's nothing to figure out. There's nothing to argue about. There's nothing to affirm or deny beyond that. It's simply a knowing because you have been living in the Consciousness that Spirit is All, and sometimes you don't have to go any further. It's better to [take] the third step, and that third step now is something I want you to take because you've done it enough so that it can become routine, a great joy, but something that you don't have to fumble to find: There is no dog. There is no boy.

If you can't face that quickly, easily, effortlessly, you've got work to do. But it can be faced that way, and then, you see, you have nothing to fight against anymore. You don't have to fight Goliath anymore. As far as you're concerned, Goliath doesn't have to die. He never existed. You don't have to cure the rabies. I mean now, this must be that Consciousness right then and there, and it takes daily living with it to be right then and there in that Consciousness. If there's the slightest fumbling and trying to untalk yourself from the problem, you've lost it right there.

Now then, if you can look at your financial problem the same way, a physical problem, your human relationships, anything in your life as an impossibility because Spirit is all there is. And stay with that for days until something in you accepts it. Something in you refuses to accept another substance in this world than Spirit when you reach that conclusion that Spirit is. And that's what Jesus was teaching, that Spirit is All there is, and that's why Spirit is invincible. That's why Spirit needs no power to overcome matter. That's why Spirit is never needing another power to overcome any material condition.

Spirit is, and the accident out there, the problem out there hitting your Consciousness doesn't make a dent, doesn't cause a reaction. It isn't that you steel yourself and your great willpower, but rather, you simply know. It just hits you, and that's the end of it. It doesn't make a dent. Now you're in a nonreactive stage, which automatically is called impersonalizing and nothingizing. You haven't done anything except you know. And we know that Spirit being All, I need no power.

Now, if we can get that far, your down escalator is going to cease to have power to bring you down. Let's stand there for a minute in the knowledge that Spirit is the Substance of God. That God is Spirit and God is All, and Spirit is the only Substance. And we're working behind the visible scenes in the one Substance which is Spirit, which is the power of perfection and love, and It is always present. It is always Self-maintaining, Self-supporting. And then the Bible says whatever you ask in my name shall be given.

Accept your Self to be that Spirit, and we're in the third step. That Spirit, which is all, is My Name, My Substance. And because that Spirit is omnipresent, and I am that Spirit, my Substance is omnipresent. I am omnipresent. My Substance is everywhere. The power of My Substance must be where My Substance is. We're accepting omnipresence of God everywhere; and therefore, the omnipotence of God must be where His Substance is. Everywhere is God's Spirit. Everywhere is God's power.

Now, these are the facts. We're not concerned about appearances. We're in the third step of the healing Consciousness. The power and the presence of God is everywhere, and that Substance, which is the presence and power of God, is my Substance *everywhere*. The fourth step puts the whole thing together. It's total freedom. The fourth step is: That Substance is here now. You take it here now in your Consciousness, and that's all you do. Here now is that Substance, that Power, that Presence, that Spirit, which is God; and because it's there, I don't have to do anything about it. It's here, and if I touch it here, I'm touching it everywhere in this Universe right now. All the Goliaths in the world can just waste their time. They aren't there!

The Substance that I'm touching here is the only Substance that is there. The Spirit that is here is the only Spirit that is there, and because Spirit is all and has no material opposite, only Spirit is there. Only Spirit is everywhere, but I must touch It here in the Kingdom of God within me. Here I know. Accept Spirit as Identity, and the power, the presence of that Spirit which is here, being everywhere, becomes the law unto me. That's the secret of no power, isn't it? What power need I have over an adversary if Spirit is all there is? And I have seen no one in this world give us that understanding of David and Goliath, except Joel. No power.

Just standing in the knowledge Spirit is everywhere as Itself, and that Self is my Self here; that heals rabies, I can tell you right now. It removes the belief in rabies right here, and that absence of belief right here becomes the absence of belief wherever necessary—wherever there has been a contact to this awareness that rabies is nonexistent, that only Spirit is. No power is needed to overcome it. None. No power is needed to overcome a problem on this earth. Though real, it is only real to the one who still has not accepted the All-ness of Spirit, the Identity of Spirit, the Omnipresence of Spirit.

And so in review, the one, two, three, four of it is this: You're doing two jobs in one. You're impersonalizing and nothingizing when you come to the place where you can know that only Spirit is. It takes some people five years to come to that: Only Spirit is. There is no material form and no material condition because of the fact that only Spirit is. You can take Jesus and see how simple it was for him, having reached the conclusion that only Spirit is, to stand looking out at every material claim and yawning, so that he only needs spittle to restore the awareness of vision. Only Spirit is. Where did vision go? Where did hearing go?

Where did all of the good things go if only Spirit is? They were lost in false belief, Goliath accepted, because the human mind is the very Goliath presenting all of the false beliefs. And so everywhere, is this condition in Spirit? Is there a cripple in Spirit? Is there lack and limitation in Spirit? Is Spirit hungry? Is Spirit poor? Is Spirit needful of something? Is Spirit suffering or dying? Is Spirit going to live just a certain number of years? Is Spirit getting older? Does Spirit need protection? And you find none of these things are true. Spirit needs none of this and Spirit lacks nothing. And you're strong. You're at the Consciousness which knows this, and so you're up to the third step. You're in that nonreactive Consciousness which can smile and say, "But only Spirit is." And you're in the third step of "And it is I. I am Spirit."

Where is Spirit? Everywhere, everywhere. Spirit is omnipresent. Therefore, that omnipresent Spirit is My Self. I'm no longer this finite material self. I am that omnipresent Spirit, which is I, and which is the fourth step: Here now. And that here now is the trigger which unites you to omnipresent Spirit everywhere, standing in the need for no power, letting the Spirit do Its own revelation of harmony and Truth and perfection. You're in the Sabbath. Rest. Stand ye still. Wait upon the Lord. Let the Lord of Hosts show forth that the braggart named Goliath is just a huge bag of wind. And that personal sense of self—which is the source of every other Goliath you're going to face—being dead—why, the source is gone. The personal sense is crucified.

You've really gone through the Crucifixion and the Resurrection with the slaying of Goliath. Personal sense slain, you're resurrected unto Reality. You hold it a while, and in your Sabbath, you ascend over the material appearance. Every time you face another so-called problem with the Truth, you go through Crucifixion, Resurrection and Ascension. So that your Crucifixion is to crucify the false beliefs by knowledge of Spirit as the All. Your Resurrection is when you stand in the Truth of Being that *I am that Spirit*. And your Ascension is when you're standing in the Lord, in the Self. In the no power of pure Spirit, you ascend above the appearance. When you keep doing this again and again and again, you find you have the weapon to meet anything with no power, and then David and Goliath becomes a very valuable teaching for those on the path to Kingship or Christing.

Now, I think the healing Consciousness should be quite clear by now. We should have solid ground to stand on. The importance of it is that when we have attained this measure of freedom, we don't waste valuable energy and thought and time pushing things away and fighting adversaries. We can devote that time and that energy to dwelling in the Spirit, to living in the Truth, to walk with God; and thereby, you find you're automatically living in cause, instead of fighting off the effects of a mortal mind. When you're living in cause, you're sowing to the Spirit. You're building with Substance. You're making a real transition in Consciousness, and the physical form is going to lose its effect. It's going to become just another Goliath as you become aware of that other body of Light, which has no outer obstructions to face, which isn't looking at the calendar, which knows nothing of the evils of the world.

Now this is the place we're all at in varying degrees, but nonetheless, this is the focus from which we're all working. Now, let's assume we had all reached the point where every Goliath in the world would meet the Consciousness of no resistance in the knowledge that only Spirit is. At that moment, you are in what may be called a point of equilibrium between the finite and the infinite, between the unreal and the real, between the Spirit and the material. That point of equilibrium is the secret place of the Most High where you walk undisturbed. And having attained it in a measure, holding it in a measure, we learn we're to live there at the point of equilibrium, which is the secret place of the Most High; and you'll find that is where My Peace is.

I give you My Peace at that point of equilibrium where there is nothing which is responding to the material world's complaints—which is sowing to the Spirit—which has built a confident assurance of spiritual Identity under spiritual law everywhere—which has accepted that God is conscious always, present always, power always, love always, harmony always, perfection always and everywhere. The miracle of Life begins at that point. That is where we walk on a new firmament, and we discover the old earth was really a symbol of our old body. The new earth is our new Body of Spirit, which is infinite; and we are that infinite spiritual Body called the New Earth.

We're on a different scale of things. There's no personal self now to be concerned about as we were before. There's no personal self to be made into a success or to protect. That's yesterday's Goliath. You'll find that David put his armor in the tent after he knew he would never need that armor to wear. The new Consciousness was formed. The armor was within in the tent. The knowledge of Self places you on new firmament. To walk in the Spirit is to walk in the acceptance that I live in the cause of Reality, and cause and effect are one.

Cause, being Spirit and being perfect, effect must be one with that cause and always perfect; and therefore, I am not concerned. I live in obedience to the impulse of Spirit. Goliath may eventually show forth again in another form and then another. But the ultimate death of Goliath is assured the moment you have reached this level which says Spirit can never be less than its own present, perfect Self in all things.

Then I would suggest that you make a little card. Get yourself a handful of index cards, and every time you come to a major truth, something you know is a landmark for you—something you've got to be able to wake up to tomorrow and be part of yourself without any effort, such as "Only Spirit is present"—when you have the realization of that, a knowledge of it, the working understanding of it, put it on your index card, "Only Spirit is present"—nice big, bold letters.

Put that card in your pocket. Put it in your purse. Keep it on your person wherever you are. Occasionally, just pull it out and look at it—"Only Spirit is present"—until this is your knowledge within, until it's carded inside yourself, until you know "Only Spirit is present" so that you can quickly look at any situation without having to intellectualize about it, and stand ye still in the knowledge that "Only Spirit is present." And then wait inside, and this is where that glorious feeling becomes the revelation of Divine Power.

Because "Only Spirit is present," you find something within you seems to move to wherever the predicament is. And right there where the predicament seems to be, even though it may be miles away from where you are, within yourself it seems such a short distance, just a foot away. And from where the predicament seems to be in the outer, within yourself that predicament seems to disappear, and something right there says, "Only Spirit is here." You have that feeling "It is done." The inner realization here, and just a little further here, "Only Spirit is here"; and that miles in the outer is just in that little space within your Self, and when you feel it is done, it is done.

All of this took place in David before Goliath fell, before he picked up the slingshot, before he let go, before it made contact. It all took place in that one little brief span of Consciousness within himself. And then, like a little microfilm shone forth on a huge screen as a moving picture, it became an outer visible thing. But the complete enactment of it was all within his inner Consciousness knowing Spirit is here. Spirit is there. The law of Spirit is perfection, and that is all that can be here. I need not make it so.

∞∞∞∞∞∞ END OF SIDE ONE ∞∞∞∞∞∞

I think we ought to go over this once lightly in the Scripture itself and look at the important spiritual points as they come up. This is 1 Samuel, chapter 17.

"Now the Philistines gathered together their armies to battle, ... And there went out a champion out of the camp of the Philistines, named Goliath, of Gath, whose height *was* six cubits and a span."

And as we read this, let's see that we're talking now about something within ourselves which is bothering us, this problem which is so big that it's six cubits and a span. And as we think about our problem, it gets bigger.

"And *he had* an helmet of brass upon his head, and he *was* armed with a coat of mail; and the weight of the coat *was* five thousand shekels of brass."

There's just no way to get through this problem. It's really an impregnable problem.

"And *he had* greaves of brass upon his legs, and a target of brass between his shoulders."

No matter where you go to wiggle out of the problem, it stands and faces you. It's a complete problem. Your human mind has no capacity to figure out how to meet this total problem.

"And the staff of his spear *was* like a weaver's beam; and his spear's head *weighed* six hundred shekels of iron: and one bearing a shield went before him.

And he stood and cried . . ."

And now your problem is beginning to talk to you. You've just been fearing it up to now. Now it's really going to get you. It's in the second stage. It's working on your emotions.

And so the problem is forcing you to meet it. The problem says, "Come on, do something." And you are trying to find out what am I going to use to meet this problem with?

"If he be able to fight with me, and to kill me, then will we be your servants: but if I prevail against him, and kill him, then shall ye be our servants, and serve us."

In other words, you know that if you lose, your life is going to change in the wrong directions. This problem is saying that it has the power to change your life for the worst. You're becoming totally involved now in the belief that this thing that's happening is happening. And unless you have got the knowledge of the presence of God, the Reality of God, the Only-ness of God without opposite, this thing begins gnawing, gnawing, gnawing deeper, deeper, deeper. And there's nothing in you that can stop it. It runs a hole right through you until you're a wreck. And finally, it just tramples all over you.

You're not meeting it with Truth. You're meeting it with argument, with fear, with worry, with the mind darting hither and there trying to figure out how you're going to escape or overcome. And all this time all that is needed is the little stone of Truth. God is here, friend. Now you go ahead and lick God if you want to fight. And that God, which is here, is my Spirit.

Now in all of Israel there's nobody to declare this. There's only Saul, the king; and Saul represents not the power of physical force, but the power of physical mind. And he's trying to figure out what are we going to do about this Goliath? He's using his mental ingenuity to try to cope with the situation, and that's what you're doing within yourself. You're calling on Saul to meet Goliath, and Saul doesn't having any answers. And you have had many such encounters in which you called upon Saul, and he didn't have any answers then either. And here is the same problem again, but there is one who is now coming through, a little shepherd boy.

"When Saul and all Israel heard those words of the Philistine, they were dismayed, and greatly afraid."

And Saul, then, is the inner mind, which is really a two-headed mind because it is presenting the problem; and it's afraid of the problem that it's presenting. It's that old double-headed snake in the garden of Eden. It fears its own problem. It's like the head turns around, looks at the tail; and they both get frightened. And they're one and the same. There has to be some order in this chaos: little David.

"Now David *was* the son of that Ephrathite of Bethlehemjudah,"

And we have a clue here right away. He came out of Bethlehem. Bethlehem means the house of bread, the house of Substance. And so we are introduced now to the thing called Bread or Substance. There's another to come out of Bethlehem later, too. And this house of Substance is the only way you're going to meet Goliath. You must have Substance. You can't do it with the intellect, the reason, the logic. You can't do it with human planning, because the very mind which is presenting the problem is going to try to do the human planning. You're falling into the trap of using he who is presenting the problem to meet the problem, and that's why we fail in our problems. We need Substance. We have to go to Bethlehem. And so David comes out of Bethlehem, the house of bread, divine Bread.

"whose name *was* Jesse; and he had eight sons: and the man went among men *for* an old man in the days of Saul."

And so Jesse, the father of the eight sons out of Bethlehem—you'll find later that Luke goes out of his way to prove that Jesus came out of the stock of Jesse, while at the same time he's trying to prove that Jesus was the Son of God, not born of Joseph. He's proving that he came out of Jesse. And that was Luke's problem. He was trying to do it both ways, materially and spiritually, trying to please everyone.

"And the three eldest sons of Jesse went *and* followed Saul to the battle: [and the names of his three sons that went to the battle *were* Eliab the firstborn, and next unto him Abinadab, and the third Shammah."]

And David was the youngest: and the three eldest followed Saul. But David went and returned from Saul to feed his father's sheep at Bethlehem."

Now, instead of sending out your three eldest sons to fight, you're being told to tend your father's sheep. All of this is before the fight, isn't it? This is your preparation. And so the feeding of the sheep is the clue that this little David is being filled with Substance, within a vision, with a knowledge of the Light of Being, that Spirit is all that is here. He's being strengthened with spiritual vision while all of the rest of the camp are figuring out ways and means to overcome Goliath.

"And the Philistine drew near morning and evening, and presented himself forty days."

Now, the forty days of the Philistine are also the forty days in which you—the David in you—is feeding the sheep. And the forty days means, then, staying in the Consciousness of Truth until it is crystallized, until the bread is leavened. Until that Substance is your Consciousness, until you are spiritual Consciousness. Then you can go out to meet this fellow, and not the way other people do. Then, this adversary, this Goliath, is going to meet somebody who knows what to do about him. Then you're not defenseless and helpless in the face of a problem which seems so unlikely to yield to any form of persuasion.

And while you're doing this, you're learning—as you are living in the Spirit, you're learning that the problem is not what you had originally thought it to be. The problem was the absence of this very Substance. The Substance you didn't have in consciousness was the reason you had the problem. It's a seesaw. The Substance is your inner Substance, your Light, and the absence of your awareness of your Light teeters your seesaw so that you see the darkness. And now Christ is rising in you, and this is the significance of David in the forty days. While the Philistine is roaring, threatening, and intimidating with his problem, in you is coming that inner Light which will so shine that darkness will be impossible.

"And Jesse said unto David his son, Take now for thy brethren an ephah of this parched *corn,* and these ten loaves, and run to the camp to thy brethren;"

And now there's more spiritual food, you see: the corn, the loaves. All this is an indication that he's being fed from within with more Light, more Light. He's being built up. And this is you. As you dwell within, you do receive more Light. If you're putting yourself out in the five senses out there, facing the problem, you're not in the Light; and you can't be fed this corn, these new loaves.

You must abide in me. And so you're not facing the problem; you're facing the within. Being fed from the Kingdom within quietly, silently to an inner enlightenment which is going to arm you from within so that you won't need outer armor, an outer spear. You're really a spiritual underground because when you come into this inner Light, the inner Light of your Being is going to be revealed as the inner Light of the Being called Goliath. You'll have him trapped from within himself, just by being in Truth.

And so we feel now that the Light of our own Being is revealing the non-reality of that which is called the problem. Goliath is shrinking before our very eyes because Light on the problem shows us God is present. Where God is, the power of God is functioning; and though Goliath still appears, the power of God wasn't shoved aside. It's there. It's functioning. In your new vision you accept that power, and Goliath becomes a dwarf. David in you is going through this. David symbolizes your new awareness that Light is the name of all Being, and you are accepting that Light as your Being.

"And David rose up early in the morning, and left the sheep with a keeper, and took, and went, as Jesse had commanded him; and he came to the trench, as the host was going forth to the fight, and shouted for the battle.

. . . And all the men of Israel, when they saw the man, [Goliath], fled from him, and were sore afraid."

Now then, there's just this one point in your consciousness, which is your hope. Everything else in you is fleeing, succumbing, letting the problem have sway as a reality. It isn't there, and only this little Light of Truth called David in you is aware that it isn't there.

"And the men of Israel said, Have ye seen this man that is come up? surely to defy Israel is he come up: and it shall be, *that* the man who killeth him, the king will enrich him with great riches, and will give him his daughter, and make his father's house free in Israel."

What is the reward for killing Goliath? Kingship. But even that finds none who are ready or able or willing in your consciousness except little David.

"And David spake to the men that stood by him, saying, What shall be done to the man that killeth this Philistine, and taketh away the reproach from Israel? for who *is* this uncircumcised Philistine, that he should defy the armies of the living God?"

He calls him an "uncircumcised Philistine," and that tells us that circumcision was a symbol of Oneness; and the uncircumcised was a symbol of those who were separated from God, unenlightened, divided. The unenlightened, by David, are called "the uncircumcised." And this unenlightened, separated-from-God man is defying the armies of the living God? The little shepherd boy is saying that. All his brothers have run away. All of the armies of Israel are turning tail, and this little something in you is saying, "Wait a minute. Did God make that fellow? Did God make this problem? What am I running for? I'm hypnotized by a mind that says there's a problem here, and I know God didn't make it."

Is there a problem in Spirit?—This glimpse of Truth. Can Spirit have a problem? What's the difference how big it appears? Is there a problem in Spirit? Can a problem outnumber or outfight the Lord of God? And now you're beginning to balance the seesaw. Spiritual vision—not logic, not reason—*spiritual* reason, *spiritual* logic is beginning to establish a place where you can come to a point of equilibrium.

"And the people answered him after this manner, *saying*, So shall it be done to the man that killeth him."

They had no answer. They didn't know what to say. And then something else happens.

"And Eliab his eldest brother heard when he spake unto the men; and Eliab's anger was kindled against David, and he said, Why camest thou down hither? and with whom hast thou left those few sheep in the wilderness? I know thy pride, and the naughtiness of thine heart; for thou art come down that thou mightest see the battle."

And so the elder brother chides the younger brother, and something in you will do just that. As this glimpse of Light comes, the very opposite will come quickly and say, "Don't be fooled. Don't be fooled now. Don't soft-pedal this thing. It's a giant problem." And so reason and logic, the elder brother's—those qualities in the mind that have been there longer than the younger brother, the memories of your inadequacies of the past—begin to say to you, "Well, wait a minute now. Don't get overconfident," or "Don't even get your hopes up." The elder brother, your past experience, chides you, this little fledgling who thinks that there's no problem.

"And David said, What have I now done? *Is there* not a cause?"

I didn't come down to here, in other words, because I just want to out of curiosity. There's a cause. There's a physical lie out here, and I am spiritual vision, and I'm simply appearing to show that it isn't there.

"And he turned from him toward another, and spake after the same manner: and the people answered him again after the former manner: And when the words were heard which David spake, they rehearsed *them* before Saul [the king of Israel]: And he sent for him. [David]."

Now, your mind and your will, well knowing that they have failed in similar situations, begins to turn to this fledgling in you, this little ray of Truth. Calls for it.

"And David said to Saul, Let no man's heart fail because of him [Goliath]; thy servant will go and fight with this Philistine."

Here's your old veteran mind, all your experience; and this little upstart inside you says, "I'll take care of this situation." Saul, the king of your will, the king of your mind is listening to the ray of spiritual vision called David:

"And Saul said to David, Thou art not able to go against this Philistine to fight with him: for thou *art but* a youth, and he a man of war from his youth. And David said unto Saul, Thy servant kept his father's sheep, and there came a lion, and a bear, and took a lamb out of the flock: And I went out after him, and smote him, and delivered *it* out of his mouth: and when he arose against me, I caught *him* by his beard, and smote him, and slew him. Thy servant slew both the lion and the bear: And this uncircumcised Philistine shall be as one of them, seeing he hath defied the armies of the living God."

Now, David says he slew a lion and a bear. Nobody knew that. You see, he did that while he was feeding the sheep. The lion and the bear represent qualities within himself that he had overcome. He had overcome the power of the lion and the power of the bear. He had overcome the belief in physical might and mental might.

He had overcome materiality. The David in you, aware of the non-reality, the non-power of mental might and physical might, has overcome the lion and the bear, the normal human impulses to go out and defend. "Oh," said Saul, "You did that. Well, that's a different story."

"David said moreover, The LORD that delivered me out of the paw of the lion, and out of the paw of the bear, he will deliver me out of the hand of this Philistine. And Saul said unto David, Go, and the LORD be with thee."

Something reaches your mind and it says, "Okay, maybe you've got new weapons I never heard of, but go ahead." That vision becomes strong enough to convince your mind to let loose, let little David go forth. Now, not by might, not by power, but by the Spirit of the Lord, you're willing to face this problem. And the old impulses are right there, of course, so David starts to put on the armor. The mind says, "Now, it's raining outside. Wear your rubbers and take your umbrella." The mind says, "There's a giant out there. Put on this armor." That's the habit of the mind, and before you know it, little David's starting to do that.

"And Saul armed David with his armour, and he put an helmet of brass upon his head; also he armed him with a coat of mail. And David girded his sword upon his armour, and he assayed to go; . . ."

That was just old habit. But then spiritual vision gets the upper hand, and says:

"And David said unto Saul, I cannot go with these; for I have not proved *them*. And David put them off him."

He's going to prove spiritual vision is power and needs no armor. David is not going to depend on material aid. Spiritual vision does not go outside and depend on the externals. Spiritual vision says, "I am self-sufficient. I have an invisible friend called the Holy Ghost. He does all my work. I need no physical power. I need no mental might. I need nothing. Oh yes, there is something I need, a little slingshot."

"And he took his staff in his hand, and chose him five smooth stones out of the brook, and put them in a shepherd's bag which he had, even in a scrip; and his sling *was* in his hand: and he drew near to the Philistine."

Five smooth stones. Not rough ones, not coarse ones. Not the five physical senses, but smooth stones—the five inner senses of the Soul—the knowledge of Truth. Not eyes to look with and see Goliath, ears to hear him. Not those senses, but five smooth senses. Inner vision was all he could use that would be of any value, and he didn't even use those five smooth stones when it came down to the crucial moment. Why? The Philistine came out and drew near David. Oh, he went into hails of laughter. "Look at this little fellow out there with a slingshot." He just couldn't believe it. This represented all of Israel.

"And the Philistine said unto David *Am* I a dog that thou cometh to me with staves? And the Philistine cursed David by his gods. And the Philistine said to David, Come to me, and I will give thy flesh unto the fowls of the air, and to the beasts of the field."

This poor little boy, David—this spiritual vision that you go out with—it seems, "Oh, am I making a mistake?" And what had seemed like an enormous thing before looks like it can crush this little bud within your heart. It gives you every kind of threat, every form of intimidation. It tells you how useless and small you are, how impotent you are. It tells you it's going to dismember you. And yet that little bud of Truth within you learns to stand there and look at it and smile and not even hate it and not fear it and not want to tear it to pieces. Not even want to go out and fight it. You don't do battle with the giant. That's your secret. You don't do battle. You know the Truth. You do what David did. You reach for one stone.

The Philistine is still ranting and raving. You've heard it all before inside yourself. You've heard Goliath's threats. It comes in the form of other people, other agencies, other institutions, all talking through your mind to you, telling you what's going to happen.

David looks up. He hasn't the slightest bit of fear. He looks at this giant who is threatening him, and he knows the giant hasn't got a chance. He has now reached the point of absolute Truth within himself. At this point David is aware that there is no giant. That the problem was a myth, a total fantasy of mind. It has completely disappeared as a force, whereas before it was all this power. The knowledge of the omnipotence of God is the growing strength of this inner Vision. It takes complete control of your Consciousness, and you know who you are; and then David in you can say:

"This day will the LORD deliver thee into mine hand; . . . that all the earth may know that there is a God in Israel."

"And all this assembly shall know that the LORD saveth not with sword and spear:" for the battle *is* the LORD's, and he will give you unto our hands."

There was a time after the forty days of David, when he was ready to go out, that he went out and said, "I am now ready to meet Him for the Lord of Hosts." And we see that the personal, individual sense of self, called Goliath, is always thinking of what *it* will do. But David represents not your faith in yourself, in your own individual power, but your faith in the omnipotence of the Spirit. Your knowledge that the power of God is what will express where you are, and not the power of the mind of man. David takes it out of a fight between two powers into the knowledge that only the power of God is present.

"And it came to pass, when the Philistine arose, and came and drew nigh to meet David, that David hasted, and ran toward the army to meet the Philistine."

Now from this point on, everything in the outer is merely the externalized appearance that comes from the newborn Consciousness you have attained. It's all automatic. From now on it's Grace. You don't make a conscious decision—just the knowledge of who you are, the living Spirit of God—and from that moment, the Spirit of God does the work. You don't. It will appear as you. It will appear as David. He will do things, but he's not doing them. He's merely the outer visible activity of the inner Consciousness of God.

"And David put his hand in his bag, and he took thence a stone,"

A stone. He had five. Which one did he pick? The five had become one. The five inner senses have become the one stone of Truth. Spiritual Consciousness is the stone. The knowledge that there is one Self. Only one Being, perfect, pure, here, now. God and no other. No problem. No one to have a problem. David is aware of himself as the Light of God. You become aware of your Self through this David Consciousness that you are the Light of God. And that knowledge becomes the stone which makes contact with the forehead of the giant.

"and [he] slang *it,* and smote the Philistine in his forehead, that the stone sunk into his forehead; and he fell upon his face to the earth."

The moment you know one Self, everything else evaporates which had been such a braggart, such a threat, such an intimidation, such a peril; and all of the consequences of it fade with it. The knowledge of one Self, one stone. The five inner senses become the one vision, the one omniscient Self; and beside Me, there is no other. And so we have most of this story. There's a little more though.

"So David prevailed over the Philistine with a sling and with a stone, and smote the Philistine, and slew him; but *there was* no sword in the hand of David."

And so we're being told we don't fight a sword with a sword. We don't fight on the level of the problem that's coming into us. We find our five inner stones. We consciously turn away from what the five outer senses are telling us. That's the meaning of the five stones. We turn away from what the five senses are telling us, and we rest within, in our Kingdom of God within—which is the five inner smooth stones—until we feel the knowledge of one Self. One pure, perfect, immaculate Being. We have now no other gods but the One, no other powers but the One. No powers to resist, to defend against. And so David had no sword. All he had was the inner knowledge represented in the outer by five smooth stones. And that's all we need, and that is the meaning of no power. That is all we need.

Furthermore, if we need anything else, we are not in the knowledge of no power, and we will not be released from that Goliath, which is our tormentor. It is only when we can accept the All-ness of God, in spite of the apparent tormentor, that we're in the knowledge of no power needed.

"Therefore David ran, and stood upon the Philistine, and took his sword, and drew it out of the sheath thereof,"

Because David had none, he took the Philistine's sword.

"drew it out of the sheath thereof, and slew him,"

And that's the end of your problem.

"and cut off his head therewith."

And now your problem can't talk back anymore.

"And when the Philistines saw their champion was dead, they fled."

Now what's the significance of David slaying him with his own sword? The subtle significance is this: That the power of evil which was so great has now been transmuted, and you find it's a power of good. That evil forced you to come to the state of knowledge that you need no power to overcome evil. That evil was good. To you it wasn't. It will only be good to you when you realize what it's done for you. Otherwise you would never reach this high level where you can stand in no power, immune to all karmic law. And there will be more and more and more so-called evil until you reach that place. Then you can do what he did.

"And David took the head of the Philistine, and brought it to Jerusalem; but he put his armour in his tent."

Finally, that has become your Consciousness, a level, a new firmament.

Now, I think we can clearly see that Samuel was telling us that there's a place called the secret place of the Most High where you can be still and the Father within speaks. And that Father within will come to you as either David or Jesus or one of the prophets, but always as an inner impulse to lift you to the place where you can stand confidently. And as we look around the world, it's very true: We cannot just toss away our national weapons because this is not yet the national consciousness. And so we're not going around to recommend to Washington that they reread David and Goliath. They're not going to get this in 10 minutes or 10 days or 10 months.

We've got all we can do to build that Consciousness ourselves, and we cannot teach it until we have it. The other day a mother said, "How can I teach this to my child?" about something; and I knew very well that she didn't understand it. So I said, "Well, I would suggest that you learn it, and then you will find you automatically can teach it. But before you have learned it, what's the point of asking how to teach it? You have nothing to teach until you learn it."

Until we are in the Consciousness of no power, there's nobody to teach it. You can't teach it to your child. You can't teach it to your brother or sister or mother or father until you are It. When you are in the Consciousness of no power, you'll find you're automatically teaching it because that's what you will demonstrate. Everything you do will be a teaching.

There will be less Goliaths in your life, and people will say, "Well, how come you're not worried about such and such a condition?" "Well, I didn't feel that God made such a condition, and so I'm not worried about it." "Well, there's an epidemic coming. Aren't you aware of that?" "Well no, I'm aware of something quite different. I'm aware that no epidemic is coming. I'm aware that there's a mental hysteria about an epidemic, but God isn't sending an epidemic. How can it come here if God isn't sending it here? Is there another power? You're still wrestling with Goliath, aren't you?"

And so, soon you're demonstrating the Consciousness of no power needed, but you're not really an ostrich with your head in the sand, pretending it's not there. That's for the one who is affirming and denying and says, "It says so in the book, so it must be true." You have made it your living Consciousness, and so for you it's the practical way. For you, David and Goliath is not preposterous. For you, any condition on this earth is just another David and Goliath condition. And then, of course, you know that Goliath wasn't just a physical thing. It's a symbol of all the other contingencies in the material world, the sum total of material consciousness summed up by the name Goliath.

Always the healings in the Bible demonstrate the power of Spirit as infallible, as indestructible in the face of every material power; but always there was the Consciousness of the Truth that matter is non-power over Spirit. And that where Spirit is recognized, realized, understood, and lived in daily; where personal self in a physical form is died to daily; where the knowledge of spiritual Identity is accepted daily; where Goliath is crucified daily and David is resurrected daily in Consciousness—that is the pathway to Kingship.

The question comes up sometime: Wouldn't it help me if I knew how Goliath gets there? What puts him there? Why does Goliath even appear? And you know, originally, I thought we were going to do some of that today; but I can see that it's going to be a very special lesson. It's really something that I have hesitated to do for a long time because it takes us into a completely different place than the kind of lesson we've had today. I'm going to call it "Cosmic Television": The method in which Goliath appears, problems appear, other forms of error appear. And although it's rather strange, I want to discuss it with you because I think we will be able to shed many of the attempts of the mind to try to understand this fellow, Goliath.

I believe you can never really reach that state of non-power until you have really convinced your mind of the illusory nature of all material form. That will be the purpose, then, of our little talk on "Cosmic Television." I don't know if it ties up with Chapter six, but I assure you by the time our talk is finished next week, it will. And so chapter six in *The Contemplative Life*. And as you read it, bear in mind that we're trying to learn through this inner contemplative meditation how to be able to know that Goliath is an illusion; that every form of problem is a form of a cosmic illusion, locally accepted. And we want to know how these illusions get here. Who puts them here? What's the substance of them? What's the background behind them? And, maybe, when we know this, this mind of ours will be still and be willing to rely on little David, who by now is grown up to be the King within us who will come forth as I, Christ.

For finally, we find here that Saul, the king, says to little David when they bring him to him after he has slain the Philistine:

". . . Whose son *art* thou, *thou* young man?

And David answered, I *am* the son of thy servant Jesse the Bethlehemite."

I come from Substance, the house of Bread. And the whole slaying of this nonexistent Philistine was by that knowledge of Truth which reveals the absence of the lie. That knowledge, which is spiritual awareness, is the Kingdom of God within you realized and lived in. And every illusion in the world—every imperfection—which is an illusion—through the Substance of your Being, when you know that you have come from Bethlehem, is revealed as nonexistence.

Then we, too, can say to Saul, to the mind, "I've been born of Bethlehem." I come from Jesse of Bethlehem, and Jesse is I Am. Everything that I am is from the root of I Am; for that I Am I am. And finally, the Christ comes forth. I and the Father are One.

The Substance is established as your Being. There is no other. And instead of being in Cosmic Television, watching images of light and shadows, you're an infinite Being without opposite. Your Substance lives Its Life.

Now, you know the four procedures, then, the four steps:

Impersonalizing means there's nothing, no one there. There's no dog there. There's no person there.

The nothingizing is: There can't be a condition if there's no person or dog or whatever there. And both of these are done by knowing that only Spirit is.

Number three: Spirit is *My* Name, *My* Identity. Spirit is everywhere Omnipresent. The Omnipresence of Spirit is My Name. Therefore, My Spirit is everywhere. Everywhere I am. No conditions, no persons, no people, no dogs, no cats, no anything except pure Spirit everywhere, the Kingdom of God. And It is where I am, and It is everywhere. I am in this Omnipresence with all the powers of that Omnipresence.

And now rest in the peace of that, and you are at the point of equilibrium. The world can turn upside down, and to you it will hardly be noticeable. My peace I give unto you at this point, not as the world gives. This peace is beyond the understanding of this world, but it is not beyond the understanding of your Self. For it is your Self that gives this peace, and this is the peace that no power is needed. The realization becomes your Self.

Every time you find you want to fight something or meet it in some way, it is because you haven't practiced the realization of no power. You can lose it in a flash, and I know that. You're going to lose it in an hour or two. You're going to wake up without it tomorrow morning, but that's where you must be. And so, therefore, you must establish ways and means for you to recoup this Consciousness until you lose it less and come into it higher, until the opposites fade away.

Get that little card. Write on it "Only God is present" or anything that came out of this talk for you. Brief it. Make it yours.

## Class 17: Has Goliath Fooled You

Over a period of time you'll have 10 cards, 20 cards. You'll find just a quick flash through—one by one—they quickly establish levels within yourself. They begin to work their silent leavening. They prepare you. And you'll find Goliath never comes to you when you are prepared, only when you are not.

Thanks again. See you next week, perhaps. The sixth chapter of *The Contemplative Life*.

Thank you very much.

# CLASS 18A

# THREE MEASURES OF LEAVEN

*Herb:* In the "Contemplative Meditation" chapter six of *The Contemplative Life*, we have a statement that is very important to all of us. It usually doesn't come out just this way except when there's a meditation. And in this particular meditation, not having any restrictions—the Father speaking within—this is what the Father within said through Joel: "God is really my Identity." And as you read this, "God is really my Identity," you're reading about your Identity. Now that is our starting point: "God is really my Identity." And then as you begin a day in any other identity, you can expect to find a conflict, because you cannot move in another identity to your true Self and expect the rhythm of God to be functioning in you, as you, through you, doing the Father's work on earth.

And so the first step is to release yourself to Identity, and in this you are releasing yourself to the will of God, which is your Identity. I release myself, then, to the will of the Father, knowing the Identity of the Father is my own Identity. And there can only be, then, one Will expressing. There cannot be a second will, a human will. There can only be one Power expressing. There cannot be a second power, a mortal or material power. There can only be one Mind expressing. There cannot be a second human mind.

We release ourselves to the infinite will of the Father, but never overlooking the truth that I and the Father are one Identity. And we reach the point where there is no twoness. We reach the point of Oneness within ourselves, the point of Oneness which is the moment of infinite Grace. Now that is where we're resting. Thy will be done. There is no other will here, no other self here, no other identity here than that Identity which is God.

And in this you discover the awareness of the power of God flowing. This established, you will also discover that the world will almost instantly challenge you upon this. And so you're prepared now, having established Identity, to look around at the world and say, "The Identity I have discovered that is my Identity here is the infinite Father, who is there. And therefore, everywhere I look I'm looking at my invisible Identity. There is no place where my Identity is not." We are not looking out at a world of divisions and separations and individuals. We are looking out only at our own Identity everywhere. We are accepting God *is* my Identity and God is infinite. Therefore, I am infinite Being; and the will of the Infinite is functioning within Itself.

Now there was a time when the disciple said to the Master, "What is the kingdom of heaven like?" And he gave them this interesting phrase:

"The kingdom of heaven is like unto leaven, which a woman took, and hid in three measure of meal, till the whole was leavened."

"Three measures of meal." Now let us take those three measures and do something with our meditation. We know he referred to mind, Soul, and body, which all must become One. But now let us take the three measures and apply them to other things. Let us take the will of the Father, and the first measure would be: "Thy will be done." But let us not stop there. Let us have two more measures. And the second measure is: Thy will *is* being done. And the third measure is: Whatever is not Thy will cannot be done.

And so now we're applying the leaven to the will of the Father in our consciousness. "Thy will be done." Thy will is now being done everywhere, and whatever is not Thy will cannot be done and cannot be there. We are coming into a oneness of Will on an infinite level and the rejection of all that is happening as an appearance, which is not the will of the Father, in the knowledge that it cannot be happening if it is not the Father's will.

Three measures of leaven. Let us take power: God is power. The second measure is: God is power *now*, and that power is *functioning*. And the third measure: Whatever is not that power cannot function because the power of God is all there is.

Always your three measures: The Truth, the fullness of the Truth, and the rejection of the opposite of the Truth as an impossibility—until you can reach the inner conviction that the power of God is now flowing where you are. The power of God is never turned off. It is *always* flowing where you are. It being the *only* power, any other suggestion of power that appears in your experience which is not the power of God is not there, but can only seem to be. And if you are accepting Identity, then that which is not the power of God cannot be accepted at the same time.

Now apply it to your back. You broke your back last winter. You have a broken back, and you're recovering, and the recovery is slow. Today we're accepting Identity. Yesterday we had a broken back. Today God is my Identity realized. What was my identity yesterday? The same. God yesterday is the same as God today. That which is true of me today is true of me yesterday. If today in God Identity there can be no broken back, could there be one in God Identity yesterday?

And so you must come to that conclusion that in God Identity, there is no broken back yesterday, today, or tomorrow. It never had happened except in false identity. The false identity never was the true Identity. Where did it happen? And now we're seeing the three measures of leaven apply to the past as well as the present and as well as the future. Can it happen in Identity? Is there anything but Identity? Is God all? Yes, God is all. Then where can a broken back occur? Only in one who is not in Identity. And therefore,

## Class 18A: Three Measures Of Leaven

where shall you remain in order to benefit by the laws of Spirit? In your Identity. Where you are now is the full power of God and always will be there.

Never will there be less than the full capacity of God. You cannot accept Identity without accepting that the full wisdom of the Father is flowing through you. All safety, all protection, all harmony is flowing through the Father. And I and the Father being one Identity, all is flowing through me. And nothing but that which is of the Father can be flowing through me. That which comes which is not of the Father is not here—is an appearance, a cosmic hypnotism. It does not belong to me. It has no Substance. It has no power.

Now your three measures of leaven, then, will apply to omnipresence, omnipotence, and omniscience. Always the knowledge of the Truth is followed by the fullness of that knowledge, and finally, by the rejection of all that is opposing to it as non-real. The power of the Father, then, should be flowing, so much so that you can now sit back in knowledge that only one Mind being present, there is no second mind to know of anything except the spiritual Universe. You rest in the Father. All that the Father hath is mine. Nothing is excluded.

And now your meditation takes a very deep turn. As I accept God Identity, there is no personal me. There is no personal him. There is no personal her. There is no personal it. There is only God Identity. There is no one else but God Identity. That means your Universe has one Identity. There are no pieces. There are no divisions. There is only one Identity, and It is God. And now you're establishing a God-to-God relationship with everyone you will meet. The Identity I claim for myself is the Identity of you, him, her, and it; and therefore, there is no person to person. There is only God to God. There is only one Mind, one Substance, one Law, one infinite perfection.

And instead, now, of looking out from a human sense of things at a world of many parts, you're accepting the one Universe as the one Being. You're not living in a personal sense of me. You're living *as* the one Universe, *as* the one Being, *as* the one Spirit. Spirit is all that is here. Spirit is all that is there. Then matter cannot be here, and matter cannot be there. All is Spirit. Material person cannot be there, for all is Spirit. Then what is material person? Material person is a mental image, and that mental image had a broken back. That mental image was sick. Are you going to improve that which is not there, or will you just change the mental image?

Now we have One, and only in this One will the power of Spirit become manifest. The power can never function except within its own spiritual Self. And when you have permitted yourself to yield to the Infinite will, to accept the Identity of the Infinite as your own, then the power—which is ever present, ever maintaining its perfect Self—becomes manifest as the power of your Being, as the law unto you, as the Mind which gives you the Kingdom, as the Mind which withholds no thing, as the Mind which appears manifest as everything that is right at the moment that it is necessary.

All needed forms must appear in the outer as this power of the One is accepted. And now the full leaven is transforming. As transformation continues, body, mind, and Soul all acknowledge the One. And so we live and move and have our Being—another three steps in the leaven—in and as the One. When this is established, your day is a different day. It is a day in the Kingdom of Heaven on earth. And all that flows in and through you and as you is expressing the Divine Will without any opposition and without the need for you to take thought, for before you ask, *I* in you shall answer: "It is *My* pleasure in you to give you the Kingdom. In *My* Presence is fullness of joy."

All those things that you had done in the outer world under your own will—all the hopes and plans and dreams and expectations—were your own preconceived notion of what you thought God's will *ought* to be. But we do not bend God's will, nor do we try to interpret what God's will is. We do not say,

"Well, certainly God wants me to be healthy." No. It is a complete, total surrender to the Will in which I have no will of my own whatsoever. For the moment I have a will of my own, I am taking myself out of the one infinite Identity; and I am separating myself from the ever-present power of Grace.

Now, there is nothing you can do to earn this power; nothing you can do to stop It. No sin on earth can move it away. It is always present. And as we dwell, as we abide, as we rest in Identity, we're in the vine. We can accept that present power, though it be unseen. We can live by that invisible power.

There are three quarters of a—well, there's about a billion people who have accepted Christianity on this earth; and about three quarters of the population of the whole world has accepted a supreme being of some sort. In spite of that, the world does not enjoy the power of God. There is still—in spite of a billion Christians, in spite of three billion who in some way worship God—we have a progressive corrosion throughout civilization on every fiber, on every level. And it is all because the belief in God is not the acceptance of the Substance of God as Identity.

Religion believes in every Bible miracle, but it cannot go forth and do likewise. It believes in Jesus Christ but forgets that he said, "If you believe on me, the works I do, ye shall do"; and religion is not doing the works. The belief is surface. The belief is an intellectual belief. It is not an acceptance of "Son, thou art ever with me, and all that I have is thine." It is not the acceptance of the Spirit of God as the Spirit of my Being. And without that acceptance, a billion Christians lose the power of Christ; and three quarters of the world loses the power of the God they worship, because the universal Christ *is* the Substance of Being. And you cannot accept unless you accept It as your Substance.

The Light, the Christ, the Substance of God is where the Power is. "I am the vine. I stand at the door and knock." When you open your consciousness to the acceptance of the present power of God as the only power that is functioning—as the only

Mind that is here, as the only law, as the only activity—you will find it possible to rest in trust, in freedom, in the liberty, in the fullness of joy, in the peace. For "I and my Father are one" in spite of what the naked eye may see, in spite of what the touch may feel; and this becomes the fact of life. Every good thing must flow and will if you will remain in the state of acceptance, not emerging once more into a will of your own.

We're told to rest in this form of contemplative meditation until a communion begins. Until instead of a you out there declaring, something inside is doing the declaring until that something inside lifts you into a place where the *I* of your Being, which is declaring, and you are one and the same; and there is no additional sense of self. There is that point of meeting, that point of contact. And this is the Divine contact which changes our lives—that point where the outer me ceases to really exist. Where the Infinite meets the inner, and the One stands revealed as the very source of Being, the Fountainhead, with no need for any external power or thing.

All is flowing abundantly. Even if there were no loaves, you know they would blossom forth. Unanticipated sources appear. Everything is touched with the magic of the inner Self released, lived in. We're not in a mind here. We're not in a mind that has a plan. Somehow that's far away. We're not in a selfhood that is apart from another self. All disappears, even the personal sense of identity. There is no you there to identify another you somewhere else.

There is only a One. And in your realized One, you're standing in the invisible at the Source of all things. Joel calls it the manufacturing plant, the infinite storehouse; and even that isn't enough. It is your Life without beginning or end. When you are in the One, you are in eternality; and there is no place where you are not. Whether it be space or time, you are there. Wherever God is, thou art because God is never separated from God. The only presence that exists is *the* Presence.

Now, this should be the way we move out into this world every day, and only in this method of release to the Will will you find that in some way you are synchronized into an invisible rhythm. Things might even happen in this state of Being that to a normal person might seem undesirable. They won't to you because only God can happen. Only the Power can express, and rather than rushing in quickly to challenge something that happens, you patiently watch as the Infinite unfolds, knowing that all is always well. All is always functioning under the one infinite Mind. Nothing can ever be wrong. Wrong is an impossibility. Right is the law, and there is no opposite.

And as the full leaven of Consciousness is completed, our transition of Consciousness takes place, and we are no longer in a three-dimensional world. For us it is obsolescent. We do not live in it. We do not move in it. We do not have our Being in it. It only appears that way to others. We live in Reality, and we are not living our lives. We are in that Identity which lives Itself. We are in that Identity which knows no beginning and no ending.

We are in that Mind which looks at a world of images without any reaction. We are in the Christ Mind. There is no darkness. There are no tears. There are no material forms. There are no material laws. There are no material identities. All is the invisible expression of God. Neither the good nor the bad in the visible make an impression. You have found another Universe behind the visible one, and you are content to let It unfold and to witness It at the Father's will.

Now, go back several thousand years and find your Spirit there. For that Spirit which is you this moment is the Spirit of Being two thousand years ago. There is no separation and no change. Move out into this entire physical world, and wherever it appears to be, you are there throughout all time. Let all of this be your realization, and it will feed you. It will sustain you. It will move this image in accordance with invisible law. Your dominion is in the realization of Oneness, for that One never knows a second one. That One never meets a second being. That One is always going within Itself everywhere, and that One is free.

Now in the Christ Mind, there is no other one. There is no place where you have to multiply loaves and fishes. They're already there as the invisible Substance. There is no place where you have to heal. There is nothing to heal. There is no place where there is a problem. There is no place to be improved, reformed, or corrected. You are in the Christ Mind of Reality above the opposites, above the need to take out a first aid kit and make a repair job somewhere. Now this is the Consciousness we want to move with in preparation for transition.

We have left behind us the need or desire or the innocence that would permit us to fall into the trap of wanting to improve our world or our world relationships in the outer. We do not paste peaches on trees. We do not clip apples to the apple tree. Everything we do in the Christ Mind is to grow from within and let the added things take care of themselves. We are in the transforming Light. There will come your moment of transfiguration when, without taking thought, without effort, you will find yourself no longer a human consciousness—no longer living from this physical focus, the sense focus. But rather, you will feel the absence of physical form even while you appear in one.

You will feel the transfiguration of Light in which you are dissolved into all that is around you. You will know yourself to be pure Consciousness. You will know that everywhere you are, but you cannot be touched by a human hand. You cannot be seen by a human eye. You cannot be measured by human standards, for you have found Identity; and you live as that Identity. In our next expression of Life beyond this present incarnation, when we have passed the point of return, we will be living in the will of the Father completely. And there, there is no choice of a second will. Here the choice remains, but here the dissolution of that second will is the preparation for living in that Kingdom where only the will of the Father is possible.

And there is no entrance into that Kingdom until we have mastered the art of living consciously in the one Will. Sacrificing all human will in ways that are very strange, but in ways that by eliminating our normal human sense of things—our normal sense of various disturbances, our normal resentments and animosities, our normal pride and vanity—these gradually disappear to the point where we are willing to sacrifice them in order to reach the higher ground where we can say, "Father, normally I might react this way, but I would rather forgo the pleasure of telling this one off or that one off and take on the garment of humility," that wonderful quality which really means the absence of me, that selflessness which is all Self. And truly, no one who has made the effort to banish self within Self and to look out upon others who are not separate selves—no one who has not done this can know the power that flows.

Suppose you accept this Universe, then, as one Being. Step out of the coat of skin, accepting your Self as that one Being. And rest in the confidence that the one Being, Being All, there's nothing to ask for, nothing to need, nothing to want—only to let Infinity unfold Itself. It takes a few measures of leaven, a few days and weeks of being willing to live this selflessly in order to invite *I* through your sincerity and dedication to lift you still higher where all things become possible in the name of *I*. You are erasing the parenthesis of mortality. You are erasing the memories that have accrued through the years. You are erasing the emotional scars, the crystallized intellectual beliefs, all of the accrued ideas that had nothing to do with the one Being; coming into the purity of Consciousness in which your Light shines.

We should be able soon to walk in the invisible, consciously knowing where we are, what we're doing, and how to do it. We should be able to walk through the material world consciously invisible, consciously letting the Father live as our Being so that we are expressing the Father's business on earth. We should be able to walk consciously invisible through every material circumstance, never separated from Source, always recognizing ourselves to *be* that Source. Recognizing that God is never separated from God; that Identity can never be less than the Infinite One; that all that *I* see *I* am.

When you were told that "The earth is the Lord's, and the fulness thereof," you were also told that "I and [the] Father are one." And therefore, the earth being the Lord's, the earth is mine. And really, we're being told that the earth is invisible Spirit. That invisible Spirit which is the earth, seen through the eyes of man becomes the material earth, but it is the spiritual Earth that is the Lord's. It is the only Earth. It is the Father. And because *I* and the Father are One, *I am* the spiritual Earth. The spiritual Earth *I* am. That is all that is here.

The spiritual sky *I* am. The spiritual stars *I* am. All that is here is Spirit, and It is *I* am. Where sky is is your Identity. Where ocean is is your Identity. Where anything is, only your

Identity is. All is your Being, and there is nothing else there. And when you walk as your

Being with nothing else there, then you are in the kingdom of miracles. For then Omnipresence and Omniscience and Omnipotence are the law of Being in action.

They're not something you think about, not something you even have to know about. They are. Grace is. Power is. Love is. Harmony is. And all these things—grace, love, peace, harmony—*I* am. There is only one Activity. And all of the things, which in the outer we see in a small measure, are all limited manifestations of the one perfect infinite Activity, which is your Being. That is why we are told to stand fast, to take no thought for our lives, because the only Life there is is our one Divine Life; and thought for any other life is separation from your own Identity.

Now you'll find the day when all of this for you is simply the way you are without any effort. It all falls in place. You wake up to it, and you know you are a different being than the one who went to sleep. It isn't you going to God anymore. It isn't you trying to find the Truth. It isn't you reaching out to discover things. It's just you being you, without corporeality, without boundaries, without a parenthesis around you. Just being You. Knowing all there is is You everywhere, no matter what might appear. And then the outer forms that you see become merely evidence to you of your unseen Self. And as the evidence changes to show forth more harmony, you can quietly know that is because I have been steadfast to the One. As you can sit in the quiet, complete, total trust of your one Being as the perfect, present power everywhere; for you It will become manifest.

It will actually show forth as the life of a friend, as the improved health of another friend. It will show forth as that which you know It to be—perfect—if you can dwell in the realization of It as a permanent dispensation. It will become the bloodstream of a child. It will become the breathing of a loved one. It will take every required form as you dwell in the one Being—knowing that the child isn't there; the one Being is. The loved one isn't there; the one Being is. Always translating everything into the invisible one perfect Being.

Now you can't do this 24 hours a day with your eyes open, but neither do you go to the gasoline station and ask for gas 24 hours a day. You get your fill of it and then you're on your way. This method of regeneration can be the first fruits, and it will take care of the rest. Every three minutes of this takes care of the other fifty-seven; and days repeated and repeated and repeated in the one Being are equivalent to thousands of years of human evolution.

Then you will discover that whereas Christian babies can be deformed or retarded or Mongoloid or blue, Christian boys can go out on the battlefield and pour away their blood, Christian adults can go through divorces and abortions, Hindus can have heart attacks, Buddhists can have brain tumors, Muslims can have migraine or multiple sclerosis—it makes no difference what the religion. Until there is the conscious awareness of one Being, you are not immune to the famines, the pestilences, the poverty, the diseases and disasters of the world. But the instant one Being is your Consciousness, for you all disaster is over. There can be no lack or limitation. There can be no karmic law.

Your pleasures are different, it's true. They are the pleasures of the Spirit. But there you are in an ever widening, ever expanding, ever new experience. The miracle of tomorrow for you is different than the routine, repetitious days of the world. And the knowledge that there is no end in this infinite, limitless expansion is not something that you have to study or rehearse. It simply becomes your consciousness. You know your eternal Self, and you know you're ready—ready to move into the sixth world—to the expression of Christ living as the perfect Son of God in the world of no opposites, learning completely how to move into the seventh Heaven.

Now the Reality of you lives in all of the seven heavens right now. All levels you are living in, and all levels come to function right where you stand in the one Being. All progression is the progression of the consciousness learning of its own Identity. Your infinite Self is always infinite. Now the reason for this today is that we have had so much truth to remember and truth to study, but we have to come to the place where *I*, the Truth of my Being, is expressing Itself. It doesn't have to study. It doesn't have to remember. It doesn't go outside of Itself to find something. It pushes Itself forth as expression. We are coming to the place of Being the perfect Truth Itself, letting It *be* Itself, not trying to pin words upon It or limitations upon It.

We're trying to really live the Infinite Way. All of the questions that come up in a human mind disappear in the acceptance of one Being. God has no questions to ask of God. Spirit has no unfinished business. Spirit has no place where It is needful. And in the expression of need, limitation, question, plan, hope, we are denying ourselves to be the one Being. Every lack, limitation, need, and problem is a denial of Identity. And in the denial of Identity, even if your questions are answered, they're of no value. In Identity just that Self Itself is the answer to all questions.

And so we might be coming close to the point where each of us is living at the core of his Being and the circumference and all between, when we can meet in the knowledge that we are the one Self, perfect as our Father, fed by the Father, living not in the mask of humanhood and requiring nothing of anyone. As we do this we have set up that Consciousness which need not fear what tomorrow may bring, and that Consciousness which need not anticipate by an hour or a day or a year the future, because that Consciousness *is* the future. It is everything that the future will be. And It being perfect, the future—being the outer—will completely show forth that Consciousness we have attained in the Inner. We have built our future in this Consciousness.

The joy of this way of life is to know that whatever comes to take me out of this Consciousness is the anti-Christ. And as I am alert, I can behold the pure, perfect, spiritual activity of the Father as I stand against the anti-Christ. This is the joy: Watching the anti-Christ dissolve. Watching the appearances reveal the absence of power that they seem to have had. Watching the miracles of each day unfold in ways that could never be anticipated by a human mind. This is the joy: Being able to say, "Thank you, Father, for that incredible action, that incredible experience. Thank you for opening new doors, new ways, new experiences, all on a level unseen by the human mind. Thank you for the peace. Thank you for the confidence, and most of all, thank you for being You."

# CLASS 18B

# COSMIC TELEVISION

*Herb:* Suppose you imagine that you are tuned in to a cosmic mind and that you are sort of a television set, and now it broadcasts to you, broadcasts to someone else, and everyone tuned into it receives the same information. If it were a radio or TV transmitter and you tuned into it, you would have an image on your screen. And any other individual would have another image, so that there might be fifty, sixty, seventy million images on screens, but all about one program. All the images would be pretty much the same, but all about the same one.

Now, as the cosmic mind broadcasts, using your mind as its TV set, the thing that it broadcasts is you. You become the image of the cosmic mind. We know it isn't a Divine Image. Now we walk around in this cosmic mind image, each of us tuned to it, supported by it, fed by it, sustained by it, each assuming this personal sense of me—this image—not realizing that it has merely been televised to us by the cosmic mind; and then it continues that program. While each of us is tuned to it, because we know no other way, it now televises a flood; and all those in a certain area, looking at the same cosmic mind, experience the flood. In another area it televises a hurricane, and all those in that area tuned to the cosmic mind; they experience the hurricane. Always, to them it seems external to themselves; and they seem external to each other, but they are all images in the one cosmic mind.

You will discover that when you look at another individual, you're looking at a cosmic mind image. When they look at you, they are looking at a cosmic mind image. But then something even stranger takes place. The image that you are is the cosmic mind image passing through your consciousness, changed by your consciousness to the level of your receptivity; and so your consciousness of the cosmic mind brings forth an image called you. And so when I look at you, I am looking at your consciousness of the cosmic mind made visible as your image. And then I do a strange thing. I make another image about your image in my mind, and so I see my mental concept of your image. And someone else comes and looks at you, and they look at the same image that I looked at; and they make a mental image about you.

I think I'm looking at you, and they think they're looking at you; but neither of us are. We are both looking at our own mental images about you. In my mind is an image about you, and that's all I can see of you; and whoever looks at you can see nothing more than the mental image that they make of you. And if 50 million people look at you, they are seeing 50 million different mental images about you; and it's important to know this for several reasons. You may think you're sick, and 50 million people looking at you will say, "She's sick," or "He's sick." But one of those 50 million might be Jesus Christ, and he would not look at his mental image of you as the rest would.

He would look *through* your mental image of yourself instead of accepting it and making a mental image of it himself, and he would see *through* the cosmic mind image which you are showing forth to the Divine. And because he would see the Divine—because the *I* of him had been lifted up to see the Divine—he would change the image of you in himself; and that image of you in himself which was changed would be the *I* of him lifting you up. And that being the higher Consciousness, it would change *your* image; and then everyone looking at you would see another image. And then they would make a mental image of that image because if *I* be lifted up, *I* will lift all men unto Me.

And the way it is done is that the image which each of us sees another in is always the same until there is one who sees from a spiritual point of view, and then sees not the cripple but the perfect whole Being and makes an image of that which is not a cripple. And that being the higher Image—the higher Consciousness, the *I* lifted up—It transforms the image of the cripple within Itself, lifting up the image of the cripple to Its own wholeness.

Now everywhere you are looking, no matter whom you are looking at, that individual you're seeing is your *own* mental image, not theirs. They are not external to you at all. They appear to be because we're all tuned to the one cosmic mind. We're all watching the same TV program and all receiving the same program from it; and seeing it on the cosmic mind, we all think we're seeing outside of ourselves. Now these mental images that we have in ourselves about other people never get outside of our own minds.

I have never seen you. I have only seen my mental image about you. But the Christ Mind does not accept that mental image about you, but knows you as you are; and that is what is meant by the transformation. And that is why we are told to die to self. We're not dying to self at all. We're dying to the cosmic mind image we have accepted as self, which is not Self.

The cosmic mind image is the one that grows, that changes, that becomes sick and well, stout and thin, young and then old. That cosmic mind image is not the Divine Image of us. It is not our Being. God is my Being. And you see, when you're not practicing the one Self, you are tuned to the cosmic mind, which broadcasts individual images to each of us, which we all form concepts about and make visible as ourselves; and then we walk around as image seeing image that isn't there except in mind. And before you know it, we have that world which is not our Father's Kingdom in which the law is not the Law of God, but is the law of the cosmic mind or the carnal mind and is karmic law.

Now that is the way one billion, God-worshipping Christians are living today; and that is the way the world is living today regardless of the religion in which they are exposing themselves. All are tuned to the one world mind. It is broadcasting, and this world that you see is nothing more than that cosmic television program made visible through the images that we entertain about it. All of it is one illusion—not many—many within the one. And we are breaking out of it by standing still. Learning that when I see an external someone, I'm seeing a lie, because the only one there is my one Being.

When I see an external condition, I'm seeing a lie. I'm looking at a television program. And if the weather changes, that is just a change in programs. No matter what happens in the outer, it is not happening in the outer. It is only seemingly happening outer. It is happening in the cosmic mind and nowhere else, and the cosmic mind is broadcasting it through images who call themselves people. But behind those images *I* am.

Behind the cosmic mind, *I* am. Where the cosmic mind and its images appear God *is*, and God is my Identity. And therefore, we learn that everything we're seeing is a picture put forth by a mind which is not the mind of God, but which is there for a purpose, that purpose being: To make us make the choice between God Being or human being. To make us reach inside and accept on faith the invisible activity of God. To enable us to walk through the cosmic mind pictures free of them, and thus develop the Christ Consciousness by this process.

As a child would depend on the parent, we learn to depend upon the Invisible even in spite of the tidal wave and the hurricane, in spite of the pestilence and the flood. In spite of every image that comes at us, we learn to depend on the invisible Self of Being; and this is how you develop the faculty of the fourth dimension. All of this is necessary that *I* may be lifted up in you, so that after a while you become aware of the trials and tribulations in the outer are merely those which are pressing us forward to the test of *I* in the midst of me until that moment when I can release myself to *I* and know that *I* in the midst of me is greater than every condition in the cosmic world of television. And then to stand in the midst of the images of the world defenseless, knowing the nothingness of all world images, the non-reality, the non-power, the non-substance. This is how you find your Self.

Now we have two passages that stress it from two different directions. In "I am the vine" in John, we see it from the standpoint of how it must be for us to stand still. Let's look at that first. "Abide in me,"—and this is a stress in John, the abiding—"and I in you. As the branch cannot bear fruit of itself, except it abide in the vine; no more can ye, except ye abide in me." Now this abiding in Me, then, is abiding in one Being in a knowledge of one infinite Self. There is no other way to stand and face the cosmic mind except in the knowledge of one Being, which *I* am.

You cannot meet it as an individual person. It's important to see that you're facing a cosmic mind, and you must meet it as an infinite Being; for that is the only place where I am greater than the cosmic mind. So you're abiding in the infinite nature of Self, and this is the meaning of "Abide in me, and I in you." ". . . I am the vine, ye *are* the branches: He that abideth in me, and I in him, the same bringeth forth much fruit: for without me ye can do nothing." When you're not in the one Self, this cosmic television is automatically taking place 24 hours a day. It doesn't matter what you are doing. If you're not in the one Self, it is functioning your life.

You can be the President of the United States or the head of a bank. You can be doing all fine things in your estimation, but cosmic mind is running you; and ultimately that will be revealed. You'll be discovered to be stripped of your power. Senility comes in. The great man becomes a doddering nobody, needing people to just sign his name for him. Why? It was cosmic mind all the time. It wasn't a president. It wasn't a chairman of the board. It wasn't an executive. It was cosmic mind appearing as.

## Class 18B: Cosmic Television

It was an image in the mind of the world. And each one thought he was looking at this one, but each was looking at his own mental image *about* this one; and this one was a mental image of the cosmic mind. That is the reason for the abiding in the knowledge of the one Self as *your* Self. You cannot meet cosmic mind from an individual, personal level. You might as well be a pebble on the beach trying to hold back the Atlantic Ocean.

Now on the other side, we see Paul taking it from the carnal mind in Romans. In Romans 8: "There is therefore now no condemnation to them which are in Christ Jesus, who walk not after the flesh, but after the Spirit." Now the flesh, then, is the mental image we entertain about self in the carnal mind, thinking that this me walking here is something, when this me walking here is nothing more than a cosmic image made visible; and in between this visible me and the cosmic mind is a consciousness called me which is interpreting the cosmic into the local appearance. That consciousness is the key.

When that consciousness is pure spiritual Consciousness, the cosmic mind comes to It and makes no impression. It comes, then, to a spiritual Consciousness, which is the Christ Mind. And the Christ Mind does not accept the anti-Christ, which is the cosmic mind; and karmic law is broken. The continuity of the cosmic telecast no longer puts forth the false image. There is a change of current, a switchover to the infinite Mind, and you are fed by the Infinite instead of the cosmic.

You are one'd with the Infinite. You come under a completely new set of laws, all of which are perfect; and transformation is underway. The physical form, which was a cosmic image, is now changed over. We are released from dependence upon it. We are released from its infirmities, from its limitations; and the Body of the Soul of the infinite Mind is now taking place. We are changing form, changing bodies, and in the process changing universes. Changing identity from an image to Being Itself. This cosmic television is the nature of the carnal mind, which Paul had discovered too.

"For they that are after the flesh do mind the things of the flesh; but they that are after the Spirit the things of the Spirit. For to be carnally minded *is* death; . . ." You see, it's really death all the way, not just at the moment of death. It *seems* to be life; it's the imitation of Life. It's the image thinking it is alive, and when we learn there is no Life in that image and can stand still, we are absent from the image and present with the infinite Mind. Paul's chapter 8 [Romans] is about cosmic television. John's chapter 15 is about infinite television. And we living in the knowledge of one Self break the law of karma for those, including ourselves, who have reached that place in Consciousness which demands transformation.

It's almost unbelievable to a human mind, but everything you see in this world is a mental image, whether it's a mountain or a river, a planet or a hemisphere, even the sun in the sky. All of it is a cosmic telecast, and the switch of consciousness is the way you switch it off. And lo and behold, here's my Father's Kingdom present all the time. I was simply in the wrong channel of thought.

Behold: One Being makes all things new. The *I* of your Being lifted up in Consciousness daily—consciously through meditation, through communion—leading to the *I* within you expressing Itself, making Its own inner statements of Truth to you, voicing Its own Truth, coming forth through you as the living Soul of your own Being. It is not under cosmic law. It is not subject to hallucination. It is not powerless before that which has no Reality. It has no disease. It has no age. It has no processes. It is the infinite Self Being Itself always, and It is *I*.

Now we must know, then, that when we are not consciously living as one Being, we are nothing but an image in cosmic television, and all we can witness is other images. We are of the world that is not the kingdom of our Father. And who is that "we" who is of the world? It is just an image that we are throwing forth

## Class 18B: Cosmic Television

from our invisible consciousness, and that consciousness is a false consciousness. We are living in a polarized sense of self which has no reality.

Death is not death. Death is the end of the illusion, but he who takes part in the first resurrection is not even touched by the end of that illusion. For now we swallow up that death in breaking the continuity of this cosmic telecast. In seeing that because I am Being, and Being is the one Mind, there is no mind here to behold that which is unreal; no mind here to behold that which is subject to pain, to suffering, to evil. And therefore, every time I behold evil or pain or suffering, what am I looking with? I'm looking with a mind that has no existence. I'm looking with the cosmic mind in me. It is looking through me and beholding the pain it put there. I'm a victim of a mind that I do not have.

You never have seen evil. Never have you seen evil. The cosmic mind coming through you as the anti-Christ mind looks out and sees the evil. But when you are in Mind, Divine Mind, Divine Consciousness, that anti-Christ mind cannot come through to see evil, because all the evil it sees is within its own mind, a mind that has been posing as yours and mine. Everything on our television set that we see in these images is in the one transmitter. We see it in our living room, but it comes from another source. We see our world around us in our mind, but it comes from another source; and that source is not God. That source is the cosmic mind. And therefore, there's one thing I've got to clear up in Joel's book. It disturbs me. It's this, on page 101 in the sixth chapter, "Contemplative Meditation". Joel is making a point, and unless you understand it, you can be caught in a trap.

Now Joel says, "God is doing all these things without our advice or petitions . . ."; tells us to trust Him. Now "If God knows enough to continue to put the fish in the sea and the birds in the air," and so forth. "If God knows enough to keep the tides in their places, ebbing and flowing . . . ." Now I want you to see that what is happening here is not God doing these things, and the reason that I'm pointing it out is that it's like God being the Substance of all form. If you mistake God as the Substance of this form, and you mistake God as the Substance of the tides and of the moon and of the river, you have not caught his meaning. God is the spiritual Substance. What God is doing is invisible. God isn't turning these tides visibly. God isn't putting fish in the sea visibly. That's our concept of what Spirit is doing.

And from what we have just talked about—the cosmic telecast—it works this way: God is being God, and That is You. And the cosmic mind is forming an impression of God being God, which translates into the visible as fishes in the sea, tides turning. But that isn't God doing it. That's cosmic mind doing it in its interpretation of God, and it's you receiving this picture from cosmic mind in your mind. And you know it's not God doing it because a storm comes up at sea, and you know God isn't bringing up a storm at sea. What is it? It's cosmic mind.

And when the Master says to the storm, "Be still. It is I," what is it? That's you standing still in the face of a cosmic image, knowing that's all it is is a cosmic image; and you're as frightened of it as you would be of a storm on your television set. This world for you becomes a cosmic image broken up into lots of pieces, and no piece of it is more real than any other, neither the good nor the bad. We're learning to walk through these images, knowing where they come from is nowhere. They're all the mirage over the desert.

God is being God, and that is *our* Name. And we stand in our Name to face the cosmic images, knowing the power of God has never gone away. The power of God is present, and that power is functioning now without opposite until the cosmic images to you are nothing but smoke. You can stop a storm at sea because there never will be one. There will only be an image there in the cosmic mind, and you'll find that's the same thing with tidal waves and hurricanes. You'll find it's the same thing with every disease on the earth. All is an image in mind put there by the cosmic mind, and it isn't God doing any of it.

## Class 18B: Cosmic Television

But God is present and only God, and the cosmic mind itself is naught but the illusion we entertain in the absence of our realization that God alone is present. The minute you step out of the fullness of God, you create a cosmic mind. It has no existence when you are in the fullness of God. In Christ Jesus, the cosmic mind ceases to exist. There's no shadow unless you're not in Reality. And so we have God Being, Self, You; cosmic mind and its images. And one of those images is you. Another is your friend. Another is your mother, father, sister, brother. We leave the images. We recognize mother, father, brother, sister as an image, which is my invisible Self all the time.

Everything is accepted as my invisible Self, and I call no man my father because God is my Being and God has no father. Everyone you see is God invisible. There is no other. There is no other Self, and every time you accept another self than God anywhere, you have denied your Identity. That's a rather fine place to come to, where all you can accept on this earth is the invisible presence of God. And yet, that is what is requested of us if we would follow the path of Truth. I and my Father are one Identity, and there can be no other Identity accepted on the earth. All is one Identity, and that's the only way you'll ever be about your Father's business.

Now I know this is difficult, the living of it.—The saying of it is easy.—The living of it. The conscious awareness of it. The practice of it. But the presence that you're to practice is your Self. You're practicing the presence of your Self *as* the Presence, of your neighbor as the Presence; and you're losing the identity of the image as your neighbor, of the image as you until there is no two of anything in the world. There is only the one infinite Presence, and that is where you're living, moving, and having your Being in order to experience *My* Kingdom, which is not of this world.

"The Dice of God Are Loaded" is the chapter for next week, the seventh. By the time *The Mystical I* is released, I'm quite sure we'll find that it is our own Consciousness that we're looking at in that book. By the way, don't any of you buy the book. Immortality House is giving each of you a gift of *The Mystical I*, and they ought to be here within a week or two, maybe even next week. I don't know. But if you're not here, it'll be mailed to you. Don't worry. We're very happy this thought came, and the opportunity to do this because it's Joel's final work, I believe. And it means a great deal to us to see his work in the hands of those who are following the greatest teaching that the world has seen in the last 2,000 years.

Well, Happy Mother's Day.

Thank you.

# CLASS 19

# YOU ARE DIVINE LIFE NOW

*Herb:* Today's chapter in *The Contemplative Life* is "The Dice Of God Are Loaded," meaning that the perfect creation is ever going to be a perfect creation; and that regardless of what we do—whether we stumble or not—Identity will never change. Life will never die.

Now in spite of the fact that God is all and God is perfect; in spite of the fact that we are all in an agreement that God is all and God is perfect, there is a universal hypnosis which compels us in one way or another to deny that fact with our action, with our deeds, with our daily activities in spite of the desire to honor the Father in all our ways. And then that frustration sets in, which says, "Here I am, doing my best, even understanding the truth; but I'm all snarled up in a lot of words and memories and quotations in spite of the fact that I've studied so many years. How much longer must I go on striving, self-doubting, wondering what's wrong with me or with the message?"

Now, this has come to me quite a number of times: In spite of the fact that every week somebody will say, "Oh, this was a wonderful class. Just marvelous! It lifted me right outside of myself."—I get those statements from people—just as well as I get the frustrated statements of why am I not getting where I belong. Today we want to establish the prime reason that we are unable to attain and maintain the Consciousness of the Father within. It only begins where the world actually leaves off. The world leaves off by looking for God "up there," and we begin by accepting God as the very Substance of my Being right here.

Now that is only a beginning. Once you have accepted yourself to be the Child of God, it is incorrect to assume that from that moment on everything you do is blessed and under Grace because that acceptance of being the Child of God usually gets no further than the larynx. We have stated, "I am the Child of God," and now we're waiting for a halo. I still call my father "my father." I still call my child "my child." I still call my sister "my sister." I still call my aunt "my aunt." I still have human relations and fail to see that having human relations is the denial that I am the Child of God. I have not left my mother, brother, father, sister. I am still calling a man on earth "my father." I am still born of woman. I have made the statement that I am the Child of God, but I still have a human mother and a human father.

And so you go on living this paradox, this contradiction; and suddenly you hit your head against the wall. The acceptance isn't quite that easy. The acceptance requires the acceptance of all of the contingencies of that Truth, of all of the responsibilities of that Truth, so that having accepted myself to be the Divine Child of God, I cannot be the human child of a human parent. I cannot be living a human life. I cannot be sowing to the flesh.

You're in an airplane. Everything is smooth, and suddenly there's a jar, a jolt. You know something is wrong. You look out through the right window. There's a fire in one of the motors. The plane is just rocking around crazily. Down she goes. You're plummeting down, down, down; and now you're a thousand feet from the ground. It seems inevitable that you're going to hit the ground. You're down to 900 and 800 and 700, and there's nothing can stop it. Nothing! And when you're almost 100 feet away from the ground, that's when we want to stop right there and reconsider who we are. One hundred feet away is death unless I know who I am. There's going to be a wreckage. There are going to be forms that never move again. Am I going to be a form, or am I going to be Life? Which am I? When that plane does hit; when those forms do not move again, where will I be? Will I be Life, living; or will I be form, dead? We have to reach the conclusion about that.

We say, "God is All." Well, then God can't be a dead form. We have been told to lose our life to gain it, and we finally learn that it means lose your concept of form to accept your Self as the Life, the Life of God. And finally, when that plane does crash, I am Life, God—not mammon, not corporeality. I am Life, and I am living just as much as before the crash of the plane.

You can actually go through that inner experience of knowing I am the Life and not the form, and you can see the division that is necessary in consciousness where you are prying apart the belief that Life and form are one and the same. You can see form dead to outer senses, but you can see Life moving invisibly, eternal. And when you are unable to accept that you are the Life and not the form, you are denying that I and the Father are one. You are accepting separation. You are accepting mortality. You are rejecting that "Now are we the sons of God." Now are we the Life of God. Now are I and the Father one and the same Life.

The same thing happens with the crash of a bomb. The world thinks of shattered forms, but the Divine Self, the Life of you, is never going to be in a bomb raid. The Life of you is never going to fall from the sky. The Life of you will never be in an accident. The Life of you will never hear about a malignancy. The Life of you is always going to be perfect as your Father.

Now, it is important to remove the belief that besides the Life of you, there is something else; and to see that form is but the concept we entertain about our Life. Life is our Name. Form is the concept with which we clothe ourselves mentally. They can have the form, but Pilate, you can have no power over my Life. This is the Life of God we're speaking about. Thou seest me; thou seest the Father, the Life of the Father. And finally, you reach the conclusion that you cannot serve God as human form. You can only serve God as Divine Life, and you identify as Life.

"I live; yet not I, . . ." said Paul. "Christ liveth [my life] . . . ." What a strange remark. Did he mean Jesus was living his life? How could Jesus live the life of Paul? But Christ liveth my life. The Spirit of God liveth my life. Why? Because Christ and Divine Life are one and the same. Divine Life is my Life, he was declaring. You see Paul, but this is Divine Life; and this Divine Life can support seven churches. This Divine Life can spread the message over the world of Truth. Paul identified as Divine Life. I live in form only by appearance. Divine Life is what is living Itself as me. This was his statement. And the Master said lay down your sense of form; lay down your life—that's your sense of form—to gain your Life, to know who you are, Divine Life.

And again, when the death of the form comes, even naturally, without an accident from the sky or a bomb or anything of that sort—what's going to die? A concept. What's going to live? That which is ever living. Your Life is going to live. Now then, why should we wait for the bomb? Why we should we wait for the plane to fall down from the sky? Why should we wait for the coroner, when all we're going to learn when it happens is that I am Life and my Life continues to be Life? Isn't this the time to be aware of it? Should we wait until we're on the other side of the veil to suddenly awaken? And once you, then, accept that the great teaching of the Master was that you are the Life that I am; and I am the Divine Life; you are the Divine Life—identify as that Divine Life. Live as that Divine Life. Reject what is not that Divine Life and see; see the difference.

And so, suppose at the moment each of us were to take and list within our mind two things we lack—human things, mortal things—two things that you lack. Just list them in your mind. You might have a dozen. List the two big ones. And then in your mind list two persons, two persons who to you are some kind of a disturbance: personal adversary, employer, government, whatever.

And then list beside the two lacks, the two persons who disturb you the most; and also list two of what you consider your major problems. Now you've got two lacks, two disturbing persons, and two major problems. And now ask yourself this: Aren't those lacks, aren't those disturbing persons, aren't those problems your denial that you are Divine Self, that you are Divine Life?

You quickly see that in the absence of the identification as Divine Life, you have no center; and being out of center, everything else must be off center. Your complete focus has to be wrong. Now there begins the pyramid of errors from that. The incorrect identification of yourself makes it impossible for you to identify anything as it is because you're the one who's now identifying. How can illusion identify Reality? And so, the entire life is lived in a compounding of the original problem: incorrect identification.

Now, take the two lacks. Whatever they may be, they are your denial that your Life is the Life of God because the Father says to the Life of God that is you, "Son, . . . all that I have is thine." Now where are your two lacks? Your two lacks are not in being that Son. You have accepted the form of you instead of the Life of you. The form of you lacks those two things, yes. But the Life of you does not lack those two things. All that the Father hath is in the Life of you.

These two disturbing persons: Christ wasn't disturbed by Pilate, wasn't disturbed by crucifixion. You're disturbed because not having identified yourself as Divine Life, these two persons to you are forms, not Divine Life; and so the form of you is disturbed by the form of them. Proper identification would say, "There goes Divine Life. Here is Divine Life," and you would find the invisible power of Divine Life making Itself manifest because *I* in the midst of thee am greater than these forms.

Your two problems—whether they're physical, social, economic—they are based upon a form as your identity. Always you'll discover that all of our lacks, limitations, problems, disturbances are really different names for the same one problem.

We have one problem, one sin, and no more: incorrect identification, the rejection of our Divine Selfhood as the invisible Life of God. We refuse to say, "I am the Life," as Jesus did. We refuse to say, "I and the Father are one Life," as Jesus did. We refuse to say, "Christ liveth my life," as Paul said. We do not *consciously* refuse. We refuse without realizing we have refused. We honor the error. We honor the evil. We honor the problem. We honor the lack. We acknowledge everything but my Divine Self, and in the absence of my Divine Self, chaos reigns. We go up, and we go down.

And therefore, the first step in living a life that is immune to the ills of this world, the problems of this world, the vacillations of this world, the antagonisms and the inhumanities is to go deep within until you can know that I have been instructed by God that my life is His Life. That the only Life I have is Divine, and if I fell in a plane crash today as a form, I would still be Divine Life. Neither life nor death, neither mortality nor the end of mortality can separate me from the love of God. And therefore, I must be living after what is called the death of the form. The only way I can do that is to be Life.

God is Life, and God is All. And therefore, Life is All; and that must be my Name. Life has no death. There is no such thing as death in Divine Life, and all that is not Divine Life is nonexistent. God being All, only Divine Life is; and that must be the only Life I am. But when I accept myself to be Divine Life, I cannot also accept myself to be human form. I cannot be divided. I cannot be Divine and not divine. Wherever you have encountered a difficulty of accepting and then standing in Identity as Divine Life, you will discover you were suffering and only for that reason. Ye are the Life. Ye are the Christ, and the Christ is the invisible Divine Life of every individual who walks this earth.

Once we have made our acceptance that Divine Life is my Life, we are beginning to come under the Grace of that Divine Life. But even though you have done that, you are still not protected by Divine Law. You can still be caught in all kinds of human problems even though you believe *you* are Divine Life. You've got to give me the same privilege. You've got to give your enemy the same privilege. You've got to know everyone in your world as Divine Life, and that means you're taking them out of form in your Consciousness. You're not sowing to the form, to the flesh. You're sowing to the Spirit. You're accepting Divine Life as the Identity of your father, of your mother, of your children, of your sister and your brother.

When you have accepted their Life as Divine and your Life as Divine, you are going to see Divine Law functioning in your Being. Why? Because when you have accepted Divine Life, you have found your spiritual center. When you have accepted Divine Life as theirs, you have found their spiritual center; and because there is only one Divine Life, your spiritual center and their spiritual center are one spiritual center. And everywhere in this Universe, then, is your spiritual center. You have included the least of these, my brethren. And as you do it unto others, so shall it be done unto you. The judgment you are now meting out is being measured back to you.

You are judging all to be the Divine Life of the Father. You have accepted the infinity of God, the infinity of Divine Life. There is no place where Divine Life is not, and only then have you accepted your Identity because your Identity is never Divine Life sitting in a chair. Your Identity is infinite Divine Life, and that is the Identity of your mother, father, brother, sister. That is the Identity of everyone you know, whether they know it or not. And when you have accepted your Life to be infinite Divine Life and know my Life to be infinite Divine Life, we are in spiritual brotherhood; for we are one and the same Divine Life. I cannot judge you, nor you me because I'd be judging myself. And then the law of Divine Life flows because you are not the Son of God until you are the infinite Divine Life. And then, "Son, . . . all that I have is thine."

Two steps, then, in your reconciliation to God: One—I am Divine Life. Two—I am infinite Divine Life. The form will move in the harmonies of that infinite Divine Life without taking thought. You'll know when to get a glass of water. You'll know when to get the cab or the bus. You'll know what to do and when because I, infinite Divine Life, knoweth your needs. I am the Kingdom of God within you.

Let's find that Kingdom of God this way. The Kingdom of God is your Divine Life. It is within you, meaning it is your Self; and when you have found this Divine Life to be your Self and have extended the truth of that to everyone you know, that infinite Divine Life is the Kingdom of God. It begins only in your conscious awareness that It is your Divine Self. It ends with your conscious awareness that It is the Self of all, and you have found the invisible Kingdom of God. Your spiritual center is connected throughout the Universe. The power of God must function in the Divine Life of God that you're accepting as your own. Now, I and the Father are one infinite Divine Life everywhere. Now you can understand, "Son, thou art ever with me . . ." because we're one and the same infinite Divine Life. Don't forget that *infinite* Divine Life.

Now, let's see what happens when we accept. We were told to forgive. Forgive our enemies. Forgive those who despitefully use us. Why? Originally, it seemed like we were being lifted out of a kind of humanhood that would hold grudges. But you see forgiveness now as the Identity of God recognized as the invisible Life of that individual you're forgiving. You're not forgiving him. You're recognizing God as the invisible Life of that person. That's what forgiveness means, then. And as you recognize the invisible Life of God as his Life, it is because you have accepted that invisible Divine Life as your Life. "Forgive us our debts as we forgive our debtors." We are erasing the belief in humanhood, in mortality there, in mortality here. We are truly accepting infinite Divine

Life as the only Life in the Universe as my Life, as your Life, as his Life.

Now, how do you fall out of the sky? How does a germ enter infinite Divine Life? By what manner does a germ kill infinite Divine Life? How do human problems enter infinite Divine Life? How do evils and errors and mistakes and miscalculations; how does lack and limitation enter infinite Divine Life? These things only enter the absence of the acceptance of God's Word that you are My Son now.

And so in order to accept I am Divine Life; I am infinite Divine Life, and so are you; you must reject all that denies it. Because we have been living in a mortal sense which, by denying individual Divine Life and infinite Divine Life, has brought us into instant karma. Instant! The moment you deny that I am Divine Life, you are in instant karma and vice versa. The moment we violate the truth that the Spirit of God is the only Substance, we are in the karma of separation from It through a consciousness that is unaware of It; and we look in vain for that Grace which allegedly is our sufficiency in all things.

But when we accept infinite Life as Divine and there is no opposite, and we deny all that says there is an opposite; when we refuse to accept in consciousness the lacks, the limitations, the pains, the problems—when we can face them with the knowledge that they do not belong to me—even a bad heart cannot belong to me because if I have a bad heart, I am accepting that I am not Divine Life. If I have a bad lung, I'm accepting that I am not Divine Life; and I'm merely perpetuating the experience of pain and suffering.

I'm facing my true trial which is saying to me, "Come on out here and be mortal. Give up that Divine Life idea and suffer a little." And I'm saying, "Willingly will I suffer." I'm accepting and acknowledging the heart with its problem instead of the Divine Life. I still believe that I have a human heart, a human liver, a human pair of lungs. Why? Because I do not believe that I am

Divine Life. And so, we still say, "I accept. I accept." But go all the way. If the Life of God is All and It is Divine, and It is your Life and my Life and his Life and her Life, why are you afraid of an atom bomb? Who's dropping it, if there's no other Life to drop it? You still have the belief that it is there. Why are you afraid of a heart attack? You still have the belief that a heart is there, and it can be attacked.

If Divine Life is All, where are you going to find Divine Life in a human form? Is it possible to pour Divine Life into a human form? Do you not see that Divine Life is telling you there is no human form; that the universal hypnosis is that there is a human form where only Divine Life is? You can't have both. Both cannot exist. You cannot be Divine Life and human form, and the universal hypnosis is that you are human form. And therefore, we sort of try to reach out and claim Divine Life while believing we are a human form. We all do it, and we all suffer for it; and this is the rise and fall of civilizations.

The stepping out, the early fumblings and stumblings in the acceptance of Divine Life grow into a certainty, an assurance, a confidence. You'd rather stumble in Divine Life than to be positive in a human form, and finally we get our stabilizer. The moment we have accepted Divine Life, we have accepted our Christhood. We're where Paul was. "I live; yet not I." This Divine Life is omnipotent. It doesn't need somebody to protect it. It doesn't need protection against the germ. It doesn't need a doctor's prescription. It doesn't need any human health.

All that would in any way endanger you is part of the hypnosis of living in a human form, and the stronger your confidence in Divine Life as your Self, the stronger you will see your capacity to reject the need for anything to improve, correct, or repair you because there's nothing in you that needs repair. If you need repair, your consciousness has fallen below the level of the acceptance that the Life of God is the Life of you.

Now then, we want to face the need for repair with that understanding: I am in incorrect self identification. That's my error, and that's my problem; and a doctor's prescription is not going to change that problem. It may change the name of it. I will still have the problem of incorrect identification no matter what human help I receive. And if a wealthy relative leaves me a fortune at the moment of death, I will still be in incorrect identification; and that Divine Life which I have not accepted up to the moment of death, I will not be able to accept after the moment of death. I will reincarnate into the flesh because unless I am living in the acceptance of Divine Life before, there is no transition. Transition is only in one who has accepted, who has lived in Divine Selfhood prior to the moment that is called death.

Every time you accept a condition on this earth that is a denial of your Divine Selfhood, you are rejecting the priceless gift of God. Now that should be made clear, then, that the way to the crown is through the rejection of every human condition as an impossibility in my Divine Life. Divine Life is omnipresent. Divine Life is omnipotent. Divine Intelligence is everywhere. Divine Intelligence is here now, but only for Divine Life.

And so when Jesus looked at Peter and said, "Who do men say am I?"—and then he said to Peter, "And who do you say I am?"—in that moment that Jesus could be seen by Peter as the Christ, Peter had seen for a second, "You are Divine Life." And doesn't that explain every miracle? Is there a single miracle that was not accomplished simply by the recognition that this cripple is not a cripple? This is Divine Life. It was a total re-Identification of everything. Divine Life, standing as Jesus Christ, looks at a cripple and says, "You're not human life. You're Divine Life." And then what happens? The spiritual center of one being the spiritual center of the other, the omnipotence of Divine Life reveals Itself.

How in the world could silver be found in a fish's mouth except as a revelation that Divine Life accepted becomes the visible, needed form through Grace? The Life of the fish is Divine. The

Life of I and you and him and her is Divine, and the resting in that knowledge becomes the law of Grace made visible. How could ravens feed a man except that the Life of the raven and the Life of Elijah are one invisible Life Divine. There was no form called raven. There was no form called Elijah. There was the one invisible Life appearing to human sense as two forms, one fulfilling the other. The forms are never there. Only the invisible Life is there, and when there is recognition of It, It appears as the necessary forms in whatever quantities or qualities are needed.

All of the healings, then, in the Bible represent correct Identification. The one who stands in the knowledge of Divine Self, who lives in the knowledge of Divine Self and looks out and recognizes nothing but Divine Self does nothing more than stand still and behold the revelation of Divine Self fulfilling Itself as perfection. And therefore, he could not accept credit. "Why callest thou me good?" Divine Self doeth Its own works. "The Father [within], he doeth the works."

Now, this is for us to see that the works that Divine Self did; the works that I do, ye shall do because the same Divine Self will do those works and greater works. Whoever will stand in the knowledge that only Divine Self exists will not accept the forms as life, but will know the difference between invisible Divine Life and visible form and know that all form is a concept we entertain about invisible Divine Life. And then forgiveness is easy. There's nobody to forgive.

If a man is insane, the state doesn't call him a murderer. If a man is under the influence of alcohol, it is realized that he had no responsibility for what he did. What if a man isn't there? Who are you condemning—a form?—a concept?—when all that is there is Divine Life. And therefore, the condemnation, the unforgiveness, the jealousy, the hate, the greed—everything directed at that form—is your denial of the Life that is there. Who pays the price? You do. Your denial of Divine Life as being the Infinite and Only is the violation which plunges you back into the good and evil of the world.

And so "the dice of God are loaded." They're loaded for perfection. Behind every door is *I* knocking, knocking, knocking, knocking. *I* stand at the door of every human consciousness knocking, and the mortal there, not knowing *I* stand there, goes right on denying Divine Selfhood, living in a sense of mortal selfhood, opening himself up to every mortal belief while freedom stands knocking at the door.

Your Divine Selfhood is knocking at the door of your consciousness. Your Divine Life is saying, "Accept *Me*, for *I* have come that ye may have Life more abundantly." And therefore, knocking at the door of your consciousness is more than just an acceptance of Divine Life. Those two lacks that you had, the fulfillment of them is knocking at the door of your consciousness saying, "If you accept *Me* as your Divine Selfhood, all that *I* have is thine." You are seeking to get rid of the lack, and here It is knocking at your door.

You're seeking to get rid of the bad health, and here's perfection knocking at your door. Everything we have lacked and needed and wanted has been knocking at our door. It is our Identity as Divine Self. The very things I have been seeking, I am; but I do not know it. And all of my fears are based upon this false identity which has not accepted true Identity and, therefore, has to go looking for the things that true Identity is knocking on my door to give me. Behind every human consciousness is the Self of God saying, "Open up and let *Me* in."

And if you fail, you'll come back and do it again. No matter how many times you do it again, ultimately there must come a time where you open the door, even a crevice. Just because we get tired of being hit on the head so often, we get curious enough to want to look and see what's behind the veil of mortal thought; and then we find the inundation of Truth. Always, nothing can prevent the ultimate establishment of God's Identity in you as You.

The delaying action in time changes nothing. "Before Abraham, I am," and that is the Truth of your Being. "The dice of God are loaded" because perfection is all that exists, and in Divine Selfhood accepted, then Divine perfection becomes the acceptance in your consciousness. Whatever is imperfect is not Divine, and therefore, in your consciousness, whatever is imperfect has no Reality.

If there's no dust on the stoop, it's silly to go out with a broom. If there's no Reality in imperfection, why go out to chase it away? You stand in Reality. You stand in the Light and let the Light take care of removing that which had appeared to be a shadow or darkness. And therefore, in answer to the questions I've been receiving—"Why do I not succeed, even though I try and am faithful; and I'm honest and am sincere?"—you cannot say, "I am Divine Self here" and turn around and say, "but you are not." You can't go to the storekeeper and think he's just a menial man waiting on you. You can't think of him as overcharging or overweighing or holding the best cuts of meat from you. You've got to see that Divine Self takes care of Itself and that there is no second self. And if you're sowing to the physical things of the world, you must accept the physical laws of the world and suffer from them.

The whole orientation, then, is to live in the conscious awareness of Divine Self everywhere. The realization of Oneness is not just where I stand. The realization of Oneness must be infinite. It's almost impossible to do this without noticing quickly that everything changes. The moment you say, "I am the infinite Christ" instead of "I am the Christ," you feel a broader base. You feel beyond a lifespan. You're not thinking and measuring in terms of 20, 30, 40 years. "I am the infinite Christ." This doesn't begin or end at a certain place. This is the infinite Christ. Forget the mask of form and now witness your own Selfhood.

All of the cluttering, disturbing fragments of thought; all of the little trepidations of the heart; all of the fears slowly dissolve because I, infinite Christ, lives only under the law of infinite Divinity. And even if you only attain 20 or 30 or 40 percent of that, it's 5 million times what you had as a human being. Because we know you can't attain 100 percent of that as long as the world is still in its universal hypnotism, but we can go up the ladder. We can actually climb the ladder of Truth so that we start with Identification as Christ, the Divine Self. We extend It to the next rung, which is Identification of Christ as the very Substance and nature of all who walk the earth.

You can look at the bird. You can look at the chicken, and you can see the form isn't what's there. The form perishes. The form is transient. Don't get stuck on the form. Sow to the Life that is there. In other words, recognize the Life which is there is not even the life that apparently goes out of the form when it's dead. The Life is never in that form. The Life is one Life. It never enters into form. The Life is simply Life being Itself, and *you* are making that form. The world mind and you are collaborating to create a form where only Life is. And get to sow to the Life, the Life, the Life independent of the form. Marvel that the Life can show forth a beautiful bird or flower, but don't think that the Life of God is in that bird or in that flower because when the heel of somebody crushes that flower, it's not going to crush the Life of God. It's going to crush only the form that we have created in our mind.

Get to see that the Life is independent of the form, does not live in the form; but It creates for us through our consciousness the appearance called form through processes too numerous for you and I to sit down and detail out. But as you are sowing to the Life, you are bringing into play the power of that Life through your consciousness. And that Life, through your consciousness, becomes the law of the form—the law of your heart, the law of your lungs, the law of your body—through your conscious awareness of the invisible Life of all Being. And then you, too, are saying, "Pilate, you could have no power over me because I have the Life. And I recognize only the invisible Life of you, and the Life of you and I are one Life." How can that one Life have any power over Itself? It needs no power. It is the only power, and you can rest right there.

Now, the work gets more exciting. As you do this and do this and do this, you find you're becoming independent of form. You're not trapped by it. You're not acknowledging form as a power because you're not acknowledging form as the Presence. The form can make all kinds of claims. It won't bother you one bit because the life that is there where the form appears is your own Life, and it's very friendly to you. You don't have to go running away from a ghost anymore.

Everything you want to do is already done in your Life, and if you will just be still and know Life is perfect and is finished, it will flow through in the very forms that are needed, whatever they may be. There are no limitations to Life because it is infinite, and *I* come quickly. The question is: Are you putting up a barrier by being a human being while claiming to be the Divine Life? Because the Divine Life can never flow into a human being. It will only flow within Itself, and if you are still on the hang-up of form as a Reality, as a living Presence, then the message of Jesus Christ for you is a dead issue. You have crucified it in your consciousness, and there can be no resurrection until you remove that crucifixion and in turn, turn around and crucify the false sense of self and let the resurrection into Christ realized become the law of your Being.

We have been given a world of images to walk in, and behind it is the invisible Life of God ever perfect, ever present, ever functioning, independent of everything that we do in these images. Occasionally one slips behind the veil of the images in Consciousness, and lo and behold, we think he's done a miracle; and he tells us, "No, I haven't done a miracle at all. You can do the same. Follow me. Do what I have done in Consciousness."

Accept the Invisible as the Divine and the Only, and take no thought for your visible form life. You will discover the power of the Invisible meets every need, but be true to It everywhere in the least of these, my brethren; and you will find the dice of God are always loaded in your favor. Perfection must manifest where God is accepted as the Only.

And as Ezekiel puts it, there's an overturning and an overturning and an overturning. And that's the overturning in consciousness as we get rid of the concepts of matter, the concepts of form until we come to that place where we can say, "There is only one Life in the entire Universe, and that Life I am." He is. She is. We are all that one Life, joint heirs in the one Life. There is no other life than the Life that I am. It is the Life of God. It needs no protection. It needs no planning. It needs no repairs, and there is no other me. Then you've dragged out of the form every concept. You're all in one piece now. You're not clinging to a Christ concept on one side and a human concept on the other. You're not divided. You're not a split personality.

You know you don't live in a form, and you know the form is but a cosmic image. They will never trap you in that form and because of it, even that form in which you are not living will walk through this world untouched because there will be a You there, an invisible Divine Being which will be the law even unto that manifest, physically-appearing form. The world is new to everyone when Christ has entered in, and the world that this atomic era has called the world ceases to have power over that consciousness which is living, moving, having Its Being in the realization that the Divine Self, I am.

Now, you might find it interesting to do something. You can go through the experience of death—not actually, of course—but you can imagine this plane crashing. You'll find a tremendous relief and release to feel yourself as Life independent of every human tragedy. And somehow when you do that, you're anticipating a day when just that thing will happen. When the realization of Life as your Self lifts you out of the earthbound mortal who's struggling along under karma—trying to figure out how to break the karma, how to erase the karma, how to nullify the karma, how to turn each little event into his advantage.

You don't turn events into your advantage anymore. You are the Infinite. You simply behold your Infinite Self revealing Itself as a better business, a better marriage, a better mother-father relationship, a better child relationship, a better human relationship. Everything that is in the Infinite reveals Itself as the new harmony of this human existence simply by standing in the knowledge that I am this Life which is independent of form.

Often you invent these little experiences within yourself just to go through them vicariously, to release yourself from the pre-concepts of the world. Then they're not as strange to you later as they come along. We should reach a place where the whole concept of death is revealed as nothing more than the termination of a false image called form. It's even possible to reach the place where you can see death as a very beautiful release into your uncluttered Self.

∞∞∞∞∞∞ END OF SIDE ONE ∞∞∞∞∞∞

Let's look at some of the statements of Jesus from the standpoint of correct identification. Jesus, of course, represents to us an individual who has accepted Divine Life and, therefore, is Christed and becomes the Christ, having died to a personal sense of self. Having died to a sense of a personal form, so that a Christed Self no longer can be crucified. It isn't in a physical form. It cannot be entombed because there's no physical form to keep in a tomb. There is only the pure Divine Life of God.

Now, as the Wayshower, then, who is showing us that we have to come to the acceptance of ourselves to be the Divine Life without corporeality, he walks through the earth appearing to us through our concept of that invisible Self as Jesus, a man. But he's consistently telling us, "I'm not a man. I am Light. I am Life. And if you believe on me—meaning if you will know that the Life that I am, which is doing these things, is the Life that is you—well then, the Life that is you will do these things where you are." And so, we're looking now at One who has done what we are learning to do, even in a small measure; who is assuring us that we can learn to do what he has done.

And now, at the tomb of Lazarus, he says this to Martha, "I am the resurrection, and the life." I am the Life. I'm not Jesus Christ, a man. I am the Life. I am the Life of the Father. I am Divine Life right here, right now. But I'm not only the Divine Life in Jesus standing here; I'm the Divine Life which is the one Divine Life. I must be the Divine Life which is the Life of him whom you call your brother Lazarus down in that tomb. I am the Life of all because there is only one Life, and that is I. That Life can walk out of a tomb because there's no tomb for that Life. In other words, that Life in you walks out of the tomb of death in you. That Life in you walks out of the tomb of a cripple, out of the tomb of a financial problem, out of every tomb. The Life that Jesus is showing is here and is the Life of all walks out of the tomb of every human problem, and there is no place where It does not walk. There's no closed door to that Life.

It's walking this earth now. It's the only Life there is. I am the Life, and I am the Life that is the Life of you. And when you accept the Life that I am as the Life of you, you can have no other Life; and that Life will show you that It is what we have called the miracle worker. It is the Savior. It is the Messiah. It is the only Life. It has no end and no beginning in time or in space. In that Life there is only the perfection of that Life, the harmony of that Life, and only the Life of that Life. It has no terminal point. And so the acceptance of this Life that Jesus is showing forth as your Life, you are doing what he called knowing God aright. Because God is that Life, and to know *that* Life is to know Life eternal.

The moment you have reestablished Identity as the Life which Jesus was witnessing at the tomb of Lazarus and in his complete three-year mission and which is the Life that he's living this moment, that Life is your Life; and you have found the Life that never ends. And the more aware you become of that Life, the more It will reveal to you the multiplicity of Its benedictions. As your consciousness opens to greater acceptance of this Life as your Life, It reveals more of its fullness.

Always in this Bible we have been given the knowledge that the Life of God revealing Itself as the Life of Jesus and as the Life of those who are called victims who had come to Jesus for healing, that that Life is always perfect no matter what concept the mortal mind may overshadow. And wherever there is an acceptance of the Life, even through one, that shadow is lifted; and the eternal, timeless, ever-present, perfect Life again is revealed to be there functioning in all its perfection. It never has gone anywhere. It is never less. It will not be more. It will always be perfect Life at every point of Itself, and It is your Life. And then we're told anything you shall ask in *My* Name shall be given to you, and *My* Name is your Life. Whenever you have accepted your name to be that Life, everything that you might ask for is already accomplished. All you need to do is sit down and watch what your acceptance will do.

Now, again and again and again Jesus made the claim, "I am the Life." He was showing you the miracle worker. And ye are the Life. And so, the miracle worker is the Life of God; and that is your Kingdom. Your function is to be the king of the Kingdom by the acceptance of the Life as your Life; and your world is to be redeemed, all of it, by the recognition that you never had a world. You had a world of images. The only world there is is the pure, perfect Life Divine. It is the only one that is present. That is where we are and who we are. The Identity of each of us is that Universe of the Divine Life. Now, whom shall you fear? What circumstance shall you fear? Or what problem can you possibly anticipate and still accept that the one Divine Life is all there is throughout what we call time and beyond, and throughout what we call space and beyond? That is all that will be here tomorrow. That is all that has ever been here.

Your acceptance of the one Divine Life, then, is the crucifixion of every yesterday that was not the Divine Life. It couldn't have happened because only the Divine Life was happening and is happening. Every yesterday in mortality is just a lingering concept. The next birthday is a concept. Your calendar is a concept. Your wristwatch is a concept. There is only Divine Life, and in it there is no time. There is no space. There is no material progression. There is no aging. There is no recovery from pain. There is no heartbeat. There is only Divine Being.

Can you stand there in the knowledge that I am the Life and realize that Life in your consciousness, so that it wells up inside you as a fact, not a statement? And that is the purpose of the meditations we are to do this week. I'd like you to each take this assignment: Take the word "Identity." Just bring it down, vertical: "I" "d" "e" "n." And with the "I," make a word up. With the "D," make a word up. Like "I am" or "infinity," but something that's true about your Identity. So that you might end up with something like "I am" as the "I," and then "D" would be "Divine," and then "E" would be "Everyone else is." I don't care if it's four or six words, but start it with the letter so that each letter of "Identity" is the beginning of a word or a sentence about your Identity. And when you get through, you'll have eight words or sentences or paragraphs, as much as you want to write, but begin it with the "I" and then do it in such a way that you remember that "I" for me stands for "Infinite." "D" for me stands for "Deny it, and you lose it." "E" for me stands for "Everyone is the same infinite Identity," and so on, until you have some kind of an inner remembrance that the word "Identity" for you means these things.

And then, in your meditations, practice those meanings of Identity for you in a contemplative way. Be still and let them take root until you are able to be in the Silence accepting Identity as Life Divine. Not life human, not life with a birth and a death, not life with an up and a down, not life with an aging process, not life with an end somewhere, not life with a Medicare program—just Life Divine as Identity.

And after you've had enough meditations on Life Divine as Identity, continue having a few more meditations on the life that you are not—I am not life in form; I am not life that comes and goes; I am not changing life; I am not life becoming better life; I am not physical life—until you know who you are. Until you can stand in front of any tomb, in front of any person, in front of any circumstance, knowing the Life that I am is Divine; and that is all there is as far as the eye can see and beyond. And for me, there's nothing beyond that to do; for It doeth Its own work. It revealeth Itself. It will blossom forth and make the desert as the rose.

There is no human me to do it. It doeth Its own work.

We have been told in many ways that as we sow to the flesh, meaning to the mortal life, we reap corruption. As we sow to the Spirit, meaning Divine Life, we reap Life everlasting. For us, there is no ending. For us, there is no beginning. For us, there is no improvement. You begin at the level of Divine perfection. You cannot improve. You accept Divine perfection. You do not start at the bottom and work your way up to it. Humanhood never becomes Divine, and Divinity never becomes human.

Now if that isn't clear, let's go over it again. Spell out the word "Identity" vertically. Make up a word, sentence, or paragraph or whatever you wish in which the first letter begins a statement about your Identity with the letter "I": "I am" or "Identity is." And then another with the letter "D" and then the letter "E" until you have finished it and have something that you can even later consolidate to a point, where for the next 20 years you can remember what Identity means to you. So that wherever you are, you can contemplate that word meaningfully. And the reason you should do this is that there is no situation on this earth that cannot be faced successfully with the knowledge of Identity.

If three wolf hounds come up to nibble at you, Identity must include their Identity and yours and right now as the one invisible Divine Self. Period. Always only one Life is present, and that one Life must always include every form that you see, whether it's the tree or the bird or the dog or the insect or the bill collector. There is only one invisible Life everywhere. And as long as you are accepting It, you are sowing to the Spirit; and you will reap Life everlasting. The conscious awareness that the Life of God I am living now, and nothing can ever separate me from It. This life and I are one and the same.

We have been going outside of ourselves to get things, but there is no outside of ourselves. Going outside to get things is the ignorance that our life is the one infinite Divine Life. There's no outside. My own life has to yield itself in my experience. There's nothing outside it to get. It is self-contained in all perfection, and that's the meaning of being a contemplative. You're accepting that your Divine Life is self-contained. It is everywhere, and it will pour forth its fruit to a place that is called your human selfhood in the middle somewhere. And this will be the fruit on the tree, but only because you're not living *as* that human selfhood. Everything will seem to come from the circumference into this center here. But there is no center, and there is no circumference. It is One.

The only Life in this Universe, then, is identified as your Life. When you meditate with that and It declares Itself within you instead of you declaring it, you will know you have reached the point where you have accepted It. You may think you've accepted It. But until It within you declares Itself—until It lifts you into a new order where your mind is no longer saying anything, but rather, receiving from the Infinite the assurance that It is so—then you will know that you have overturned and overturned, and He has come whose right It is to sit upon the throne. There is an infinite acceptance. You have reached the realm of the fourth dimension of Consciousness where the Spirit within you says, "Yes, *I* am come."

This is out of your hands now. You're not in human government, and don't try to retrogress and go back into human government to defend against things. Don't try to get things. The government of God, the government of Spirit is infinitely perfect and infallible. It doeth the works. It performeth. It perfecteth. Just *know*. Know you are the Life. Rest in It. Accept It in confidence, and Its peace will envelop you; and Its peace will give you that peace which the world cannot give, the peace of Grace and fulfillment.

You will find yourself looking out at the relationships of yesterday, and they will change before your very eyes. The very substance of them will feel different. All animosities quickly fade. The usual things that pressure us become the sting of the serpent that no longer has power. When they caught us in the low focus of a human selfhood and we met them all on their own level, we were seeing two powers. We were witnessing good powers, material powers, mental powers, powers that overcome other powers; but in our new elevation of Consciousness, we're in the one Self that has no need to overcome anything, for all that is on this earth is an imitation of that one Self that you have discovered. You never have to use a power over the imitations. You never have to use a power, period, because the one Self is ever maintaining Its glorious perfection where you stand and in all that concerneth you.

Now this little pour of a class, learning of its own Divinity, is being prepared to walk forth within the consciousness of the world where two powers are accepted, knowing that there is no power on this earth other than perfection in all things. We walk with our hands behind our back. We do not worry about faltering businesses. We do not worry about any condition. We look through the form, through the appearance, through the shape, through the size, through the density, through the condition; and we accept that one, perfect Life is the only Presence; and It is *I*. It is the Life of the horse. It is the Life of the dog. It is the Life of the bird. It is the Life of the cat, and I have no need to assist that Life. I merely must recognize It, and Its perfection will manifest where I stand.

The Life recognized becomes Identity Infinite recognized, and that becomes Grace manifest—not just in 60, 70, 80 years–but unto eternity. That is why "the dice of God are loaded." There is no power on this earth that can alter the Presence, the perfection in all things of Reality. Every individual that you are willing to see in this Light with this Consciousness, you are lifting up, redeeming, improving, to lift them out of their mortal sense of self. Not with words, not with arguments, but with the recognition of one Life. You never proselyte with words. You never become a great missionary, but secretly and sacredly you are lifting the consciousness of the world.

Now take those two lacks, those two problems, those two disturbing people; and after you've completed this Identity chart for yourself, apply it. Apply it to everything you consider wrong in your life, and if you do it correctly, you will see that there is nothing wrong in your Life. Absolutely nothing wrong in your Life, not one thing. You simply had the wrong life. You hadn't accepted Divine Life as the only Life. And living in the false sense of life, you even inherit things that are wrong in the false sense of life. Then you can look out and crucify that false sense of life, and watch your garden grow.

Next week we'll do chapter eight in *The Contemplative Life*. But always as we walk into another chapter, we must remember that the book, *The Contemplative Life*—as all of the writings of Joel are—are about your Life, are about the Christ of your Being, about the Christ of Jesus Christ. And always the Bible becomes a very central source of refreshment for us. Yes, we want to read the books, but that Bible must never be forgotten because you can take any inspired statement out of the Bible and go all the way with it.

The Bible must still be an important part of your weekly reading, and if you've been neglecting it, it isn't necessary to read chapters. A phrase, a word, a situation, anything that emanates from an inspired Consciousness like Jesus Christ has to be important. And really, a week gone by without something from him is an opportunity wasted, even if it's just a sentence. If you only took "I and [the] Father are one" and brought it into this chart of identity and worked with it for a day or two, think of the priceless opportunity to work with "I and [the] Father are one" about your own Identity, knowing that these words were spoken from the Source, were spoken *by* your Identity. Is there a better teacher, a more dependable one?

So, bring that Bible back into your weekly work, even though you read next week's chapter eight; and work out your assignment. Look at the people around you with the knowledge that their Identity never was any different than yours. Look at the birds and the trees and see that their Identity is never any different than yours. All is your one Life. It is all You. There's nothing in this Universe that is not You. Don't you see? You *are* the Life of the Universe, and the Life of the Universe is You. There's no place where you stop and someone new begins. It's all your Self, and only when you recognize your Self everywhere will your Self everywhere come and pour its abundance where you stand.

This infinite Self recognition takes you out of persons and personalities. You're looking at your Self everywhere, and this must become a ringing Reality. Identity. That's the story today, and it will be as long as we walk this earth. "Thou shall have no other gods before me," no other Life before me. I am the Lord thy God. I am Life, and besides *Me*, there is no other one, no other life.

We have all been slaves to form, when we have freedom in Life. The slavery is the slavery to the mental idea of form, to the material idea of form, to the material things. We are slaves to forms that have no existence, when our freedom lies in I and the Father are one Life. You and the Father are one Life. Everyone and the Father are one Life, and there is no other life than I. I am the only Life on earth. Whom shall I fear? What condition shall worry me? I am the only Life on earth.

Do you see how you pyramid yourself up? You step up the ladder step by step until you can come to that place: I am the only Life on earth. I am the only Life in all the universes that exist. There is only one Life. And every time you're fearing or doubting or wondering or trying to improve, you are saying, "I am not the only Life." And you are having other gods before me.

## Class 19: You Are Divine Life Now

Now, you can't just make the statement, "I am the only Life in the Universe." It will be very hollow. But build your ladder and climb it slowly and carefully up your eight steps of Identity. Do it yourself, and next week bring it with you or whenever we get together again. I'll try it; I'll bring mine with me. We'll see what we have come up with, what we can put together and all agree on—one Identity that we can all understand. That will be our strength.

I'm sure that when Jesus stood upon this earth and looked out, that Spirit which stood where we saw a form, that infinite Consciousness knew It was the only Life. It was Life knowing Itself everywhere. There was no other life It had to worry about. There was no other being but It, and It is you and me. I am the only Life everywhere. That includes my client and my employer, my brother and my sister. These are the masks of forms. The Life is I everywhere.

Wherever you go, you are. When you try to jump into that realization without building your ladder, you can't hold it. But as you build step by step, you'll find you can hold it for a little while. Then you have to go back again and hold it again and again until one day it takes root and you don't have to go back to the first rung of your ladder. You're on the second as a permanent dispensation. Maybe someday you'll reach the third rung. You never have to go back as far, and you wake up with the knowledge there's no other Life on this earth than I am. Practicing *that* Reality is practicing the Presence, and Grace does flow in the measure that you attain the pure Consciousness that the one Life is your Name.

Thank you very much.

# CLASS 20

# YOUR IDENTITY ALREADY WALKS ON WATER

*Herb:* Good afternoon. Before I forget it today, before you leave, pick up your gift copy of *The Mystical I* at the desk here.

We have an interesting subject today. Although it's about a man walking on water, it has a great deal of meaning to us now that we have come to the place of Identity where we are ready to stand on Identity. Looking out at the world, regardless of what it presents, and knowing that Identity is invincible, without opposite, without a need to protect Itself—ever present, ever functioning, ever perfect. Needing no help whatsoever to defend Itself, to improve Itself, to correct Itself; for It is All that is here.

Once we have to a degree made this our starting point, walking on the water becomes a very significant event. Religiously, we only say, "He walked upon the water"; and there it stops. It does no good for mankind whatsoever. Scientifically, we say, "He didn't walk upon the water" because it's impossible." And so either way, whether you happen to be religious and say he did, or scientific and say he did not, you're stuck with an event that has no significance in your life; and it would be ridiculous to assume that the Wayshower would be functioning in such an abnormal event without a purpose.

Now, it is then insufficient for us to believe he did or didn't, but rather to know why that took place. We're given several clues, and even the Gospel of Matthew misses the major clue. While it reports the event, it does not report something significant which John caught; and so we have to compare the same event in two Gospels. We find in Matthew it goes this way:

"And straightway Jesus constrained his disciples to get into a ship, and to go before him unto the other side, while he sent the multitudes away."

They had all just been fed, 5,000 of them, with invisible loaves and fishes.

"And when he had sent the multitudes away, he went up into a mountain apart to pray:

and when the evening was come, he was there alone."

Now, the significant thing here is that after this seemingly supernatural event, why did he go into a mountain to pray? You know that prayer is the activity of Consciousness in oneness with God, and you know that in order for loaves and fishes to appear to feed the multitudes, he had to be in that kind of prayer. And therefore, having been in prayer, having produced through prayer the visible requirement of the moment, why would he now retire to a mountain to pray? Now, this is not given in Matthew. In a moment you see the ship is in the midst of the sea, tossed with the waves; and so he skips right from Jesus going to the mountain to pray to a ship tossed on the sea. And to even a very studious reader, there's no indication here of why, after the Master feeds the multitudes with loaves and fishes, he should retire to a mountain to pray.

But we're given this instantly in John, and because it is so different, I would like to do the John version of it. Now, in John, after they had gathered their baskets and eaten:

"Then those men, when they had seen the miracle that Jesus did, said, This is of a truth that prophet that should come into the world."

Now, this is where John differs from Matthew:

"When Jesus therefore perceived that they would come and take him by force, to make him a king, he departed again into a mountain himself alone."

Now, the significance there is that he had perceived that they were personalizing him. They were seeing Jesus, a man, a Messiah, one who could feed multitudes. This was the man who would free the Jews, and this was dangerous because this was not his mission. His mission was to present the universal Christ as the Substance, the Identity, the Law, the Activity of every person on the earth. Here, a segment of the world seeing his miracles was ready to crown him king, a person, a man with supernatural powers; and so he had a problem.

What was he going to do about it? How could he make known to them the Truth that he was not a man; that he was the Light? That the Light of his Being was the Light of their Being. That they were one and the same, and that all that he did they could do. So he went to a mountain to pray. Just as you and I, confronted with an insurmountable obstacle will sit in the Silence, standing still, waiting for that inner Self to emerge and take dominion; he had reached the point where doing miracles was not enough.

He had to reveal to them the Source of every miracle. That the Source was the Infinite Self, which was the Self of All. That he was not one selected alone; that the messiah in-dwelt every individual. And he needed guidance. And it was in this moment while he in deep Silence, waiting for the Voice, was confronted by another situation; and yet, this very situation was the answer to the guidance he sought. The ship on the sea was in trouble, and it was miles away. There was no time now to catch another ship. There was no time now to be that man which the world saw as Jesus. He had to be miles away now for his disciples who were on the ocean. They were on that lake out there, and it was an ocean to them.

They were fishermen. They were skilled in all the maneuvers on the lake. They made their livelihood there. And here, in spite of it, they were in trouble. They were rowing frantically, and the turbulence was upon them; and they needed help. And this was the answer to that which he was meditating upon. What shall he do to show the Source is not the man, but the Spirit which is the Substance of all men? And now, he had to be somewhere else now. He had to be Spirit in action.

And so they saw him walking upon the water, and they were surprised, undecided, frightened. Surely, this was a myth, some kind of a hallucination. They didn't recognize him in the slightest. Even when he got on board, they didn't recognize him. It doesn't even say here that he got his feet wet. They saw this apparition walking on the water, and religion says it really happened. Period. It happened.

Now, you try to go out and cash that at the bank. You try to use that to make yourself feel better. You try to do something with the fact that it really happened. See if that will keep an atom bomb away from our country or away from this world—unless we see what *happened* when they saw that apparition walking on the water.

And so, we're staying with John on this instead of Matthew, because John gives us the reason that the event took place. It was a response to an inner need for guidance to show the world that Jesus was not a miracle maker, but that the Spirit of God had answered every need before the need arose. And always, where there was One in Consciousness receptive, yielding, humble, trusting, confident—One who had stepped out of mortal identity—the answer would flow, not just as a casual suggestion, but as an activity in Consciousness. And here that activity manifested as the disciples frantically rowing on a turbulent sea, needing help; and there was no man who could give them help for such a situation, only Spirit Itself.

". . . The disciples . . . [then] entered [the] ship, went over the sea toward Capernaum. And it was now dark, and Jesus was not come to them."

There's a symbolism in "dark." Day is always the spiritual journey, and night is always the material journey. For them it was night. We know it was the fourth watch. We know that there are four watches beginning at 6 p.m., three hours a piece. And so, this was between 3 and 6 a.m. Actually, it was before sunrise; and that again has a symbolism. Just as the sun falls in the west, which is death, and rises again in the east, which is resurrection; so they were in the darkness just before dawn. And now we're preparing for a resurrection, for a sun coming up, for light to take them out of darkness.

"And the sea arose by reason of a great wind that blew. So when they had rode about five and twenty or thirty furlongs, they see Jesus walking on the sea, and drawing nigh unto the ship: and they were afraid. But he saith unto them, "It is I; be not afraid." Then they willingly received him into the ship: and immediately, [*immediately*] the ship was at the land whither they went."

The instant he stepped on the ship, it was no longer in the sea. It was on the shore. So we have some fantastic things happening there in response to the inner prayer to shatter all material concepts.

Now, there are many levels to walking on the water; and if we can take an in-depth study, I believe we can come up with much that will be of advantage to us in the days of revelation that lie ahead of all of us. For one, I think you may find that this event, coupled with all other events in the complete demonstration by Jesus Christ, is a preview of your new consciousness. In your consciousness of Truth right this instant—not tomorrow but this instant—the fact is revealed that your spiritual Self is now walking on the water. You might catch up with your Self eventually to realize that, but it is a fact now.

The Christ of each of us is walking on water, which means it has overcome the first birth. If you go back to John the Baptist, you will see that he is a symbol of the first birth. ". . . I, he said, "must decrease." "[And he who follows me] whose shoe's latchet I am not worthy to unloose. . . . He must increase."—The second birth. The material man, the spiritual man.

And then John, the symbol of the first birth, is also the symbol of water; and so he baptizes with water. He even baptizes Jesus with water, but it isn't long before there's an inner baptism of the Spirit. And then we see the meaning of baptism with water and baptism with fire. The second baptism, the baptism of fire, is the baptism of light upon the water. And we see many, many other symbols. We see water as a symbol of mortality, water as a symbol of the human birth. Each of us comes into this mortal sphere the same way—actually come out of a water bag, and this is the baptism of the water; and now we must be reborn of the water and the Spirit.

Now, the early Christians were in their first birth; and so they were called little fish. And these little fish were in the water, but they were really trapped in the water. They had to learn to come out of the water. And now we find this spectacle of the man called Jesus Christ walking on the water, which means he had risen from the first birth of water. He was no longer trapped *within* the water, but he was now standing on the water. He had come out of the little fish stage. He had come into the rebirth, the resurrected Self to whom water is no longer an obstruction, an obstacle, something that can drown you; but rather a harmonious expression of the one Self.

And so, the symbolism of the water and standing on the water, walking on the water is mortality being dissolved into immortality. It is the symbol of the new age of rebirth. All who come into the conscious awareness of the indwelling Christ are walking upon the water, dissolving mortality into the illuminated Consciousness of immortality. And this is the now fact: Never is there a physical form that walks upon the water. You will not physically walk upon the water. Jesus did not physically walk upon the water. No one anywhere at any time in the human form will walk upon the water on this earth.

Now, let's take him for what he said. "I am the Light . . . ." You have seen light shine upon water. Does it drown? Does it go under? It's right there on top. I am the Light. I *am* the water. I *am* the wine. Always, the knowledge that Light is the Substance of his Being, and light is the substance of all that we call matter. And there's Light upon light—not form of man upon physical water.

Consciousness one'd with Itself externalizes. Always, that which is in Consciousness is made visible. You're not seeing a physical form walk upon physical water. You're seeing the infinite Consciousness made visible as one harmonious activity of two different kinds of form. You're seeing a third-dimensional form called ocean or lake or water and a fourth-dimensional form called spiritual body. The fourth-dimensional body of the Soul made of Light appearing where there is a three-dimensional concept called water. And they appear to be in contact, but it is the Consciousness of One being made visibly manifest, the Consciousness of the Christ.

Peter wants to do that, just as anyone would want to do that. And the mistake, of course, is that this is an external event; that there is someone *doing* it. And no one is doing it in the outer. The activity is all taking place within the Consciousness, and unless there is an inner activity, it cannot be made visible as form walking on water. Peter, not knowing this—thinking you can just go and do it—wants to do it, but he hasn't had the inner activity. Peter is still a man. Jesus is the Spirit. Peter is still the mortal being. Jesus is the immortal Self. Now, for you and for me, the message of walking on the water contains within itself all that we have to know about ourselves, our Identity, what we're doing here, and why and how we are to do it.

Now let us see, without flinching from fact, that if water is what science tells us it is, and if the physical form of Jesus was what science tells us it was, that there could have been no walking on the water. And therefore, if it happened as it is reported here, then it broke all of the material laws of science. And naturally, science would be outraged because it cannot acknowledge this as a fact because it cannot explain how he could shatter every material law. What is science going to do now? Once it acknowledges this as a fact, it cannot explain its material laws anymore. The law of gravity was broken. You didn't pick up the morning paper and see that somebody walked on water. You don't expect to. Science doesn't expect to. But here somebody did, and there's no explanation scientifically. There's no explanation religiously, except God did something supernatural.

But there *is* a scientific explanation, and it is shattering—but not to those who dwell in Identity. If we take science's word that man is formed of the atom and the water is formed of the atom, then scientifically what you have is atoms walking upon atoms. But we know that there are atoms that would fall through that lake and drown. We know that when Peter tried it, he almost drowned, except that Jesus reached out to grab him. We know that the boat they were in, which is human safety or the symbol of it, was not safety for them at all.

We know that everything there is a symbol. These are all props to teach us something. There's water, and there's a ship which is a symbol of safety; and there's a shore that they're rowing toward. And yet, all of these things—the oars, the symbol of safety called a boat—are helpless in the face of material law called wind and rising water. And yet, something comes along with no props to help it and saves them. We are being shown that the external struggle, the external belief in the power of matter to help us is a sham. There is no external help, and the help comes not from something external. It comes from the inner Consciousness of One who is sitting on a mountaintop miles away. That's where the help comes from, not from the boat or the oars.

And then suddenly there's no wind. And suddenly there are still waters, and gradually we begin to conceive within ourselves what really happened.

What we're learning is that the complete outer picture was first a series of mental images in the minds of the disciples who were rowing upon the lake—not hallucinations, not visions, fact as we see it today—but revealed by the Master as a cosmic hallucination. Not just that storm on that day in that sea, but every storm on every day in every sea is revealed as as much a cosmic hallucination as that one. And the same power that sent a form called Christ moving across the water then is here to do the same for every storm at sea today.

"If you believe on me, the works that I do, ye shall do."

And this is the challenge: That there is a Christ form to move out and walk across every sea and every ocean into every part of the Universe—where there is a storm, where there is a turbulence, where there is a wind, where there is a whirlwind, where there are men frightened by the elements—where there is a witness of the omnipresent Spirit as the only living Presence. And there was One who had just fed the multitudes. And that One without any visible support defied the laws of space, of time and of matter and of motion. Defied everything that science has drawn around us as a fact, and without a word of explanation demonstrated that time is not what we think. Space is not what we think. Matter is not what we think. Material form is not what we think, and material condition is not what we think.

In fact, none of them have any power in the Presence of that Spirit which walked out upon the sea, clambored upon the ship and instantly took it to the shore. What had happened to change the complete picture? The law of externalization. The unilluminated consciousness outpictured one scene, which we have learned to call cosmic television; and the illuminated Consciousness outpictured another scene, which we have called Infinite Mind television. That is what happened. Two different scenes.

But I, if I be lifted up, take you out of the cosmic mind scene into the Infinite Mind Reality of perfection. And so, demonstrated there that day on that sea was that matter is a mental image, whether it's a calm sea or a turbulent one. That a ship is a mental image. That the conditions of a ship on a wind-swept sea are all one mental image. That all material form is a mental image, including the person.

And the hard teaching was that man is Spirit. And just as man is Spirit and not physical form, the ocean is Spirit and not hydrogen and oxygen; and wood is Spirit, not wood. But science says it's all made of atoms, and there was one picture of atoms changed by the Master to another picture. And so, if we accept the atomic structure of things, how could he change it? You see, this, too, blasts the atomic theory; and science is left completely without any theory at all. Just dumbfounded. There's nothing it can say except, "Show us how to do it," or "It never happened."

Now, while science says, "It never happened," and religion, not knowing why or how it happened, we are left without a God. We are left without spiritual power. We are left at the mercy of a cosmic mind, and consequently, in a state of cosmic hypnotism. We are left in a situation where a boy comes home from war, and whereas before he went to war, he was as his father called him, perfect. In today's paper, the comedian Jerry Lewis: He doesn't think war is very funny. He had a boy who was a perfect boy, a rock band leader. Everything about the boy was just the way a father wanted him to be. One thing got in the way. He was drafted. And when he came back, instead of this vivacious, alert, eager, enthusiastic boy, there was someone who not only couldn't adjust but didn't care. His father would say to him, "You've got to put your head back on your shoulders," and he'd say, "Well, why?" He'd seen something. He had seen a futility, a helplessness, a purposelessness called war in which nobody wins. This is cosmic mind.

You take away the incident of walking on water, and you're stuck with that cosmic mind which outpictures war. You take away the incident of walking on water, and you're stuck with this world. What's the answer to it? Well, this comedian, Jerry Lewis, has an answer to it. It's running away. He says they won't get another one of my sons. He says, "I've got one now who's fifteen and a half. If this war is still on in two-and-a-half years, there's going to be a Bekin's truck pull up in front of my house; and we're all getting in it, and we're going straight out to the water and we won't stop."

Now, you see, there's a better Way. We can't all get into a Bekin's truck. We only do that when we do not understand Identity. The Spirit of you walked upon the water that day. The Spirit of Jesus and the Spirit of you and the Spirit of me are one and the same, and the Spirit said, "Be not afraid. It is I. I, the Spirit. And where I am, there is no storm. You're looking at an illusion. What were you worried about? Where was your faith in the Identity of your Being?"

The Spirit said to them, "Am I not the only power? Have I not been telling you that I in the midst of you am mighty? Have I not been telling you that I am the activity of God in you, and that I am not material? I am pure Light. I am the Substance of infinity. I can never leave you. Right here out on the sea, I am; and that sea that you're looking at, It is I. Be not afraid. It is I. All that is here is I. I am the sea. I *am* the water. I am the ship. I am the individuality of each one of you frantically rowing away. I am the Only. I am the One. I am the omnipresent Spirit and besides Me, there is no other. Of course, I walk upon the water. I *always* walk upon the water. I'm not walking on the water any different than I walked upon the land. It's just that when I walked upon the land that you did not notice that I wasn't walking like others."

If he hadn't walked upon water, they would never have known that he was walking the same way on the land. There is no obstacle or obstruction to I, the Spirit. I, the Spirit lives in an unobstructed Universe. I, the Spirit, walk through steel. I, the Spirit, walk through walls of concrete. Why? Because Light is like the x-ray. Doesn't the x-ray show certain things that you cannot see with human eyes? The x-ray itself is but a counterfeit imitation of I, the Life, the Spirit, the Essence. And so, one standing in Identity overcomes a whole sea, a sea of illusion. Is it any different than a common cold or a backache? I walk upon the water, walk where every germ seems to be, where every ache seems to be, where every bit of suffering seems to be. It is only I. Be not afraid.

And they followed him after this. They still didn't know, and they thought he was now surely going to free the Hebrew nation. So he had to make it still clearer, although he knew nothing would except disappearing from the tomb. He had to make it clear what he was teaching: that matter does not exist. It does not exist. There was no sea there. There was no ship there. There was only the invisible God there, only the Spirit. Where each of us stand is the Spirit. And if it's a room instead of an ocean, nothing has changed. No appearance changes the fact of Reality.

Your chapter in *The Contemplative Life* was "Contemplation Develops the Beholder." And contemplation, it turns out to be, is not pondering. It's not sitting there in deep thought. Contemplation is that capacity to behold all appearances—lakes, mountains, storms, tranquility—and as Joel puts it, to watch them all as you would a sunrise or as you would a painting. You don't get out your brush. You watch it. You don't go out there and push the sun up and down. You watch it. You behold. And then in contemplation, you not only behold, but you develop the capacity to let God within—*I*, the Spirit—interpret *My* Universe to you.

As you dwell in the silence of contemplation, beholding as you would behold a sunrise, only in that stillness of beholding are you opening the mind to let Truth emerge, interpreting Itself, free and independent of the five-sense interpretation. The five-sense kingdom of this world showed a raging sea. But the beholder standing in the contemplation of that raging sea, letting the invisible Self interpret Itself, discovers that the sea ceases to rage. The wind ceases to storm. And even time stands still and space diminishes into nothingness. And they stand now on the shore because in God there is no space and no time and no whirlwind, no raging sea.

If you believe on me, the works I do, ye shall do; which means that this was not an event for one, but that the Consciousness which can behold the raging sea and the whirlwind, which can step out of time and space is part of the property of all who are joint-heirs in Christ. You and I, as we develop the capacity to withhold judgment, not saying this is bad and this is good, but just to behold and to let the inner Spirit interpret to us, discover the law of Grace is functioning.

Often, someone says, "Why shouldn't I call something good?" Because the moment you designate it as good, you only do so because it's better in your eye than something which you didn't designate good. And therefore, you have fallen into the trap of something that is good and something that, by your unwillingness to designate it as good, means that you think it's bad. And so, you've got a duality, a double consciousness. You've got the belief that there is a good and a bad.

When you magnify that, you'll find it's the difference between a sea that is calm and a sea that is turbulent. Always, the outer expresses the inner. Matter is not there. Matter is a mental image. Therefore, what's in your mind becomes more important than what's out there. And as the world tries to conquer matter, what is it conquering? A mental image. And so, we're told, "Withhold your judgment. Don't conquer the world. Don't conquer matter. Don't seek a victory over the things of the world. If you must seek a victory, realize that the outer world is nothing but the expression of mind; and therefore, let's get back to mind."

And then, if you want to go further still, the mind that outpictures evil isn't the mind of God. Why try to conquer it? Don't conquer matter, and don't conquer mind. Conquer nothing. Be still. To know that mind and matter are not of God is your victory. To look at that which mind and matter conspire to produce and to know it isn't there, this is the beholding. This is the contemplative life. To look at all material things—conditions, objects, persons—with no judgment that it is good or bad. This is the contemplative way.

It's a self-denial, and many people aren't happy unless they can spend their hours telling you about someone else who has done a foolish thing or someone else who is stupid or someone else who is wicked. Always the discussion takes the turn of a third party who isn't there. And we all know that third party who isn't there is either foolish or stupid or a cheat, and this becomes the way of conversation among mortal beings—never realizing that we are judging ourselves.

We are falling into the trap of a consciousness which is dual. All mental concept, whether it's good or bad, is a trap. When you say, "Margie is good," you're saying someone else isn't. Always the subtle implication that this one is better than that one is falling into the trap of materiality. And the hard teaching, the teaching that enables you to walk upon the water of Spirit, is that materiality does not exist. It can neither be good nor bad. And every time you violate it, you'll find that the teaching of walking upon the water has eluded you.

Now then, contemplation, the withdrawal of judgment, the awareness that only Spirit is present would seem to leave you with nowhere to go. You remove all of the material world, and there's nothing left. Seems like a stalemate, a blind corner; and where do you go from there? Unfortunately, you'll never know until you get to that point. Those are the terms, and that's why it's a hard teaching. The price you pay is complete annihilation of the belief in matter, and then you don't seek matter. You don't strive to win or earn matter. You don't struggle to possess matter or to hold matter. You don't love matter. You don't hate matter. You don't fear matter.

You're making your transition to where you are coming out of the birth in water as mortal being, out of the fish trapped in the tomb of a natural birth in matter. And now you're leaping above the water—above the material world, above mortality, above every concept of the past, above every concept of the world—into *My Kingdom*, which is not of this world but is here. And when you are willing to walk upon the water, which means to erase the concept of matter in your consciousness, then you are coming into your transitional experience in which the keys to the Kingdom are given to you; and that which has been invisible is opened up.

There were two steps in the work of Jesus. The first was always to bring harmony. He didn't take them into the invisible, spiritual Universe. He brought material harmony first. In other words, he first obeyed the law of normalcy in this world. He took it out of the abnormal situation into the normal rhythm of goodness. And having brought harmony, he then was able to take it from sense to Soul. Now, all of us have sought the harmony without taking the next step from sense to Soul; and you know how many people drop out of this work when the harmony comes. But it always becomes discord later again because they have not been willing to erase the fullness of the belief in matter. They've been willing to postpone their belief in matter just for a moment to lose the problem, but they don't walk upon the water.

Now, as you behold all material worlds, all material objects, all material things in your non-reactive acceptance that the invisible Spirit alone is present as my Identity—the Identity of the water, of all who are here—in this quiet contemplation you have opened the way for Truth; and the Truth is what quickens you. It quickens you out of death; matter and death are one and the same. Out of mortality. And that quickening breaks the law of the atom, the law of karma. That quickening puts science right back in a cage. That quickening breaks every physical law because that quickening is what changes the images.

"He leadeth [us to] still waters. Cease ye from man, whose breath is in his nostrils." Recognize the spiritual Identity. Every disciple had forgotten that I and the Father are one, and I can never leave you. The Spirit quickeneth, and for that reason Paul could say, "In spite of all the infirmities that besiege me, I am not moved by them." He was a contemplative. Now you know that Jesus didn't behold this scene in one instant and become a contemplative. This is part of the discipline.

*We* are those disciples rowing on the turbulent sea. Each of us has his own turbulent sea. Each of us is struggling frantically to overcome it, and it isn't there. The hypnosis is that it *is* there; that we are in a form. And that the material world to us is a turbulent sea, and each day we're struggling to overcome part of it. To build a little place where we can call our sanctuary, our peace table. To put up a little nest egg. To maintain our health. If you walk upon the water of Spirit, you'll stop all of that.

Identity tells you you are Spirit and only Spirit. Are you trying to maintain the health of Spirit, or isn't trying to maintain your health a denial of spiritual Identity? You're putting up a nest egg. Is Spirit requiring a nest egg? No, that's a human mind doing it, isn't it? Start to think about all of the things you're doing mentally, physically to deny your spiritual Identity; and see what is stopping you from walking upon the water of Spirit. How in one grand recognition of the spiritual nature of the Universe we know that all matter comes under subjection. For there, walking in defiance of gravity on water that can never hold a solid man in a windstorm on a rising sea, all is suddenly peaceful and calm. All of the material world on one lake is brought under the dominion of one invisible recognition of spiritual Identity as the Only.

Every heartbeat, every backache, every pain, every lack, every limitation is taken care of in that one second of spiritual Identity as mine and yours as a universal fact. Nothing left to do. The hypnosis is broken, and we discover that atoms—which allegedly are the substance of matter, which can be fashioned into a bomb—atoms are not there. Atoms are images in the mind, just as matter itself is an image in the mind. We never drop a bomb. We drop images. Those same atoms which in matter cause what we call decay, degeneration—they are not present in the presence of *I*, the Spirit.

All of the power of matter is built upon the *existence* of matter. And here the Spirit proves the nonexistence of matter, and thereby, the non-power of the matter which has no existence. Matter is built upon the atom, and the Spirit proves that there are no atoms. The power of matter, matter built upon the atom; all are nothingness in the illuminated Consciousness of the Christ. There is no atomic world, no material world, no material power in the world. There is only *My* Spirit, and that covers every ache and pain and lack and limitation in the world.

And then, when religion says it happened but has no meaning for it; and science says it didn't happen, we are deprived of one of the greatest demonstrations of enlightenment, which explains the passage in Genesis that man was given dominion. *Spiritual* man was given dominion. And your dominion lies, then, over land and over sea and over air because there is no land; and there is no sea; and there is no air. And your dominion over them is because they are nonexistent.

Only *I*, the invisible Spirit, exists; and that is the difficulty of that teaching of walking on water. They proved the nonexistence of the water, of the material world, and of the conditions in the material world. And we who are trying to live in Identity discover that this is true. Whenever there is an inner awakening, when the Identity speaks, when in the stillness the Voice utters Itself, the sea of the world is melted. The earth is melted. The problem is melted. There is something that bubbles up and bursts within, and in that quickening, in *My* peace, we are literally walking on the water.

You don't see Christ walking on the water, but the Infinite is walking throughout Itself on the waters of Spirit, revealing the perfect Presence that is ever here. In Identity, you never waiver between doubt and faith. You don't pray and doubt at the same time. In Identity, perfection is the law of Being. Any imperfection is rejected because it denies Identity, and Identity never changes. Identity is always Identity. Spiritual Selfhood is always spiritual Selfhood, and everything that declares something is wrong is telling you you're not spiritual Selfhood. And so, you're not trying to make anything better. You're trying to recognize the hypnotism of what isn't there, the hypnotism of the rising sea.

Now, it may seem difficult to the rest of the world to try to understand that a sea isn't there, a boat isn't there, or a person isn't there. Only God is. Only Spirit is. Only Identity is. But ten thousand healings by Jesus and twenty thousand by Buddha and ten thousand by Joel and five or ten by you and me is enough to tell us.

∞∞∞∞∞∞ END OF SIDE ONE ∞∞∞∞∞∞

The symbolism of the ship being on the shore instantly, of course, is that when you have the Christ realization, that's the end of all inner turbulence. However, this does appear in the outer. This isn't allegory. This is the visible expression of infinite Consciousness through the Christ Mind appearing visibly as event. Now, the very next day he's disappeared again. Doesn't say that he had a ship or anything. He just isn't there. The disciples have gone in their ship, but Jesus didn't go with them; and he isn't there either.

When they finally catch up with him on the other side, there's no explanation. We must presume that he returned as he came, and now he chastises them for following him just to receive more loaves and fishes. And he tells us to labor not for the meat that perisheth. He's giving us the clue to what he just did. Labor not for material things. That's the meat that perisheth.

Now, I find it easier to accept the non-reality of matter when I combine the spiritual teaching that there is no matter with the scientific explanation of what matter is. Then it seems to reinforce, and they agree. We know that matter is mental and that this mentality is not the Mind of God, but the cosmic. And we know that all matter consists of cosmic thought, and therefore, these are images in mind. And that's the only place where they exist, and that's the only place where they have power.

But when we insert the idea that these images in mind are atoms, then we have a clearer-cut picture of why they seem to have power. Because now you take that which is called the visible sea: How do you see it except through your visible eyes? And so, the visible sea and the visible eyes—both being atoms—when you see something turbulent, you're seeing the reaction of the atoms of your eyes in their reaction to the atoms of the water. It's atom to atom which causes the appearance of disturbance.

Every problem that you see is the activity of that which is the problem or the cause and your reaction to it, through your eyes, to that physical thing which is causing the problem. But because matter is atoms, the atoms of the thing and the atoms of your eyes are in a reaction; and the atoms of your eyes are as much in the cosmic mind as the atoms of the thing. And so, the atoms of your eyes are cosmic thought. The atoms of the thing are cosmic thought, and it's all a self-contained lie. All of our world, from the atomic standpoint, is the reaction of the atoms of your physical self to the atoms of the world around you; and that creates the appearance of your world.

And so we have a cosmic radioactivity, and this is probably a scientific explanation of the word "mist" in Genesis. The mist that covers this earth is cosmic radioactivity, and it doesn't bother us normally to live in radioactivity because that's all we are. We are radioactive atoms, and the things we see are radioactive atoms; and the difference in the vibration of one against the other makes all of the things we call time and space and motion and shape and size and texture and density. Everything is the relationship of one set of atoms to another set. And every object that you call tin, wood, or gold is nothing more than the relation of its atoms to your atoms, your sense atoms.

Remove the atom, and there's nothing there; and the Christ Consciousness does just that. It removes the belief in the atom, and there's nothing there. The material world is gone because all it consists of is atoms responding to atoms. It's a sort of relative radioactivity, cosmic relativity. But God made nothing to decay, to degenerate, to die. Spirit is Itself, and Spirit is one continuous Substance. The atoms are not only separated from each other, but separated within themselves. They're mostly empty space.

In other words, we have electrical energy; and our reaction to electrical energy creates the appearance called matter. And when we overcome the belief in this invisible electrical energy, which appears visibly as matter, we discover that neither the matter is there—which is our concept—nor the electrical energy is there either. It, too, is a concept of the cosmic mind. And the entire foundation of the world is that mist or thought, invisibly an atom which is empty space, nothing but a cosmic mental image. And the multiplicity of these nothings and their reaction within each other creates our radioactive universe.

When something gets out of whack, then, we really start to worry about real problems in radioactivity. Otherwise normal radioactivity passes for this world. And the myth of it, the veil of it was pierced when the Master said, "My kingdom is not of this world." Well, they didn't want to learn anything about atoms. They didn't want to learn anything about the myth of matter or mortality. They wanted more bread. And so they followed him, and he said, "No, you didn't want to learn anything. You just want more bread. That's not my function. My function is to reveal the Kingdom of Truth, of Heaven on earth, of Reality, of the one continuous Substance in perfect law, ever maintaining Its own perfection as the only existence here."

The conflict between the atoms of your vision, the atoms of your hearing, the atoms of your sense organs, and the atoms around you becomes an inner conflict that becomes an outer conflict; and every conflict in our outer world is a result of this inner conflict. And we are not made of atoms. We are *not* cosmic thought. That's the appearance world of us. That's the form world of us. That's the material appearance of us, but it isn't our Self.

And until you step out of the concept of the world—which is that we are made of atoms—until you consciously step out of the scientific belief that this is an atomic universe, you are standing in the midst of cosmic radioactivity; and it is moving you. It takes you from birth through death, and then it brings you back again and repeats the process. It moves you through land and space and air in a false identity, in an up-and-down, good-and-evil world, which is not the invisible present Kingdom of perfection.

And only in your Identity, as you stand and face the invisible atomic world, knowing it to be a nothingness—a very clever counterfeit of your Reality and the Reality of the Kingdom—only then are you aware of the hypnosis; and that awareness of the hypnosis breaks the hypnosis. Then you're not trying to get more loaves and fishes. You don't follow the man for the loaves and fishes. You follow the indwelling Spirit, which is the cause and Source of all; and It is not under the law of radioactivity, of atomic relativity, of material forms, of material laws of gravity, of storm, of flood, of fire.

All this is exposed as the veil of atomic illusion by that *I* which can never leave us. And that *I*, appearing as Jesus Christ, is revealing its power in a preview of your Consciousness, which must be your Consciousness at the moment that all of the material universe is dissolved. There will be such a moment, in a dissolution of the material universe, where you will be standing in the midst of a turbulent sea. There will be gnashing of teeth. There will be frantic effort. There will be material effort with material powers to overcome apparent material powers.

And in the midst of that, we shall stand upon the still water of Identity without oars, without physical effort, without material belief, in the knowledge that God is not in the atom. God is not in the windstorm. God is not in the flood. God is not in the fire. God is in no material thing. And yet only God is present, and that is My Being. And It is the invisible Being where all of the frantic effort of the world is taking place. This is a preview of the end of the world and the Consciousness that will stand in the midst of it.

That is why he couldn't permit them to settle for just another repeat of the miracle. He was building the Consciousness of Christ on earth; the Consciousness of the invisible, perfect Universe; and these were but signs that such an invisible Universe could be brought forth in the midst of turbulence when no human hand could do it. And instead of recognizing that he was revealing what is ever present, they said, "You're doing wonderful miracles." And he kept saying, "No, no, no! I'm not doing miracles. I'm showing you Reality is here for anyone who can accept it."

Seek ye not those things that perish. The material world and its possessions perish. Know who you are. Extend your knowledge of who you are to your neighbor. Hold that Identity as the infinite Reality of all that is, and you are sowing to that which does not perish. You are in that non-conflict which is the acceptance of the One. And though the world won't see it, this externalizes in spiritual manifestation as your Being walking on the water. It experiences Itself as Oneness within and Oneness without, so that form and water are one—one harmonious activity. The same way you will walk in the sky as one harmonious activity. The same way you will walk under the ocean in one harmonious activity. It will be an interactive Consciousness expressing without obstruction. The dominion is in Identity.

Never do we try for the external event. That's what perishes. We don't go out on the water to walk on physical water. We don't go out to improve or correct or heal. We walk on the inner surface of the water, in the invisible Spirit, in Identity accepted with no opposite, so that in your Consciousness you are in the Kingdom of perfection now regardless of what you see. Your Kingdom is perfection, infinite. Your attention is turned away from the five-sense world to the invisible Kingdom of perfection.

You're laboring for that which does not perish, and therefore, you are in oneness with It. And that oneness with It is the power, because now there's no division within. And therefore, when you are seen visibly walking on the water without, there's no division there. Yes, only One was able to show that—no division within, no separation within—always one, invisible, perfect Self everywhere. And so it's really the same miracle repeated all over, whether it's loaves and fishes or walking on the water or healing the cripple: One, invisible, perfect Self made visible through that knowledge.

There are four elements: water, earth, air, and fire. There used to be a belief that we have four bodies, one for each element. We have a body of water, and that symbolized the emotional state, the body of emotions. Always, water symbolized the [emotional body]. And then the earth symbolized the physical body. There was the body of emotions, the body of physicality; and the air symbolized the body of mentality. And finally, the fire symbolized the body of Spirit.

So you had these four bodies, and your center of focus would come from one to the other; and it would all be spasmodic. You wouldn't linger in one, and some would overlap. And so you'd find that you were through your water body living in the element of water, through your physical body living in the element of earth, through your air body living in the element of mind, and through your spiritual body living in the element of spirit or fire; and each body could only interpret its world. Each one was limited to its own world.

And then two were unified in Genesis, so that the water and the earth were unified as the lower firmament, and the air and the fire unified as the upper firmament. And then it became water and fire—water standing for water and earth, and fire for air and fire. And so, always, we had two births: The birth in the water, which meant through those two bodies; and then in the fire, which meant through the air and the spirit. And so, often you read in the Bible about the fire on the water: "There shall be no more sea. There shall be fire on the water."

And because two births were necessary, there had to be the two baptisms. That was the reason for them, the baptism first in the water, and then through the dove's spirit, which was the birth through fire. And we should be past the point now of the first birth, coming out of it into the birth of the fire, where we are self-sustaining, spiritual Entity; and where all of the so-called four bodies are one. Where you overcome the limitations of having a body which only knows the world of water, another which only knows the world of earth, another which knows the world of air, and one which knows the world of fire.

The integration into One appears as the man walking on the water. It is the symbol of the new age in which all separation within is resolved into the oneness of Spirit. Everything is absorbed into the One, and that One is the spiritual reborn Christ Self in which all else is gone. Nothing else remains, and that is how the dominion comes over land, sea, and air. The fourth, the Spirit, the fire, takes dominion over the other three; and we're in the upper firmament, the Living Waters.

Now, toward the end of this eighth chapter, I think it's the eighth or the sixth of John, we find that he reveals what he has been doing. He's been showing them where the fields are white with harvest. Right here, where you had seen no food, there was food all the time. Right here, where you had seen a turbulent sea, there was calm and peace. What had externalized was the human conflict. The conflict within each man's mind externalizes as the outer conflict, sometimes on a limited, human, personal scale; sometimes on a complete community scale. But right there, the fields were white to harvest. The Kingdom was present.

Always where you are, regardless of what you're experiencing, the fields are white to harvest. The Kingdom is right where you are in your Identity as Spirit. And he says it another way over here. I shouldn't try to do this without having a note on it. When he says to them My Kingdom is not from hence, he is telling us that his Kingdom is present and that his Kingdom is spiritual Identity. Now, this is the place where everybody left him except his disciples because they just couldn't swallow the idea that there's only a spiritual Universe. And if they hadn't left him, we might not be sitting here today. But they left him, and then the church formed and left him. It has not accepted a spiritual Universe. The church is part of those who said, "It's too hard a teaching for us, too."

And that's why today we have veterans returning, wondering whatever they accomplished when they went out to shoot or be shot. They were going through the futility of living for the meat that perisheth. If they won, they'd gain nothing; and if they lost, they'd gain nothing. But you don't have to go to war to discover that by winning you gain nothing. Living mortally is the same. What do you gain living as flesh and blood if the flesh profiteth nothing?

All you gain is a sort of a temporary parole in which you can persuade yourself that you're doing good things for people; that you're serving; that you're living a normal, sensible life. And you're playing right into the world mind, which one day puts us all on that sea because we were fooled into laboring for that which is not forever. And we did it because we identified as a person and identified the world around us as made of people. We identified matter, and we read books in science that told us about electrons and protons; and we said, "Isn't it marvelous that they're getting inside the atom?"

And here before it all happened, Spirit proved to us that there's no inside to get into. There's no atom. Anything that perishes; anything that changes; anything that deteriorates; anything that decays and degenerates; anything that can exhibit any form of imperfection exists only as the reaction of one group of atoms to another, having no relationship to Reality. It is not of our Kingdom.

Now, if tomorrow were that moment when all matter dissolves, it would be very important today to be in the Consciousness of Truth. And because this is the kind of Consciousness you don't build in a day, we are given sufficient time to establish it. Sufficient information to make us contemplative beholders of this massive hypnosis called matter. To take the hard teaching and not to say, "I understand it." Not to say, "I agree." But to consciously pierce the veil every day until your agreement deepens into that conviction which says, "I have the key to the non-reality of matter, and I can prove it at will. I can step out of material belief and watch harmony take place before my eyes. I can step out of material belief and watch invisible harmony from far off move into the visible area with the speed of light."

But I am not standing in two places. I'm not saying I believe it, but I'm waiting to find out if it's really true. Because that mind that's waiting to find out if it's really true is not living in the spiritual Universe. *It* is the barrier. It's still living on the other side of the fence in the veil, and it is standing between the very activity of Spirit that we wish to behold, and therefore, must be eliminated. We must catch the mind in all of its little traps.

Every remnant of anxiety, concern, worry, doubt, fear is the trap. Every moment of unbelief is a trap. And every time you're caught in the swirl of reaching out to protect physical things without recognizing first the spiritual nature of all that is around you in this Universe, you will find you're struggling on the sea with an oar; and the wind is really blowing—when the easy way, the *only* way is Grace manifest through the Consciousness—which is not a material you; not a material brain; not a material body; not a material, mortal person going about your daily life—but that invisible, living Spirit.

Now, if some of you have brought in your little charts or notes on Identity and feel you can put your name on them and put them up here and let me look at them and return them to you next week; that'd be wonderful if you care to do that. I'll put some comments on them. And what we're going to do, you see, is take all of these and sort of make a collage of them and come up with the best ones. And you'll find that you'll end up with not one little formula called Identity that way, but you'll have one to overcome one barrier; and you'll have another one to overcome another barrier. You'll find at various levels and various barriers a certain one about Identity will do better than another one. And you'll find that Identity—being infinite—there are many, many wonderful things you must know about it:

*I* can never leave you.
**D**ivinity is your Substance.
**E**very moment *I* am with you.
**N**ever, never are we separated.
**T**ime cannot separate us.
**I**nvisibly, *I* accompany you wherever you are.
**T**his day *I* am with you.
**Y**ou are my Son.

Now, that's just one. Just think of the millions that are possible, and as you keep working with this, you'll find you have a complete Bible. Identity is your Bible. Identity is every textbook that will ever be written, and Identity is the key that turns the lock and lets out the illusion of matter and lets the Truth seep into consciousness.

Every moment you spend working with that Identity, either in the manner I suggested or in any manner you deem suitable, you will find it sticks. It sticks. And there will be a time where you won't be saying, "Well, matter isn't there." Identity within you will proclaim it. Identity within you will go before you. Identity will prevent material disturbances from entering your household. You'll discover the magic of it as it becomes living Consciousness. It has never seen a storm at sea. The Identity called Jesus Christ saw no storm at sea. ". . . it is I; be not afraid." There was no storm to remove, you see. There was only false identity, and out of false identity can only come a false appearance; but true Identity reestablishes the Reality of harmony.

I'd like to keep those for a week, if I may, whatever you put up here. And then I'd like you all to accept this book as a token of our appreciation to you. Everyone who's here has a book here, and thanks very much.

# CLASS 21

# TOTAL RE-IDENTIFICATION

*Herb:* We know that when Jesus walked upon the water, a phenomenon occurred in this world that is not understood. And last week, together we saw that this unusual experience was a preview of an experience that all of us are inevitably going to discover for ourselves. We found that there was an event on the sea, and although not present there at that time, being somewhere else, that which was called Jesus suddenly appeared walking upon the water. And as we rested in the Consciousness of the Father, we learned that this was not a physical form walking upon water. But rather, this was the Divine *I* made visible as a form of the Soul; a fourth-dimensional body appearing and not being obstructed by material laws such as gravity or matter. And instantly, without taking thought, this occurred; and instantly as it occurred, all the laws of time and space were pushed aside.

And so you and I in our bodies of the Soul will discover that when we are not in thought, we are moved. Moved in such a way that wherever we are needed, we are; and whatever we must do, we are doing. Because I, the Spirit in the midst of us, is greater than any external-appearing event in matter. *I* within us dissolves that which appears to be the discord, but only because we're resting in the knowledge of Identity, not standing in the knowledge of a personal self in a material form in a material world.

Now, prior to this, Jesus had demonstrated other things. The Spirit, released through the absence of a personal self, had also calmed the sea at another time. And we who are at that level of consciousness that is *capable* of overcoming the belief in a material universe are still wondering why, even though we feel the peace—even though we even feel the Presence—we find ourselves sometimes unable to throw off the material discord *in the face* of the Presence. *In the face* of the inner peace we are still confronted with discords that somehow remain to torment us, questions that remain unanswered. And I think we can today face that with a better understanding because of these demonstrations in the Bible, once we understand walking on water was the activity of a Soul body, not of a person with supernatural gifts.

Once we understand that stilling the storm was not the removal of material laws, was not overcoming nature, but was the revelation of the nonexistence of the storm—then we begin to see that just as a storm is not an individual experience but a group experience—it's not one person's consciousness outpictured, but the consciousness of many. And in similar fashion, we discover that our problems that we call "my personal problem" is never that at all. And when we try to overcome "my personal problem" on the level of "my personal problem" and still cannot do it, it is because we have not seen the nature and the source of what we call "my personal problem." We have not overcome the illusion of *world* mesmerism, the *universal* mesmerism.

And so I want you to see it this way. The boy has a bloody nose, or the woman has a dizzy spell, or the man has a weak heart. And so the mother says, "My son has a bloody nose." The woman says, "I can't walk. I have a dizzy spell." And the man says, "I can't get up and go to work because my heart is weak." Each considers this a personal problem. And undoubtedly, each of us has considered our problems as *personal* problems. And then you go into the Spirit. You touch your center, you realize the peace; and you still have the personal problem. And you say, "I thought

I was supposed to do these things, and it would dissolve." It's the same way when a cancer is cut out. It comes back sometimes in a year. Why? What did we cut out? Did we cut out the cause? When you have not cut out the cause of your personal problem, that same cause will manifest as a continuation of it or as another problem. And always, the cause is **not in you**. And when you say, "This is **my** problem," you are placing the cause in **you.**

And you will discover that when you place the cause in the world mind and realize the problem is only *passing through you*—passing through—not **yours**, not attached to you, passing through—presented to you from the world mind at the moment you become aware of it. And it's up to you at that moment to see that this is not my problem. This is a world mind problem. This is not **my** bloody nose. This is not **my** weak heart. This is not **my** dizzy spell. This is a world problem. It doesn't belong to me at all.

And strangely enough, once you locate it as a world problem, you find a depth of inner peace you hadn't known before. You have faced the world mind. You have located the cause of that which is trying to manifest in you, and had you accepted it as *your* problem, you would have nailed it down. And the moment you recognize it as world problem, you find a missing dimension. A weapon which enables you to see I am not unemployed. I do not have a false appetite. The world has a false appetite. The world mind is unemployed. The world mind has a weak heart. The world mind has every problem, and that is where every problem is found, in the world mind, never in an individual. It is merely presented to the individual for acceptance or rejection.

Your rejection is the recognition of its source. The moment you know that its source is not God, you know its source is the world mind; and in that moment, you have seen that the snake is not there. The recognition of it not being there is the end of the hypnotism. That's the end of your weak heart. It's also the end of your unemployment. It's the end of your dizzy spell, and it's the end of your bloody nose.

The minute you locate where it's coming from and know that **there is no world mind**, you have located the mirage—and the mirage which is the source of the mirage. You've pulled the rug out from under the problem. And I don't care what your problem is. When you can face it and locate its source, and then know that the source is not God, and therefore, nonexistent; you're on your way home free. Always, the problems that irritate us the most and that seem the most persistent are those that we have accepted as "my" problem; and you have never had a problem in your life. You have accepted world problems and made them "your" problem, and you have grappled with a shadow. Now, you will see the power of this when you do it. If you have done it, you know the power of it.

As we look at the Master, we see him faced with an unusual situation. The sea is rising. The sea is actually so high that the waves are over the ship. This isn't the same one as when he walked upon the water and when the ship was on the land instantly. This is another one, an earlier one. And yet this earlier one was necessary for the later one to take place.

He was sleeping on the ship. But before he was sleeping, he had given us the Sermon on the Mount, which incidentally, is almost word for word the code of the Essenes. He had given us the Sermon on the Mount. He had healed the son of the centurion. He had resurrected the dead boy at Nain. And now one of the scribes came up and said, "This is marvelous. I'll follow you over the earth. Wherever you go, I want to go." And he looked at this eager scribe, knowing that he wanted to follow a man. That's where we're going to begin our Bible lesson. He wouldn't let this scribe follow him as a person. He had to tell him and all those who are so eager to follow a man that his name was not man, Jesus. His name is never the head of a religion. "You cannot follow the person," he said to the scribe. And he said it in his own words, which we shall see here.

"Now when Jesus saw great multitudes about him, he gave commandment to depart unto the other side."

Always the other side has a symbolism: out of matter into Spirit, higher.

"And a certain scribe came, and said unto him, Master, I will follow thee whithersoever thou goest."

This is the material mind willing to follow the man.

"And Jesus saith unto him, "The foxes have holes, and the birds of the air *have* nests; but the Son of man hath not where to lay *his* head."

The Son of Man, the second birth. The first birth was the son of woman. The rebirth makes him the Son of Man. He has no place where to lay his head. Why? He is not material form. I am not form. I am Consciousness. I am infinite Consciousness. How will you follow me in the flesh?

And so he's telling the scribe, who could not understand, "Follow the Christ of your own Being." That's how you follow Me, because that's My name, infinite Christ; and *I* am in the midst of you, not standing out here. There's no place to lay My head. I am not a physical creature. Those miracles you saw were not performed by a physical creature, and the miracles you are about to see will not be performed by a physical creature. No physical creature is going to raise the dead or walk upon the water or heal the cripple. The Spirit of God in you is the Messiah."

And so he first qualifies what is about to happen by telling us don't be confused and personalize the event. Don't say, "Oh, what a great man Jesus was." But realize that Jesus is your name, walking there as the invisible *I*. This is You. This is your Self. This is the invisible Christ made visible *as*, and every word that Jesus says is your invisible Self speaking. Every activity that you see engaged in by Jesus is your invisible Self moving in Consciousness. This is the *I* of your Being demonstrating Its Presence and Its perfect power. Whatever Jesus said is the Truth of your Being. Whatever Jesus did is the Truth of what your Being is always doing. And when you are in Being instead of out of Being, you will find that your Being is doing precisely what He did.

And so if he's now going to save a ship at sea, we must see that *I* in the midst of me saved that ship at sea. *I* in the midst of Jesus, *I* in the midst of John, *I* in the midst of Peter, *I* the One, the Only in the midst of all am greater than he that walks the earth. *I* in the midst of you am the power of God. This is not the man. This is *I* in the midst of you about to show Peter and the others that where *I* am realized, the inner conflict, called storm in the outer, is no longer there. And so he sets the stage. But here's another, even before they can go any further.

"And another of his disciples said unto him, Lord, suffer me first to go and bury my father. But Jesus said unto him, Follow me; and let the dead bury their dead."

And so we see the word "dead" as applied to those who are dead in the material sense. Dead in the belief that they live in the flesh. Dead in the belief that the world is material, that bodies are material, that life is material, that birth and death are material, that possessions are material, that we live in a material universe. These are the dead who are not alive to *I* in the midst. Dead to Christ, dead to Reality. Dead because they believe that what happens between the cradle and the grave is life. Dead because they have not seen life as a continuous, uninterrupted, perfect continuity proceeding from God, through God, in God, and never leaving God—and so, dead.

And now they're ready.

"And when he was entered into a ship, his disciples followed him. And, behold, there arose a great tempest in the sea, insomuch that the ship was covered with the waves: but he was asleep."

Now, the "tempest in the sea" is always an outpicturing of the inner consciousness of a group of people. The whirlwind is the outpictured consciousness of that area. Always, the visible, material world is the inner level of consciousness that has been attained by individuals collectively. And so our material world is the level of consciousness which we collectively have been able to reach, and now it is externalizing as a storm and a wind blowing the waves.

If we were to say Jesus stopped the storm, it would do us no good whatsoever. But he's introducing now a new element. He has shown us that the dead are those who are dead in matter. Now he's introducing a new element called motion in matter—the great, powerful storm moving; the waves rising. If matter isn't there, how can it rise? If matter isn't there, how can it blow? So matter in motion is a double illusion, no more real than a stone or a pebble lying in the street. No more real than a dizzy spell or a bloody nose. Matter cannot move because matter isn't there. Therefore, the movement of matter, however perilous it may appear to be, is recognized as the impossible. There can be no motion to nonexistence.

God is not in the whirlwind, and however horrible the tempest may appear to the frantic disciples, he is asleep, completely unaware of any such occurrence. Why? Because there isn't any. The collective consciousness is outpicturing a storm. Now we're being told that weather is not an act of God, are we not? The world believes it is. The world believes that all weather is a God activity—that beautiful Hawaiian weather—the beautiful sky, the beautiful mountains, the beautiful water, and the countryside lavish with flowers. Certainly, all this is of God. And then suddenly the typhoon, the tidal wave, the ship swallowed in the sea. Is that of God? What changed it?

Neither the good nor the bad were of God. Weather is a material illusion. We make our own weather collectively and individually, and the disciples have made their weather. They have made their storm in a conflict, in a turmoil, in a fear. All of the conditions of weather which are unfriendly represent the externalization of the world mind, accepted individually. And then we say, "This is the weather in San Francisco. This is the weather in Marin. This is the weather across the bay." It isn't. It's the consciousness outpictured of those who dwell there. It is world mind fooling, with its cosmic hypnotism, those who still believe in a material world; and the disciples are among those. They are still dead in matter. They're dead in the wind. They're dead in the water. They're dead in the motion of the wind, unaware that *I* can never leave you. Unaware that *I* am all there is. Unaware of Omnipresence. Unaware of the power of divine Love. Unaware that only One is present. The Lord our God is One.

And so the cosmic hypnotism, the universal mesmerism, becomes an individual experience for each one who is unaware of it; and they come to him frantic, plea for help.

"Lord, save us: we perish."

They are Life eternal, and they expect to perish; and so he chastises them.

"Why are ye fearful, O ye of little faith?"

There's only waves a hundred feet high, and he says to them, "Why are ye fearful?" What is he saying when he says, "Why are ye fearful?" of those waves that are a hundred feet high? Because they're matter, and matter is only mortal thought; and the motion of the matter is only the motion of mortal thought. You're looking at your own thought.

You mean there aren't any waves out there? That's right. There are no waves out there. There's only mortal thought appearing as waves. What about all the oceans in the world? Same thing. Cosmic mind appearing as oceans, mountains, rivers, lakes, seas, grass, flowers. The material world is mortal mind externalized. That's what he's teaching. Not just this wave on this particular sea—but all matter, all solids, all liquids, all gases—all are the denial that Spirit is All. The germ, the infection, the contagion is a denial that Spirit is All. The whirlwind is a denial that Spirit is All.

And how does it get there? It doesn't. It only appears to be there. All matter appears to be. He is teaching the nonexistence of a material universe. And as incomprehensible as that may be to most of the world, every time that we are able in our own small way to experience the non-reality of matter, and consequently the non-power of matter, we are reliving this incident on the sea with him. We are learning that *I* in the midst of me is the living Spirit of God, and *I* am infinite Spirit. There is no place where *I* am not, and *I* have no opposite. Only *I* exist. As far as the eye can see and beyond, *I* am. And the roaring sea or the calm sea—neither is there. *I* am. Neither the good sea nor the bad sea, neither employment nor unemployment are there. Neither good health or bad health are there. *I* am.

The invisible Spirit is all that is here. There are no goods, and there are no bads. There is only invisible Spirit, and the outpictured material universe ceases to have power to make us seek the good in preference to the evil, to make us choose between one or the other. Rather, we rest in the knowledge that as I find my own Substance, that as I can say to the scribe within me, "There's no way to follow Me. I have no place to lay My head. I am not form, and I accept no form. I am that Spirit, which is the all. I am infinite Consciousness." And therefore, as you stand in your true Identity of infinite Consciousness watching the world pictures, *I* in the midst of you—not you, but *I* in the midst of you—It is *I* who dissolves the world pictures. It is *I* who adjusts and brings forth the invisible harmony. *I* in the midst of you overcomes the world.

And so they are of little faith because they're panicking. They're really looking for another material power to overcome this material power or some supernatural power. They're not looking for the Spirit to present Itself as peace, tranquility, harmony, absence of discord, presence of God. They cannot stand in the center of their own Being, and so they are of little faith. Now you know that a few of us are faced with situations that are more difficult than the one he is bringing to our attention. Really, everything we face is of the same nature. It is a material condition, a material discord, a material lack, a material threat; and always, the problem never exists because only God is present.

"Then he arose, and rebuked the winds and the sea; and there was a great calm. But the men marvelled, saying, What manner of man is this, that even the winds and the sea obey him!"

The winds and the sea did not obey him. He was demonstrating that the storm was a cosmic illusion. That universal mesmerism outpictures as good weather and bad weather, good health and bad health, prosperity and depression. He was telling us: Do not seek the good things or the bad things because they will both change, and they will both perish. He was inviting us to walk in Heaven on earth.

And so today is just that: walking in Heaven on earth. We've all made out our little charts. Some of you have turned them in about Identity. I'd like you to hear some of them. They'll show you the level of the class. There is a definite strength among the students. We have all come to a place now where we know Identity intellectually. I'll show you what I mean. Now, you couldn't write these things unless you had the intellectual awareness of Identity.

This student took quotations, and that was a very good choice.

"**I** and my Father are one."
"**D**estroy this temple, and in three days I will raise it up."
"**E**very kingdom divided against itself is brought to desolation."
"**N**ow are we the sons of God."
"**T**ake no thought for your body."
"**I** am the bread of life."
"**T**hou couldst have no power at all against me except it were given thee from above."
"**Y**e are the temple of the living God."

And that spells out **identity**, and a person could use this to remember and practice a meditation from this until it becomes Consciousness.

"*I* and the Father are one."
Deny it to another, you lose it yourself.
Everywhere I am.
Now is God's power.
Total surrender.
"I can of mine own self do nothing."
Trust.
Yesterday's Identity marks tomorrow's harvest.
You see, we have Substance here.
**I**: *I* am God. *I* am Life. *I* am Love.
**D**: Destroy this temple, and I will raise it up in three days, Jesus said.
**E**: Even if ye walk through the valley of death, God is with us.
**N**: Never be afraid, for God is with us all the way.
**T**: The tree of Life has never been moved and is still there in the center of our Being.

Now a person has to feel something like that to say it: "The Tree of Life has never been moved, and is still there in the center of our Being."

**I**: "In the beginning was the Word, and the Word was with God, and the Word was God."
**T**: "The light shineth in darkness; and the darkness comprehended it not."
**Y**: Yea, "Be still and know that I am God."

Now, these are all an experience for the persons who have done these, and there are others; and they're all very good, which was a very pleasant thing to see because it means we can go further.

Now, one thing that is noticeable among these statements about identity is, number one: That we are all claiming what we are, and this isn't good—I am this and I am that, and I am the other thing. Rarely do you find one in here that says, "I am humble. I am a true witness. I am listening. I am meek. I am waiting for the will of the Father to express. I am glorifying the Father." It's all about "*I*" and is still saying identity on a higher level of identity than the human sense, but is still very close to a higher *I* than this I. And it's not the witness who's quiet, learning how to let the infinite *I* do Its own work through a me

And so, identity is a beginning. And you know, when you come to identity as a fact that you're going to live with, you find it necessary to do something else; and that is what may be called to re-identify. To re-identify the world around you and to re-identify yourself. Because even though you have just said I am this, that, and the other thing; you can't throw away a half century of being something else just because you made a declaration; and so all your old habits continue right on up. And while you're saying, I am this, that, and the other; you still think you're a material form. You still think you're going to go to work tomorrow or not. You still think you're going to do the same human things you've been doing. You're still thinking in terms of mortality. You're still buying insurance.

You're still doing mortal things, and so re-identification is now this: You have come into intellectual agreement about Identity. Fine. Now we must come into spiritual agreement about Identity, and that is re-Identity. That is going within with this new Identity you have accepted intellectually and abiding there. And there are about six or seven levels that require re-identification because they control all the rest of the levels. Now let's see, then. We're re-identifying as the Identity which we say we are. And if we are what we say we are—the Son of God, the Spirit—this is Heaven. And so in your re-Identity, you are saying the Kingdom of Heaven is at hand, and this is It. *I*, Identity am moving in Heaven here and now. That's part of re-Identity. Now that must be done until you can accept that Heaven is where you are.

Heaven is everywhere you're looking, and it makes no difference what world pictures are being presented; Heaven is where you are. And until you're in *that* awareness, you'll find you're walking in two worlds: one intellectually, claiming to be in another; and then going right out, jumping over puddles. And so Heaven is here, and in Heaven you cannot find any germs. You cannot find any discord or distress. When you do find germ, discord, distress, evil, error, sin, etcetera, what are you finding? You're finding that you're not in Heaven. You haven't re-identified your location. You are in Heaven, and therefore, only that which happens in Heaven can happen in your Consciousness.

There's no time in Heaven. The only time in Heaven is now. And so now becomes a new time for you. That's part of your re-identification: now. And there's nothing in Heaven ever becomes something. It *is*. *Is* is the only Reality in Heaven. There is no future. Everything *is*. And so, when you are in the Consciousness of Being in Heaven, you're in the acceptance that everything *is*. There's nothing I have to seek, nothing I have to pray for, nothing I have to struggle to get. Everything *is*, or else I have not accepted that I am in Heaven. Everything *is*, and now is the only time. There is no tomorrow. And because everything *is*, tomorrow *is*—today. Tomorrow is today.

However strange that may sound, Eternity is today. Every tomorrow is already now here. And that's part of being in Heaven—the knowledge that everything is now here. That's the acceptance of your fullness. This is part of re-identification, and then you're in the continuing Consciousness of *is*. Now, here, Heaven; where All is perfection. Any imperfection is hallucination. And there's only one power in Heaven: Love. Divine Love is the only power, the only law here; and so what have you got? You've got a complete re-identification that Heaven is where *I* am here and now, and the fullness *is* because perfection is all that can exist in Heaven; and Divine Love is the only power, the only law. Now you're really accepting Identity, and because of this Identity, you can be in a state of humility.

There's nothing to seek, strive, and struggle for. Recognizing Identity as Spirit; recognizing power and love as spiritual Presence right here, I rest in the Word and let the power of Divine Love manifest its own Universe, glorify Itself. You're in the vast peace which has nothing to seek, nothing to strive for, nothing to remove, nothing to get rid of, nothing to correct. There are no mountains in Heaven to be removed. You rest in the Word. You have all kinds of scriptural authority for this:

"Cease ye from man, whose breath is in his nostrils."

Cease from the form, the material form.

"My kingdom is not of this world."

And that's the cease ye from time and space.

"It is I; Be not afraid."

That's the acceptance of spiritual Identity.

". . . the glory which I had with thee before the world was."

Is still mine. That's the assurance that spiritual Identity is forever, always.

". . . all that I have is thine."

That's the assurance that nothing is withheld. It is present. It is thine.

And as you go through your Bible mentally, you discover that everything in there is an authority for you to live here now in Heaven, in the Is. You have an Is which is the perfection of God expressing, and there is only one Is. One infinite Is. One infinite Consciousness expressing. But it appears *as* because between the Is and the *as*, there is a cosmic mind. And as Is moves through the cosmic mind's interpretation of It, you get the multiple expressions which appear to us as this, that, and the other thing.

You're looking at the *changing* universe which is *as*. But always behind it is the one perfect, Divine Love expressing as the Is and the acceptance of now *is*: Now is the Father. Now is Divine Love. Now is fullness. Now is All-ness. Now is all that God *is*. Everywhere God is being God. Everywhere God's perfection is present in all things. My Grace is thy sufficiency in all things.

We rest in the knowledge that this is Heaven now, and there is no condition in Heaven other than the perfection of Being in all things. And when you rest there, you're in Identity; and you will discover that your own spiritual Substance will readjust for you that which had appeared outwardly as the unemployment, the lack, the limitation, the overweight, the underweight, the germ, the contagion, the infection, the problem, the discord, the unhappy relationship. Everything that it appeared to be was cosmic mind universally expressing, accepted in your most vulnerable spots, appearing as your personal problem because you were not standing in the knowledge, the Truth of Being, not in the Universe of God.

All of this is part of the re-identification, so that you walk through this world of "as" looking at everything that appears as this and as that, knowing that it isn't that at all. Only Is is there, appearing through cosmic mind as this, that, and the other. You live in the Is in the now and experience the "as"—but not accept it because Heaven has no "as." Everything in Heaven is perfection Itself expressing.

Now, whenever you've got a problem, then, you've taken yourself out of Heaven and out of spiritual Identity; and you have merely read Bible verses as some people perform calisthenics, some kind of a physical exercise or some kind of memorized prayer. The points given to us by these biblical events are to free us, to purify us of material thought. The unreality of matter is one of the prime purposes of these biblical events, to teach us the unreality of matter. And even though something in us stubbornly clings to the reality of matter, that isn't even your mind doing that. That's the world mind refusing to give up.

Always there is the world mind telling you: *But matter is real.* And until you face that—until you see that Jesus was demonstrating matter is unreal, nonexistent. Storms are not there. There's no water to walk upon. There's no cripple to heal.— Because these things do not exist in heaven, and earth is our material consciousness about Heaven. When you are out of your material consciousness about Heaven, you discover Heaven was where you always were. There is no other place.

And so because of these very nice papers that you submitted here, it's clear that we are ready. We are ready to spend another portion of this year losing all remnants of material thought. And it leads us to a place where we can look at those who talk about projecting the Soul body through space, and we can see that we will not have to project a Soul body. Rather, we will discover that I am in my Soul body now. I have no other, and the dropping away of that which is not my Soul body reveals that I have ever been in it. My Soul was never in a body that decays, in a body that dies. My Soul was that which is my eternal Life and is now here.

And that Soul has Its Body, and I am not going to project It. It knows what to do, where to do and how to do it; and It's doing it all now. And when we start to move through the Invisible, it will not be because there is a will in a human being projecting a Soul Body. It will be because we are experiencing the actual activity of the Soul, which instantly could move from a mountaintop to water to appear where a ship was drowning. And you will be moved, and I will be moved in such a way that we are where we belong at the right moment always. *I* in the midst of us will be the projector, not a human mind.

But first, all material remnants must be purified. We must re-Identify, and we must look at everything that appears *as* and re-Identify it as Is. It cannot be what It appears *as* because It appears *as* matter. We must re-Identify It as invisible Spirit through cosmic mind in an individual mind appearing *as*. And then we can look at the whole world and know that everyone is seeing their level of consciousness. But I am not bound by *their* level of consciousness. I am not bound by what *they* externalize. What they externalize is just as nonexistent as the waves at sea which threatened to bury the ship.

Always what appears *as* is the camouflage of the cosmic mist, the cosmic thought atoms. But behind them and where they are—above them, below them, and in them—where they are is always the now perfection of Spirit, of Being, which *I* am. This should become our daily Consciousness. It should be our daily rebirth. Every day we should have a second birth. Every day the son of woman should become the Son of Man. Every day we re-identify our Universe and our Identity. Every day we come to the second birth and let that be the beginning of our day, to live in the Heaven of now and Is.

Now let's just dwell on some of these things in a contemplative meditation for a moment. Because through your contemplative meditation, you're preparing the way for your listening meditation. You're clearing out the density of thought. You're letting yourself relax from the pressures of thinking, of planning, or trying to remember things. You're willing to walk out on Truth alone, knowing It is power. It is present. It is activated by love. You don't have to direct It; you can rest in It. And then just let go, standing in the knowledge of infinite Substance, which spins Itself into whatever forms are needed, wherever they are needed and whenever. My Substance is my God.

My spiritual Essence is the Father within. It lives now, here in Heaven, in the Is; and I am never going to leave the now. I'm never going to "become." I'm never going to stray one second from now, because only now am I that Essence. Never tomorrow, never yesterday, always now. Now never had a tomorrow, never had a yesterday. Now is infinitely and eternally now, and that is my home. Never fooled into moving out into time. Now accepting Is. God Is. Only God Is. Only God's perfection Is. I care not what appears *as*. Only God's perfection Is. And be sure that My Soul is where It belongs, always.

[Silence]

Now, if I were to tell you that your son's nose is bleeding, you could quickly dismiss it, knowing only perfection *is*. I am faced with a cosmic image. I will not accept it as belonging to my son. It is not a local Truth. It's a cosmic image presented to me, and in this state of knowing Is now, whatever is not of God is not now. And that's all I have to do. Stand still, rest, and watch the spiritual Essence of Being adjust the outer picture and show you no nosebleed, no dizzy spell, no this, no that. Only *I, I, I* am present. There is no other. "The Lord our God is one . . . ."

But you must be at this place always. And all that is is the preparation for moving as Soul through the Universe unimpeded by material obstruction, by condition, by material concepts appearing as form—free in Self. Be thankful, then, that everything that comes at you forces you to rise to the higher ground. It would be so easy to relax and say, "Oh well, we've got it." But we haven't. We'll never have it until transition.

[Silence]

Suppose we rest a little and come back in about five or ten minutes and see where the Father takes us then.

∞∞∞∞∞∞ END OF SIDE ONE ∞∞∞∞∞∞

We're told in this ninth chapter that we are to do certain things every day. He calls it a daily habit, and the first was to become consciously aware of the presence of God. Now, without the presence of God we have nothing except our human selves. With the presence of God we are prepared to open ourselves to Divine infinite Law, and to become conscious of the presence of God means to accept that presence as the Substance of my Being. I cannot be something apart from that Presence. No matter how important I may think I am humanly, if I am apart from the Presence, then I and the Father are not one Identity, one Substance.

Occasionally in the world we find many important people who are unaware of their unimportance, and they're marvelous people on this human level. We read in this morning's paper that Frank Conniff was the top man with the Hearst chain. He's the fellow who went with Hearst and Kingsbury Smith over to Russia, and no one had been allowed behind the Iron Curtain to interview Khrushchev; and he was smart enough to get the assignment and the okay from Khrushchev. He did some marvelous things in the journalism field. A very handsome, charming, intelligent man; the kind that everybody loved; capable of real power in his field. But why at 57 is he gone? Why at 53 did he have these massive heart attacks?

It wasn't overwork. It was the inability to know that the Kingdom of God is within me. It was the belief that I am this fellow you see, and somehow, somewhere there's a God who loves me; and this is separation. And it isn't enough to know that isn't true. That isn't enough. You can know it on Monday, but that won't help you on Tuesday. It must be a continuing consciousness, and this is the meaning of Joel's caution that part of your daily experience must be the conscious *awareness* of the presence of God as a continuing fact. And the awareness of that Presence means here, now where I stand.

And then because of the presence of God here, now where I stand as my spiritual Substance, I am under spiritual law—no other. These things shall not move me that are not spiritual law. That presence of God which is my Substance needs no defense, and therefore, the only protective work you do is the knowledge of that Presence. You don't have to look over your shoulder. The knowledge of the presence of God as the Substance of my Being—extended as the Substance of all Being, as the infinite Substance—this is our daily requirement. That's the whole point of his chapter. He calls it "Daily Preparation for Spiritual Living," and I want to read this paragraph:

"Since God constitutes the law of my being, I am governed by spiritual Being, spiritual Law, spiritual Light, and spiritual Truth." [The Contemplative Life, p. 151. Acropolis Books, Publisher]

There must be an inner acceptance. And then, because of the inner acceptance that spiritual Law is all that governs you, you cannot say I am under the power of lack or limitation or anything else. You're only under spiritual Law, and for you the only Law that exists is perfect spiritual Law. There are no other powers.

This is daily, daily, daily until it's my Consciousness. I know God has never been paralyzed, never blind, never deaf. I know God never had indigestion. Spiritual law prevents the possibility of these afflictions. If I have them, it is because I have within me a belief that there is another power besides spiritual Law, and that belief is showing forth as my affliction. Whatever my problem is, it is the visible evidence of my belief in another power besides spiritual Law. And when I rectify the belief—when I come home to spiritual Identity, and therefore, only spiritual Law is acceptable to me—then there is no place for the world mind to express in my Consciousness, and it cannot externalize as these afflictions from which the world suffers.

He [Joel] goes on to say this, "If we engage in this daily practice—and we must—we shall soon find that we have received in our inner being the secret of the universe, the secret of harmony, the secret of the Holy Grail. We shall find that we have the secret of life, once we know that the consciousness of the presence of God is the only reality unto us and there is no two-law universe. There is only the spiritual-law universe of God. When we have that, the discords and inharmonies will melt gradually, but certainly and completely." He speaks from his experience. We have seen that everywhere the Spirit of Christ walked in the form called Jesus, this was true. And all of us have experienced that wherever the consciousness of perfect spiritual Law is, the non-powers of the world are exposed. In some miraculous fashion they lose the ability to imprison us in false belief.

Now, as Spirit, conscious of the presence of God *as* your Spirit, you must further accept that you are completely Self-contained. That means there can be no lack in Christ of any kind. And so we bypass all physical evidence because the physical evidence will always tell you that you are not Self-contained. And the question comes in those who have not had the experience yet: "Well, if I am Self-contained, what do I do about these appearances that I'm supposed to bypass?" Even though we have lesson after lesson on that very subject, you will find your mind saying, "What do I do, then, about this thorn in the side?"

And that's just exactly what he's telling you to do: Rest in the knowledge that only spiritual Law is here. That which is not spiritual Law is the universal hypnotism. It isn't here. That's the meaning of hypnotism: It isn't here! You don't try to overcome what isn't here. Even trying to overcome hypnotism is tightening the noose around your neck. It's the recognition that it isn't here. You can never suffer from Reality. You can only suffer from unreality. Every form of suffering is a cosmic hypnotism. That's the great revelation of the Infinite Way—every form. And there is no power to cause it. It is being caused by that which is a seeming power to one who is not aware that only the power of God exists.

The non-problem is caused by the non-power which you accept *as* a power, and therefore, as a problem. And this is apply named, this chapter: "Spiritual Exercises To Be Practiced."

[Chapter 9 is now entitled "Daily Preparation for Spiritual Living."] And the reason for the practicing of the Presence and the spiritual Power without opposite is because we are learning to accept the inexhaustible resources of our own Being. We are learning not to go outside ourselves; not to make the mistake of thinking that in my own Being something has been withheld. There is no thing, no person, no condition that you need that is not within your own Being now. The mere thought that it's possible for what you need to be outside of your Being is to lose that which is yours. You might as well lose it because even though it's there, you have no use of it.

Now this brings you, then, to a level of Consciousness which is more aware of who and what you are and of the limitlessness nature of your Being. We have discovered within ourselves that every time we know the Truth of our Being, that we never have to pray for a need. But before we ask, in the mere knowing of the Truth of Being as Self-containing all that we need, that which we do need does appear as form, as condition, as thing, as person, and as place.

The miracle of spiritual Existence is that which we need, being ever-present, It always externalizes itself in the three-dimensional material world—provided we stay there in the Now and Is of spiritual Presence as the One and the Only; and let the Father do, through your transparent Consciousness, that which the Father is ever doing—being God here, now, and everywhere. Everywhere in this Universe, God Is Being God, fulfilling God.

Now, many of us talk to people on the level of people, and I'd like you to consider a little exercise to practice with yourself. It's very difficult, very challenging, and very rewarding. Now we know that matter has no intelligence, and yet we all talk to matter all day long. We talk to the boss. We talk to our employees. We talk to our friends. We really talk to matter as if it had intelligence. And sometimes we don't think it's very intelligent, and we even say so. Well, it isn't! It has no intelligence whatsoever.

Suppose we try to see, too, that the mind which is in that body, or in which that body is, is not the Divine Mind. And there's no point really talking to it either, because it's as much illusion as the material form that it externalizes. Then why talk to it? Now, here's a test of your spiritual development. See if you can do it for one day or even for an hour. Establish consciously that you're not going to talk to the physical form or the mind of an individual. You're going to talk to the Divine Mind. Even though there's a person there, you're going to address your remarks to the Divine Mind, as if for you the person had no existence. And to do that, you're going to talk from your Divine Mind—Divine Mind to Divine Mind.

And you've got to do this in such a way that the individual doesn't know you're doing it. That you're talking from Divine Mind to Divine Mind and looking straight at a person as if you're talking to a person, so that the person thinks you're talking to me, to him, to her. You try that for a while as an exercise and see what it does to you. You begin to feel some of that which was happening when Jesus spoke to his disciples. He never spoke to "them." He was either speaking to the cosmic mind or the Divine Mind in them. Never was he speaking to an individual mind.

When he said, "Peace, be still. It is I," do you think he was speaking to Peter? He was telling the cosmic mind, "You have no power here, friend." When he said to Pilate, "Thou hast no power over me," he wasn't speaking to Pilate. He wasn't speaking to a lump of flesh which had no intelligence. He wasn't speaking to a human mind. He was letting us know that this cosmic mind, which is pretending to have power, has no power. He was showing us the universal mesmerism we must face, not the individual. When you conquer that universal mesmerism, you'll find something in you saying, "Right, I have overcome the world," not the individual. There are no individuals. There is only a world mesmerism.

And so dwelling in the consciousness of the Presence until you can re-identify not as a person who has found the Presence, but *as* the Presence. The Presence that I have discovered I am. The Truth that I was seeking I am. In your re-identification now, all that you had seemed to be—a corporeal person of a certain size and weight and density, a certain age, a certain sex—all must be re-identified. There are no corporeal beings in Heaven. There are no men or women in Heaven. There are no sizes and shapes in Heaven. There are no material conditions in Heaven. There are no backaches and heartaches. Deny thyself.

When you are consciously accepting the Presence, you are consciously rejecting thyself, the mortal self. You're putting off the old man. And so Joel's commandments to us have a double-edged sword. I can't just sit here and say, "Oh, the Presence is here."

That won't do me any good. Everything that the Presence *is,* is here. The Presence is all, the fullness of the Presence, the infinity of the qualities of the Presence. Can I say, "The Presence is here, but I'm unemployed? The Presence is here, but I am paralyzed? The Presence is here, but I am sick?" Then I haven't done my homework, because only the Presence is here; and the Presence is not paralyzed, not unemployed, and not sick. Only the Presence is here. This is the practicing of the Presence. Only the law of the Presence is here. All else must be hallucination. All else must be the false mind, the non-mind.

Self-contained is the acceptance of the presence of God as I and the Father, One Self, and therefore, Self-contained; and this is your preparation for the activity of Grace. When we do the chapter on Grace next week, number 10, if you haven't read *The Contemplative Life* lately, you may have forgotten that at the end of the chapter, there is a list of other chapters in other books, which Joel had called the "must chapters." I know that since that was written, there were other chapters that would have been included had this book been written later. But nonetheless, there are seven or eight, or—I don't know how many chapters in other books that are listed; and it wouldn't be possible, perhaps, for you to read them all for one class. But we're going to have to do those in a measure, sort of double up on ourselves.

The important thing is that because God is present here where you are, and God is in Heaven, you must be in Heaven; and you cannot violate the laws of Heaven and expect to remain in Heaven. You cannot violate the law of perfection, which is spiritual Law. As a matter of fact, it cannot be violated by anyone. You do not have the power to violate it. That is an illusion. There is no power on earth to violate the Law of Heaven.

Only the will of the Father is being functioned in Heaven now. Only the will of the Father is functioning where you are. And that will being your perfection, everything that denies it must be unreal. As you dwell in this, you will be out of the body; for there's no physical body in Heaven. There is no physical body where the presence of God is realized. There is no physical condition where the presence of God is realized. There is only My Kingdom. And when you are out of the body, through your daily practice of the presence of Spirit as your Presence and the ever-presence of Spiritual Law as the only Law, you will lose the illusion of a temporary life.

You will know as certainly as you know anything that all temporary life is illusion. There is no such thing and never has been. It is part of the universal mesmerism. It simply has no existence. There is no such thing as temporary life. The temporary life that we are all so concerned about doesn't exist. Take no thought for your temporary life. It isn't there. The only Life you have is the perfect, forever Life. And in your absent-from-the-body experience, dwelling in the Essence of Being, that false belief will fall away. With it will fall away the concerns about that temporary life. You will see that Life is ever Itself. All Life is ever Living, ever Being.

You have never been separated from Life anywhere in this Universe. All Life is One. I, being Life, all who I know being Life; neither this human sense of life nor death can separate us from Life, for that is our name. We must know these things so well that the complete freedom of Being Life, finding Its way through our Consciousness, releases us from the limitations of a temporary life. For those limitations are as unreal as the temporary life. The false horizons created by the cosmic mind, accepted by the human mind—the false horizon of a beginning and an end, the false horizon of an absence of this or that—these are all false horizons. The false horizon where there's a beginning of a pain; there is no such place.

We are Self-contained in Christ, and we are to live as pure spiritual Being, enjoying the fruitage of It. This is the glimpsing, the living, the awareness of the Soul realm, where all the horizons vanish. There are no horizons. There is the limitless Self, and all

## Class 21: Total Re-Identification

good flows in through that limitless Self and appears where the corporeal form seems to be as the sustaining influence of that form. When you're in your limitless Self, your infinite Being is flowing to a point called the human self. That's the point where the infinity of Being is made visible. That's the point of Grace, and ultimately it's the point of release from corporeality.

We should be in that Consciousness which says, "I'm not concerned about an end of the world because I know there was never a beginning of the world." The false horizon of the beginning of the world and an end of the world has no place in spiritual Consciousness. The Lord our God is One, and we have no other gods. No other identity, no other being, no other power, no other belief. The perfect infinite Consciousness, called God, is the perfect infinite manifestation, called God; and that manifestation is Son of God. That manifestation is *I*. When we are feeling this limitless Self, the fruitage of it is quickly visible. There's no attachment to person, place, or thing. There's no clinging love. There's no fear of loss. You're in Spiritual Consciousness. You're in your illuminated Self.

Now, if we've learned anything from walking on water, from stopping storms, we have learned that matter is a mental obstruction with no Reality in God. We have learned that the conditions of matter are purely hypothetical and hallucinatory. They are mental energy appearing *as*. We have learned that we are invisible Self, made of the pure Spirit of God without boundaries, and that there are no margins in Heaven. This is our Living Consciousness.

We are not here to glorify a human being. We are not here to seek status. We are here to let the will of God, which is perfect, express Itself as our living Being. We are here to let the mortal sense of self step aside and behold that Living Will of perfection making manifest Itself in all things. We are here to hold the line against the belief that the power of imperfection is present where we dwell. We are here to be faithful witnesses of the all power, the all knowledge, and the all presence of the spiritual Father called God.

And when you have accepted that your function is to be a faithful witness, all of the need and struggle and striving to do and be something is taken off your shoulder. The responsibility is not on you. The government is on the Spirit Itself. Your function is to witness that activity, denying your human selfhood. In setting forth our identities, because we're still unformed in that Identity in our Consciousness, we have all tried to claim certain things for ourselves. And now we will learn that there's nothing we need claim because we *are*, and we can humbly let our Identity express to glorify the Father. If we will glorify the Father and not a human personality, we will find that all that is required of us is present in infinite measure. My Will be done. *I* in the midst of thee am greater.

So Infinity is now moving in our consciousness as our Consciousness to the degree that we have humanly seen the folly of mortality, the false horizon of birth and death, the cosmic mist which comes forth *as* appearances. And we are facing all claims, not as **my** claim, but as a universal claim, which I refuse to accept as **my** claim. Standing in my Identity and watching spiritual Substance dissolve its suppositional opposite called material problem. Everything you do this way is under law, under Grace, under the Will of perfection. You need not press a button. You need not pull a trigger. You need not lift a sword. Stand ye still.

Next week we'll discuss Grace. And if you will, I'd like you to do with "re-Identify" just what you did with Identity. You did Identity. Now do the same thing with the word "re-Identify." And I'd like to hold what you've already done until you've done that so that you're not guided to repeat yourself. Come up with a complete new feeling about it, and then you'll see yourself within three weeks after you've done the first one how far you've developed. However, if any of you want to still take whatever you've done back with you, you may, of course. So I'll leave them here. Anyone can take the one that they want, if they want to take it. If you want to leave it, leave it.

Try it now with "re-Identify." "R" "E" "I" and so forth. Make up your crossword, paragraph, thought, sentence—whatever you wish—until you get this feeling of being in Heaven. In the Is, in the Now, in the law of perfection and Divine love, where no opposites can possibly occur. That's the re-Identify. That'll prepare us for the experience of Grace.

Thanks so much.

# CLASS 22

# HERE IS NOW

*Herb:* We'll take a look at Burroughs' poem in this chapter.

"Serene, I fold my hands and wait,
Nor care for wind, nor tide, nor sea;
I rave no more 'gainst time or fate,
For lo! my own shall come to me."

Now those are very reassuring and comforting words to hear, and many have heard them. They put us in a momentary sense of peace until the little mind begins to say, "Well, how long do I wait for mine own to come to me? And is there something I can do in the meantime? Where shall I look for it? Shall I prepare? Shall I make some plans?" And before you know it, we are lured into the trap of what may be called the mental universe.

Now, we have today something new to do together. And in order to do it successfully, we have to first get down into the jungle, the jungle of the mind. We have to know why. We have to answer certain questions for the restless mind. You might say we have to go into the lion's den in order to really come face to face with the lion and overcome the belief that there is power there over the Spirit of God.

Now, if you were to put your finger on one word that covers every problem in this world, it would surprise you what that word is. And strangely, it was named so that it even pronounces like "Adam" in Adam and Eve: "A" "T" "O" "M." We're going to put the finger on the atom and say, "*There* is the cause of every problem." Yes, we can read about Grace and mine own will come to me; but we're going to say that mine own will not come to me through the atom. And as long as the atom stands there—as long as I have a belief in the material world of which the atom is the basic ingredient—mine own is not going to come to me, and Grace is going to continue to be a word in a book.

We want to look at this atom. We want to see how it has fooled us. How, because of the atom, religion has been able to give us a God who cannot stop germs, a God who cannot stop pain, a God who cannot stop war. All because of the atom and the mind which perceives the atom and forms its own impressions, and then makes up its kind of God based on what it knows nothing about. We want to see how science, too, can find the cause of every problem in the world and not even know that they have discovered it.

We have a universe today which is slightly different than it was 20 or 30 or 40 centuries ago. This universe was unknown at that time. We had a physical universe, and we had it in three levels. We had a mineral universe; we had a vegetable universe; and we had an animal universe. And out of it came a human universe. Always there was a progression on the physical level. And so these four components of the physical world were unaware of the next world, which became known to man as it came over the horizon; and man found himself in a mental universe, a mental world. And today we live in that mental world, comprehending it as a physical world, unaware that behind the mental world is still another one coming over the horizon into consciousness. And so whereas we were given the right to be a king in our Kingdom, we remain servants and slaves in a mental world.

Now, the components of the mental world have been discovered as the atom; and all that an atom comprises itself to be in our world is the material substance that we have mistakenly called our physical forms: the forests, the oceans, and the rivers and the mountains, the sky, the air we breath. All that we have called matter is the invisible atom. And so we reach out to grab a handful of this matter. We reach out for a handful of atoms. We think our security lies in matter, and we're reaching out for atoms.

Always, whatever we do is based upon that invisible atom. Even our senses—the eye, the ear, the nose—made of the atom. And so you have eyes that are physical, and the substance of them is the atom; and they look out upon a world made of atoms. And all you've got is the inter-reaction of the atoms of the eyes with the atoms of the world—atom reacting to atom—and from it comes human experience. Then we have bullets, and they're made of atoms. And we have bombs, and they're made of atoms. And we have germs, and they're made of atoms. And soon you get the idea that God did not create the atom. Science discovers the world is made of atoms. Truth discovers that God did not make the atoms that the world is made of, and Jesus reveals it in "My kingdom is not of this world."

You find your problem is that you are reaching for atoms. You are trying to preserve a life among atoms. You are building security and safety and everything in life on the basis of an atom that you have never seen. And all of the karma that we call the cause and effect of this world is based upon the inter-reaction of the atoms of your physical form—your physical brain, your physical eyes, your physical senses—with the atoms out there. And as you face this situation, the Spirit within informs you that the world, which you have said is outside there, is not there at all. You have built it by the inter-reaction of your atomic brain, your atomic mind, your atomic senses to the atoms out there. Atom reacting to atom. But how can an atom react to something if there is no atom?

If God did not create an atom, what is your eye made of? And then you face another Truth: If the eye is made of atoms, and God did not make the atoms, I do not have a physical eye. If the ear is made of atoms, and God did not make atoms, I do not have a physical ear. I do not have physical senses because God did not make physical senses. God did not make the atoms that are the substance of physical senses. And you go in and out of your body, and you find your heart is made of atoms; but God did not make atoms.

There isn't a bone or an organ in your body that is not made of atoms, and yet God did not make them. And then you come where Jesus finally stood: I have no material body, and the atoms of my senses which are reacting are an illusion. And what they are reacting to must also be an illusion because that which is not here—the senses that I do not have—cannot react. The reaction is illusion too. There is no world outside of me. There is no physical universe outside. There is no external world. And finally, there is no physical me; and so I am not on the earth.

And we reach that plateau, then, of consciousness where I physically am not on this earth; and there is no material earth on which I can be. That which says I am is the sense mind, the atom mind—that which reacts to what is not there and which itself is not here to do any reacting. You're in the lion's den of Truth, and slowly your atomic universe dissolves. Its only reality is in the atomic mind, in the atomic brain, in the atomic senses that God did not create. There never was a world of atoms. And the whole material world which we have worshipped is based upon atoms that are not there. The illusion isn't the matter. That's only a secondary illusion. The illusion of matter is based upon a reaction of nonexistent senses to nonexistent atoms.

And then, when you finally can accept that the world of atoms is not the Kingdom of God, is not the creation of God; when you can divest yourself of every belief in a physical you with physical senses in a physical world—then your only problem is how, then, can I overcome the atom? And the mind will struggle with that for a long time. If it accepts that it wants to overcome the atom, it will strive to do so; and it will set up all kinds of barriers to the success of overcoming the atom. It will say, "God, help me. God, bring me this. God, I seek your help to overcome the atom."

And the mind will try to build an improved sense of mortality. The mind will try to correct situations. The mind will think, "Well, I have all this karma behind me that I've got to write off first," unaware that karma is only in the atom, and that all an atom can control is another atom. All the power of atoms lies in its power over atoms. And finally, it dawns upon you there is only one way to overcome the atom; and that is to know it isn't there. You cannot overcome it if you believe it is there because that is the trap. Before, you were trying to overcome matter, which is visible. Now you are trying to overcome the atom, which is the basis of matter, which is invisible. And when you know the atom is not there, then all matter based upon the presence of an atom is equally not there.

The overcoming of the atom is the knowledge that there is no atom to overcome. Science, which gave us the atom as the substance of the material world, gave us a substance that is not there; but it is the invisible substance of matter. It proved the nonexistence of matter when it gave us a nonexistent substance as the substance of matter. All of this to Jesus was nothing. And so "I have no material body" was his final conclusion about himself and about every person in the world. To him there was no person outside, no form outside, no thing outside, and no human condition outside. He lived in an unobstructed universe without atoms.

And now you're in that place where to overcome the belief in the presence of an atom and the secondary belief in the presence of matter—which is based upon the atom—you find that you cannot reach the state of nonresistance as long as you strive to do it mentally. Now think for a moment of the ramifications involved in this. You seek financial security, and that takes the form of money. Money is matter. Matter is based on atoms. Atoms aren't there. What is money? It is a concept, but yet you're seeking that concept. You seek a home. A home is based on matter. Matter is based on atoms, but there are no atoms. What is a home? A concept. You seek health. Health is based on good matter. Matter is based on atoms. Atoms aren't there.

Every physical problem is based on some kind of disruption in the relationship that we entertain in mind between the atoms of our body and the external world. We don't mind being made of atoms as long as they're harmonious. It's only when the discord enters in, when the ratio between one set and another set is discordant, that we're concerned. Then we're willing to look at the ultimate Truth. The ultimate illusion, then, is that me which is made of atoms. That is the basis of the dream world. That is the basis of every condition from which we suffer. And as long as you try to overcome that condition with your mind, you find that you fail; and there are many reasons that the mind fails.

We know for one thing that the mind you are trying to reason with has its own built-in set of logic, which is not divine logic. The mind reasons, "This is a bad condition. Certainly, God approves of a good condition." And you're wrong. God doesn't approve or disapprove of any human condition, good or bad. The mind is not the Mind of God. This is the mind that identifies evil. The Mind of God does not identify evil. The human mind, which identifies light and dark, good and bad, is in the tree of the knowledge of good and evil. It is a mind separated from Reality. It is based on five senses which are based on invisible atoms, which are based on nothing. All atomic thought is is cosmic thought. And you come right up to the cosmic mind, which is creating the illusion of cosmic atoms; and you find there is no cosmic mind there.

And so as long as you try through this individual human mind, you will try to channel, to outline; to seek person, place, thing, improvement, correction; and it won't work. Be still and know. And there's the paradox we come to. If I'm still, how can I know? If I'm not thinking, how can I know anything? What can I use to know with? And I know that's the paradox we all go through. They tell me to be still, and they tell me to know the Truth. Now, which shall I do? If I know there's no atom, I'm using my mind. If I know that everything is illusion, I'm using my mind to know it. So I'm always in this paradox of trying to know the Truth that makes me free and also trying to be still in the mind that is supposed to know the Truth. That's why today's class is so important.

There's only one way to get out of the dream of the atom world. Be still, yes, in the mind; and know in the Soul. And the secret of Grace is when you touch the Soul realm in the stillness of the mind. Then you are not in the atom universe. Until then, the mind, which itself is an atomic creation, is trapping you into perpetuating the very conditions you're so eagerly striving to lose. Be still in the mind *until* you open the bud of the Soul. Until that Soul says, "Now, you have been still sufficiently to touch the fourth dimension. Now, *I* in the midst of you will reveal all that you were seeking in what you thought was an external world of atoms."

There *is* no external world of atoms, and everything you sought in that external exists in the midst of you. The Kingdom of God is not external. It is within your Soul, not in your mind. And every religion in the world that has God in their mind finds that it has a God with no power. A God who cannot heal a flea. A God who has no concern about his so-called children, even though they worship him. A God who will not stop an assassination. A God who will let mothers die in childbirth. A God who is completely indifferent to this world. Why? Because it's not a God at all. It's a mental image, and the world is worshipping that mental image called God.

You cannot know God. You cannot know Spirit. You cannot know Reality. **You cannot know Truth with your mind.** You can only know the mental universe, the world in which the invisible atom has fooled the religions and the scientists of the world. And everyone is running around trying to improve the world, and there is no world to improve. It is all based on invisible atoms that aren't there. And as long as you're trying to find your security in the world, in your mortal selfhood, you are in the illusion that you are going to improve something; and even the improvement is illusion.

Always, we are chasing shadows. But when you touch that realm which the mind cannot touch, which is the realm of the Soul, which is the fourth-dimensional Universe—then you touch the infinite Essence, which is the Substance of all that you have been seeking. Then the infinite Essence, touched through your Soul, pours through, flowing as the Grace that forms Itself; and the law of Self-fulfillment is brought into your experience. There is no karma. There is no being a servant to the cosmic mind. There is no chasing shadows. There is only being a beholder of the Reality.

"I have come to glorify the Father," he said. "All thou hast given me, I have kept in thy name." We are never a witness to the invisible glory of God with our human minds. All of the hosannas we sing, all of the words we speak, and all of the hopes within us are false human logic—fooled by this invisible little fellow that has been fingered by science and unknown to religion—the atom, which makes the atom man, the atom world, the atom condition, the atom lack, and the atom limitation. From that little atom comes the heart attack. From that little atom comes the belief in cancer. From that little atom comes every disease in this world, all of them based on a change in a condition called matter. And none of it is there. But to the *mind* it's there.

We are brought now into the realm of Grace, the Soul. The fourth-dimensional Essence which is not touched by the natural man who receiveth not the Essence, the things of God. Our Grace never flows because we deserve it. You can fast or sacrifice or do good things. That isn't what brings Grace to you at all. The only thing that brings Grace to you is like the overcoming of the false belief in the presence of the atom or matter: You overcome the false belief that the Grace you seek isn't here. It always is here. You never go out to attain it or acquire it. You learn to be still in the mind, alive in the Soul so that Grace may reveal Itself. You don't pray for It any more than you pray for sunlight. You don't seek It any more than you seek sunlight. You rest in the knowledge that here Grace is.

Now, what we want to do today is establish a very firm foothold in Reality. We want to recognize when we are in the mental universe and when we are in the Soul Universe, so that we are not deceived into perpetuating the illusion while we think we're coming out of it. We want to know when we're seeking what isn't there. We want to know when we're doing the Divine or when we're doing the human. You will discover that when you're in the mental universe, you're always in a state of time. Somehow you are drawn out into hoping tomorrow will be better.

When you're in the mental universe, you're always in a place. You're in a chair. You're in a trolley. You're in a car. You're in a theater. You're at a lecture. That's still the mental universe. Always, in the mental universe you go from here to there, and you return from there to here. You go up or you go down, or you travel at a certain rate of speed. None of this exists in the the Universe of Grace. And to say, "Mine own will come to me" is beautiful. But it will only come into your experience when you have moved aside all of the mental barriers which prohibit Grace from becoming active experience. If the shades are down, the sun, which is ever there, cannot come through. If the shades are up, the sun shines in. If the shades of your mind are pulled down, Grace can be present; but it will do you no good.

Now there are certain qualities, then, that are necessary to make a radical change so that you are not just improving your mental concepts to improve your mortality, but walking consciously in the Soul Universe. Living in God, moving in God, having your Being in God through Soul realization, not mental realization. Ultimately, we want to come to a place where we're doing something we never dreamed we would do. The first is to establish that level of Consciousness which you recognize as a Soul level. Something that you can put into activity, into action, and hold regardless of what appearances try to draw you away.

Now let's get these four or five or six key ideas down. The word **Here**, the word **Is**, the word **Now**, the word **One**, the word **Perfection**, the word **Love**. Now, these are all part of your Soul Consciousness. In mind you have *here* and *there*. In mind you have *was, is,* and *will be*. In mind you have *yesterday, today,* and *tomorrow*. In mind you have *many;* you have *multiples*. But we are going to see that in Soul everything is **Here**; everything is **Now**; everything **Is**; everything is **One**; everything is **Perfect**; and everything is **Love**.

Now, when you're not in those understandings, you are in the mind; and you're not in the Soul. That's how you will recognize that you have slipped into a mental universe. And the moment you do that, you can be sure that your continuity of Grace has been interrupted. The moment you slip into the mind, you are literally turning away from all that you are seeking.

God is **Here**. This never changes. And to the God of Hereness this earth is not broken up into little places. This earth is Here to God. And therefore, this earth, which is Here to God, is also Here to the Son of God. And by Here, I mean not there but Here. The word "there" drops out of your vocabulary in the Soul. Every "there" ceases to exist because to God everything is Here, and *I* and the Father are One. "The earth is the Lord's and the fullness thereof" Here and Now.

The significance of this will become apparent in a moment. You have identified your Self as infinite Being. You have said: "*I* am the infinite Invisible. *I* am the Divine Child. *I* am That *I* Am." Fine. Now you're going to be held to *being* what you said you are. God never said, "There's a rock here, and there's a rock there" because everything is within God. And therefore, everything within God is Here to God; and therefore, everything that is within the infinite Invisible is Here to that which *I* am. The moment you have a there, not a Here, you are denying Identity.

So it was very important on these little identification charts we've been making up not to put down words, but to put down your proven Consciousness, something you can live by. When you say, "*I* am the infinite Invisible; *I* am the infinite Christ," that means to you everything is Here. You can be sure if everything wasn't Here to Jesus Christ, there would have been no miracles. "Here *I* am," said the Voice when Moses wondered why the bush was not consumed, though it burned. "Here *I* am."

Whenever there's a laying on of hands in the Bible in the physical appearance, it is because the one who is laying on hands is recognizing the invisible Identity of another. And the invisible spiritual hands that are being laid upon the other is the recognition of Here *I* Am, *I* which is in the midst of thee. *I* is in the midst of him and her. *I* am Here. *I* am Here. *I* am Here. *I* am in a thousand places. Here *I* am. The *I* in the midst of you is in the midst of everyone else. Here *I* am.

One day you will hear that when you look out at another: "Here *I* am." And this is the secret of the ages when it's understood. For that "Here *I* am" in another and the "Here *I* am" in you are one and the same. You have thought of yourself as looking out of these two eyes and living in this form while trying to become aware that you are the infinite Christ, and that step must be taken now in Consciousness: "Here *I* am." You see that bird on the tree? When it says to you, "Here *I* am," that is your Self where that bird appears. And when it says "Here *I* am"; when you know that *I* in the midst of you is *I* in the midst of the bird, you will come to another secret: That *I* in the midst of everyone on this earth is You, and that is the infinite Christ. And that is how you will know you're in the Soul realm.

To declare it in your mind is nothing. For It to declare Itself in your Soul is everything. As we sit here now, *I* in the midst of you am the *I* in the midst of every individual on earth. It is important to reach a plateau, which may never have occurred to most of us, to listen so intently within that *I* in the midst of the bird, that *I* in the midst of the ocean, *I* in the midst of the sky, *I* in the midst of everything on this earth declare that *I* am in the midst of you.

And where *I* am, *I* am one with the *I* in the midst of you because I *am* you. And therefore, *I* in the midst of the bird am Here to you. When *I* am in the midst of the bird, *I* am no longer *there* to you. *I* am Here. For the Hereness of the *I* in the midst of the bird is the Hereness of your own Being. When you catch this, you have your Consciousness out of the trap of being in a body.

The Voice actually declares from the bird, "*I* am Here," and that Here means Here to the person who hears it even though there is distance between them. It shows you there is no distance. "*I* am Here," and that may come to you from another century. And that Here is also Now. When *I* declares its Hereness and its Nowness to you, It is telling you about your Self. It is removing the mask of matter, the mask of atoms, the mask of time and place.

It's important to practice the knowledge that *I* am a hundred feet away, two hundred feet away, five hundred feet away; and that five hundred feet away is Here. That thousand feet away is Here. Every place in this world is Here because it is *I*. It is *I* who is in the midst of you. And you're catching the true mysticism when you know that *I* on every planet am Here. *I* in every century am Here, and that *I* is the only *I* you will ever be.

That is why you can say, "*I* am not a person on this earth. *I* am *I* in the midst of all that appears on this earth. *I* am not this fragment in the form. *I* am the infinite *I* everywhere." And everywhere is Here because everything in the Universe is Here to *I*. There is no place in the Universe that ceases to be anything else except Here to you. Alaska is Here. New Zealand is Here. Home is Here. Wherever you are the Universe is Here, and this is the turning. As you dwell with this, as It registers, you find you're not in mind. And that's how you know it's registering. Because it begins to give you a sense of expansion, of immediacy.

You begin to see why everything was Here to Jesus. There was no "there" in his vocabulary or his Consciousness. "There" did not exist. *I* is everywhere. And everywhere, therefore, is Here in *I*. There was never a second's lapse of time. *I* is always Now. And before there was a second of time to lapse—stretch forth thine hand, thine arm. Always there was a Now and only Now. There wasn't an instant hesitation.

Now *is* the perfection of *I*. Now *is* the perfection of love. Now *is* the power of the Divine. And what comes forth? *I* do, for *I* realized is Grace. *I is* the Essence Now. *I* know thy needs. *I* perform. *I* perfect. *I* am the bread. *I* am the Way. *I* am the bread out of the sky because *I* am Here. *I* am the Divine manna. *I* am the Life. *I* am the Way. *I* am the Resurrection.

Always it is *I*, and it is always *I* Here and Now, perfect. It is the Consciousness of *I* Here—not just Here, but *I* of the Hereness of everywhere—which brings forth Grace. If you think *I* is Here, only Here—No. Here is infinite. *I* is *infinitely* Here, and the distinction is the difference between the manna that flows and the manna you hope for that never seems to arrive.

As you sit in a room consciously aware that there is nothing in the Universe but *I*; that *I* is the infinite Spirit of God and that is your name, and that *I* comprises within Itself all of the Father; that the *I* within you and the *I* within everyone you know is the same I, all indivisible, One Self, same *I*; then you know that the *I* within everyone you know is the only Being on the earth. That *I* is who you are, not this me; and that *I* is One with the Father.

When that *I* is your Identity, then this Universe is Here to you; and this Universe is Now to you; and everything is Is-ing Now Here to you. Then you're in your Soul. Now this is going to become standard Consciousness. Here, universal Here, is Here. Eternal time is Here Now. There are no more tomorrows. There is nothing going to happen tomorrow that isn't Now Here in Spirit. You have your infinite Nowness, your infinite Hereness, your infinite Isness; and that becomes the permanent Consciousness of your Soul. Whatever would draw you out of It, you meet Now instantly with a recognition that I don't have to wait till tomorrow. It's what I know Now in my Soul that is going to be the human tomorrow. It's what I know Here in my Soul as the Isness of God, not the future of God. Here is Now God perfect; and there is no other power.

As long as this remains your Consciousness, you're not separated back into mind, which again separates you from Reality. The conscious Awareness of God is Here Now, and the meaning of those words, "Here is Now," includes the infinite Eternal. There is no action on the face of the earth that to you is not Here because your invisible Spirit is where the action seems to be, and your invisible Spirit, which is where the action seems to be, is Here as well as to a human there. One Spirit, and that brings everything Here where you are; and when everything is Here where you are because your Spirit is everywhere, It must flow. It flows only through that Consciousness.

We may not do it today, but we will have to look at every one of the healings of Jesus and see that never once, never once did he move outside of God is Here Now. And that Here didn't mean where he stood. It meant where the fellow was 300 feet away or 300 miles away. That was Here to the *I* of Spirit. And that's why he said, "Now is your son well. Now sit down and eat." There's no other time. The perfection of God is always Now Here. The moment you have found some way to accept this, you'll find yourself relaxing. That's how you'll know you're moving out of the mind universe. The moment you feel that, "Oh, oh, I can relax then." Then you'll know your Soul is coming forth.

As man has progressed through the various universes into this mental one, still unaware of a Soul Universe that is now coming over the horizon, he's striving to improve his situation; when all he needs do is stand still, and the Soul will reveal that there never was a world of good and evil; that all lack is in an atom that isn't there. All limitation is in an atom that never existed. All hunger, all poverty, all war. All of these are atom images made into visible images through the reaction of sense mind to the invisible, nonexistent atom. And as we stand still, all of this action and reaction ceases to be. The Soul coming through the horizon of the new Consciousness reveals the fourth-dimensional realm, swallows up the third, and into your life pours Essence to fill the forms. Light to remove the darkness. Truth to remove division and duality. The Hereness of you becomes manifest.

The Love of the Father becomes the Light of the world. This new Consciousness of Soul, resting in Here is Now the fullness of God everywhere, is brought right into Here; and you are truly a king in your Kingdom instead of a servant to the cosmic mind, instead of a mortal trying to find solutions to problems that only exist in a mental universe. Then mine own comes to me because mine own is realized as being Here Now. Here is love. Here is friendship. Here is companionship. Not in atoms.

The moment you insert your mind to find out how to build a friendship in the atoms, a friendship or companionship in atoms or security in atoms, you are trying to channel the Infinite. And it would be marvelous if it worked, but it doesn't. And if it worked, we would only short-change ourselves. It doesn't work, and we have to ultimately come to the higher ground of Soul. Now you may still think that you're going to enter Soul with your mind, and you cannot. The crucifixion is there. The resurrection of Soul, bringing forth the infinite Universe of Truth, depends completely upon the crucifixion of the mind which has falsely conceived a world of atoms. Grace becomes the permanent dispensation of Reality made visible.

The substructure of atoms is removed in our mentality, and with it goes the mentality that gave it birth. Then the peace comes, the peace which says, "*My* Peace is evidence that I am come into your Consciousness. *My* Peace is evidence that you have died to the mental realm. *My* Peace is evidence that you have found the meaning of spiritual righteousness." Your righteousness now exceeds all of the scribes and the Pharisees. It is the righteousness of total mental surrender. Everything you seek, you put in one great big bag and throw it away. Your Soul is seeking nothing, and if you are still seeking, you haven't found your Soul. If you are still seeking, you have not *trusted* Identity. *I* contain the seed of all that exists. *I* am the Tree of Life, and *I* grow my own fruit. The external world gives you false fruit.

The Kingdom of God within you is God is Here Now, and Its fruit is the fruit of the vine. The locusts cannot eat Its fruit, and all the lost years of the locusts are broken when you grow the fruit from the vine of the Kingdom within so Jesus could say, "I have glorified Thee." We are learning how to say, "I am learning how to glorify Thee." I am learning how to be a witness—not in a human mind—not a false witness. As you stand in the Truth that God is Here Now and that around the corner is Here to you, the accident around the corner means that God is Here Now; and therefore, there is no accident around the corner except in the mental world of atoms. When there are two or more who are not in the mental world of atoms, the accident disappears.

When there is one who is not in the mental world of atoms, the manna falls from heaven. When there is one who is in the Hereness and Nowness and the Isness of perfect Love, in spite of every appearance to the contrary, you have the fourth dimension of Heaven on earth. And so, ultimately, we can say when I am in the Isness, the Hereness, and Nowness of God, earth for me is the earth spoken of when we are told that, "The earth is the Lord's, and the fullness thereof."

The earth of man is the earth of atoms. The earth of God is the invisible Spirit which to man appears as a world of atoms. That earth which is the world of atoms is not God's. Its fullness is deception, but the earth that is the Lord's is Heaven. And man, looking at Heaven, recreates it into his own mental image and calls it earth. Earth Divine is Heaven, and that earth is the earth that is the fullness of God; and that earth is the earth you live in in the Hereness, Nowness, and Isness of God. Then you experience the earth is the Lord's and the power of the Lord and the glory of the Lord; and the Kingdom is come into experience, into living experience. We are then walking in a new Universe, the Universe of Reality; living in It in the Soul, and we are not in a corporeal form. We are in a new form. We are in the Soul body. We are not in a form made of atoms that perish.

Now, you cannot cling to the old and have the new. You cannot be around the corner and call that Here and still be in a physical form. To be infinite, you must be *out* of a physical form. To be infinite, you must be spiritual form. To live in the Soul Universe, you must be Soul form. Be ye perfect as your Father, in that form, in that Soul which lives in the perfect Universe of Grace.

In these human years ahead, there are those who will be still struggling to step out of the problems of the body. Their struggle is as much an illusion as the problems. Whoever will accept the Word of the Father, that *I* am Here, as an infinite Truth, will find that neither the problem nor the struggle is necessary. In your Soul Consciousness, you will be making your transition out of the world that God did not create. You will find there is no need to seek any improvement. In fact, it is a disaster to seek an improvement in your human life. It is a perfect way to turn away from the very thing that God is saying: "Take It. Here is My Kingdom. It is my good pleasure to give you My Grace." But the natural man receiveth not, only that Consciousness which is open to its own Soul.

∞∞∞∞∞∞ END OF SIDE ONE ∞∞∞∞∞∞

Today we're more concerned with the mysticism of this message than the metaphysical side, and I believe this will be the way we will have to go in order to attain a Consciousness of Truth, which is not a mental consciousness. As long as you have the capacity to sit back and think about whether it's this way or that way, we're not in Christ; for in Christ there are no thinking processes.

Now in Christ, there's no inside and outside; and we've reached the part of our journey where the inside and the outside are one. When you apply this to any of the healings, you'll notice quickly that when Jesus looks at a paralytic, he's not seeing it from where he stands as the world sees it who reads about it or as any of us would see it if we were looking at a paralytic ourselves. We see Jesus there, the paralytic here; and they're both illusion. And even us seeing the two, we're illusion too. There was no paralytic outside of Jesus. Infinite Christ has no outside. There's no paralytic outside of you. There's only one outside of your "person," but that's the wrong consciousness. In your true Consciousness, there is no paralytic outside of your infinite Self; nor is there one inside of your infinite Self because It's perfect Spirit.

You can't find the paralytic outside of infinity or inside of it, and the reason is because you're looking at a mental image called a paralytic. And this which is Jesus looking at the paralytic is a mental image that we entertain too. But Christ isn't there standing in one form looking at another form. Christ is *I* am in the midst of both images. *I* am the Life, not an abstraction. *I* am the real Life of that paralytic, and if *I* am the Life, there's no paralytic there. There's *I* am, not reaching the visible sense of human consciousness because there's no one to see *I* am. There's no Soul Consciousness there to see *I* am there; and over here, this isn't Jesus anymore. This is *I* am.

*I* am where Jesus appears. *I* am where a paralytic appears, and *I* am all that is behind both images. There's nothing to heal there. There's just the realization that *I* am. And fortunately, this over here called Jesus *is* the realized *I* am. And therefore, this over here which is not the realized *I* am becomes the realized *I* am; and the paralysis disappears. Now, you stand in Jesus' shoes for a moment and even look at a paralytic outside of your personal self with Here is Now. Over there now is not a paralytic because there's no "over there." That "over there" is *Here* to Christ. Therefore, *Here* Christ—meaning that realization is there—then the power of Christ automatically is made visible.

Now, think for a moment in silence with me; and let's see if we can get a noise from the outside that we could hear. If we hear a noise out there, the minute you hear the noise, let your mind register "Here *I* am"; and you'll begin to get the feeling of the *I*-ness of you, which is Here. Usually we get the noises. Now we don't have one. As I speak to you, this can be the noise. As I speak to you, let your conscious Awareness be that the *I* of you is right Here where this voice is speaking, and that *I* of you which is Here is the Hereness of your Being.

Whenever you hear a sound anywhere, quickly register "Here *I* am" in your Consciousness; and you'll see how it shows you what some day will be a permanent automatic thing without you taking thought about it. Wherever a sound occurs, "*I* am Here"; and that means the You that is sitting where you seem to be are where that sound is. You are where that sound is. The Jesus standing there looking at a paralytic is where the paralytic is. Right where the paralytic is "Here *I* am." Do you see how there's not two separate places? There's only one, and it's all Here. That's the very same principle on which you have read about people who in their high states, they're able to walk out of one body and leave it somewhere and go somewhere else.

We heard about this minister in earlier centuries who was very adept at living in the invisible Self, and he was at one sermon, right on the pulpit making a sermon, when he remembered that he was committed elsewhere to be in the choir right then. And so he said to his congregation, excuse me, and he just stood there and lowered his head, quiet a few minutes; and then he resumed. And right at that moment in another church, he was singing in the choir. This is very incredible to the human mind because it thinks of two places, but you see, the Truth of you is that You are right now in more than two places; and we want to get to know that. The bodily you is here, but that's your mental creation. The Soul Self is everywhere.

And so the You of you is in many places right now without having to move a muscle, and you must become conscious that you are in every place because that is infinite Consciousness. You don't have to stop the congregation and go Soul traveling somewhere to be in another place. Because "*I* am Here," and "*I* am Here," and "*I* am Here Now." And how valuable this will be is quite evident when someone tells you your brother or sister in another city is sick or something of that nature. "*I* am Here" will be your instant Consciousness. You won't have to go into a deep meditation. You won't have to know a lot of Truth and a lot of memorized formulae. There will be that Consciousness that "*I* am Here," which needs take no thought for your Life, which has no outside, but which is the infinite Hereness. And then you won't waste your time trying to do something "out there" when there is no "out there." There is only your Self where "out there" seems to be.

Now, we won't all become mystics overnight, but we do have to rise above this third-dimensional world of matter and atoms. We do have to prepare the way for the journey into the higher Self. All healing that is any value is by Grace. The human self does nothing, but the Soul realization is made manifest as what we call the healing. All supply that is truly supply is by Grace. All good fortune that is truly good fortune is by Grace. The health, the peace, the harmony, the prosperity, the cordiality, the graciousness, the wisdom—all that flows out of the Soul—making Itself manifest in our so-called visible experience, comes by the Grace of a Consciousness which is always perfect—the infinite Consciousness which manifests Its perfection on the holy ground where you stand.

Now, there is no place where holy ground is not. There is no such place. Even where the mortuary appears to be, only the invisible Heaven is. That's one of the supreme illusions of this world. The appearance of death and lack and limitation and disease and suffering and pain is all in the mental universe. Our new horizon takes us into the Soul Universe, and the mental universe will slowly dissolve. The new law that takes over is the law of Reality.

Now, we have read in this chapter something that we had probably not noticed before; but it begins to sneak into our consciousness now with greater meaning. And so when you see this: "*I* in the midst of you will raise up the temple of your Body." A whole new Body! That we had easily passed over so many times. We thought that our old body will be made new, improved. But no. *A whole new Body.* Why? Because this isn't the body we're going to live in. The body we're going to live in is our Body, our spiritual Body; and It is not consumed in the fire. It is not a paralytic. There's a wonderful thing you can do in the mind while you're waiting to attain more of the Soul realization, and that's to know that if God didn't make something, it isn't there.

Even if you were a person looking at a paralytic and not in the Soul, you can look at a paralytic and say, "Did God make it? Did God make a paralytic?" Where is it? It isn't there? Did God make poverty? Where is it? Is there another source, another creator, another cause than God Cause? Where are these things that God didn't make that we see? And so we have a simple little way of identifying anything as Reality or unreality: Did God make it? Did God make poor vision? Did God make bad hearing? Then why do I have bad vision and bad hearing? Because I live in the mind, and I live in the mind that God did not make because God didn't make a human mind.

The mind which God did not make; how can it have perfect vision? How can it have anything perfect? It eventually gives up the ghost for that reason. And as long as I live in the body that God didn't make, why should the laws of God apply to it? That's why the brain has its tumors, and the heart has its attacks because in my mind self, I perpetuate my mental creation. You know, there's even a place where just in a second you have this glimpse, and you can't hold it; but you realize your whole physical form is nothing but a series of mental impressions that you have received, conveying to you the form of you. Hundreds and hundreds of thousands of mental impressions have left you with the impression that you are there in a form.

But once you peel away each illusion, you'll find some of it is a visible illusion; some is a touch illusion. Every sense has been involved in recreating your Christ Self into this illusion called "the me," which is the ultimate supreme illusion. There never was "a me." There was only *I* infinite. And when you catch that second in which you know that all I am is a lot of sense impressions glued together in my mind, you begin to get that vastness of looking out in a universe which is not obstructed by forms, by matter, by invisible atoms. You clean out of your mind all belief in anything atomic or visible or tangible or material. You live in your unobstructed, perfect, infinite, invisible, One Universe.

And now there's the paralytic. It's instantaneous: There wasn't any paralytic to be there. This cosmic image in time and space, you see it for what it is without taking thought. *I* am there Now. The full Godhead is there. I don't have to think about it. It's there, and It knows, and It does, and It maintains, and It supports Itself. It creates and does not permit any variation from Its perfection. This is your Soul Consciousness. You see the bird, and instantly something in you says, "This is *I* invisible." And all of the space between the bird and your physical form disappears in your Consciousness because it is all *I* invisible, and you rest. You're not worried about that bird being hurt anymore. The moment you find yourself giving up fear, concern, doubt, distrust, suspicion, you'll know you have caught the Soul realm.

And that's how this whole new Body begins to be part of your Awareness. You're not forming It. You're becoming conscious of It because this Body is bigger than this room. This Body you become conscious of is the Body that is from here to the bird, and from that bird to the next bird and throughout the Universe. You become conscious of your infinite Body. Just think, as you multiply this sense of body into an infinite Body, how that infinite

Body is fed by an infinite Mind and how that all flows to where this visible body seems to be. Do you see how Grace, then, is only what you yourself cast out upon the waters, coming back? As you become conscious of your infinite Self, your infinite Self becomes Conscious expressing; and the Tree of Life puts out Its own fruit that way.

All that you begin to experience is nothing more than your own expanded Consciousness. And so that's why when Joel says something here, it begins to have another meaning for us: "The sun, the moon, and the stars up there in the sky are all under God's government." Ah, now we can see what he was getting at. The government that is there is the invisible living Spirit that we are seeing as these atomic stars, this atomic moon, this atomic sun. The invisible government is there as God. What we are seeing is our visible concept of it, just as we are seeing the visible concept of ourselves. But behind it is *I*, and *I* am here. *I* am here in the sky. *I* am here as perfection now *Being*, perfect, loving, Is-ing. And all of that that he's speaking of as the *I* behind the sky, behind the moon, behind the star—this is the *I* of your Being. To be conscious of this *I* is to bring your Universe into visible harmony. You're getting out of finite me.

At the back of the chapter, you have noticed the six, seven chapters he refers to: "New Horizon," "God is One," and so forth in the other books. We won't do those specifically next time. We'll do "Supply and Secrecy," chapter 11. But you can see what's happening. We're preparing to make the Mystical *I* our Consciousness. Not a book that Joel wrote, but our Consciousness as It was his. As It was the Consciousness of Jesus Christ, as It was the Consciousness of Saint Teresa, as It was the Consciousness of Buddha, as It was the Consciousness of all those who had discovered the futility of the logic and the reasoning power of man's mind as he struggles to improve a world which is based upon the nothingness of the atom.

And if science did nothing again in its discovery of the atom upon which we have based our mental universe and our material universe, it has proven the Truth of the statements of Jesus Christ while it is denying the Truth of them. It's almost like Pilate, who did us all a great turn while he was making possible the crucifixion of Jesus, because he was part of the Divine plan to reveal the nothingness of that crucifixion. There had to be one for us to know the nothingness of it. Science, which is largely atheistic, is proving the presence of God. Pilate, who couldn't care less about Jesus Christ, was proving that the eternal Spirit cannot be crucified.

And all this is Now. *I* in the midst of Pilate; *I* in the midst of Herod; *I* in the midst of Caiaphas, the High Priest; *I* in the midst of the rabble who were spitting; *I* in the midst of all those who participated—*I* am showing you there is no power in form. For in three days that same form will be there because *I* in the midst, *I* am the power Now. And that *I* is the *I* of You Now. Before Abraham was, that *I* is the *I* of You Now. That *I* of You restores the lost years of the locusts that have eaten the false fruits of a material world. That is the Mystical *I*. It is the Self, and it will never be crucified. It will never be in pain. It will never be lacking. It will never be limited. It is the perfect Self of God, and It is your Self; for we are all that One Self.

When you remove all that appears, there *I* am. And when you put back all that appears, *I* am still there where the visible lie seems to be. When you are that *I* instead of this me, then there is no place where You are not; and all of You is infinitely perfect. Now, that's our Soul Consciousness. If you have the time and the inclination, pick up your Bible anywhere; and in the New Testament, you look at any so-called healing. Put yourself in the shoes of the healer and stand there in the knowledge that this that I am looking at, this form in this problem over there, I will face it with Here *I* am. Now *I* am. Now *I* am the Is of God, *Being* God, perfect. One infinite *I* here and none other, and then rest in the Word. Be still and know that this *I* which you have declared is God.

Ask yourself then if *I*, that God, made this condition; and you will be able to say, " No." And therefore, shall I improve that condition? If God didn't make it, shall I improve what God did not make? If God didn't make it, can I correct it? If God didn't make it, is it there or am I under the atomic illusion? And if it is not there, what is my solution? Be still. Let the mind which sees it there be still. And then the Soul will tell you this Truth which makes you free, revealing only *I* am there, whole, complete, and perfect.

You apply these simple little rules to any of the healings in the Bible, and you will see that the power of *I* in you is the healing. When you will stand on those, you will be walking in the Soul Consciousness; and the Grace that flows will be the sign to tell you you have attained that Consciousness. It will be quick. It will be sharp. It will be powerful, and it will be glorious. And It will pave the way for many new mansions of understanding.

Now, "Supply and Secrecy. And we don't yet know why secrecy is used with supply, but there must be a reason.

When we meet again, I'd like to know that in your re-identification, you are including that all time is included within the *I*-ness of your Being Now; that all space is included within the Hereness of your Being Now; that all past, present, and future is in the Isness of your Being Now. That you have taken all that has ever existed and is and ever will be and put it into a One that is Now Being perfect, and that is You. That is your Self. And if you will even work with that in a measure, you will see the power of Self-revelation, of Self-expression, of the Divine Being made manifest as the Word brought into human experience as living Grace.

If any of you care to rework your re-identifications, fine. If any of you wish to put what you have up here, fine, either way. And then before we get into *The Mystical I*, we all want to start with a proper re-identification of Self as living Soul.

Thank you again.

# CLASS 23

# DIVINE SUPPLY

*Herb:* We're in the eleventh chapter of *The Contemplative Life*, and although the subject is supply, it would be like discussing one little finger on your hand to leave it at that level. We have to see the Allness of Being in order to realize the nature of supply, and so we'll be reaching out to other elements of this work. Next week we will complete this book, even though it's a chapter about Christmas. Christ *is* next week as well as at the 25$^{th}$ of December, and so we'll do that chapter next week. And then on the following Sunday, which I think is the 27$^{th}$ of June, we will begin *The Mystical I*, the new book of Joel's, for at least 12 weeks into early October probably. And so that's the continuous program. There'll be no interruption for the Fourth of July.

We know that a fish never struggles to swim, nor does a bird struggle to fly. These come naturally. And we want to learn why the Son of God seems to struggle for supply when we are told that we are to take no thought for our life, what we shall eat, we shall wear. In other words, supply is just as natural to the Son of God as swimming is to a fish or flying to a bird. It's the very nature of our Being. Perhaps as we look at supply and see that we have a concept about it, we begin to notice that we have limited supply down to what we believe finitely. We think supply should be money, dollars, homes, investments, income; but this is the concept of the earth man.

And although the Father knoweth our needs, and although it is the good pleasure of the Father to give us the Kingdom, we somehow think that we have to decide in what way the Kingdom should come to us. And before we know it, we have split away from Truth. We have entered into concept, into the perception of the senses, into the world illusion. And soon we say, "My supply has been limited," and then we face what we consider financial problems. And so we find that one out of every hundred may be immune to this or maybe one out of a thousand, but everywhere we go we find financial problems, limitations, and lack even though the Son of God is unlimited.

When we do mental work to correct this, we go through the illusion that with the human mind I can permanently improve my condition. And so we take Truth, and we try to apply Truth. And alas, we discover that you cannot apply Truth. Truth is Truth, and Truth is Self-fulfilling and Self-acting. The moment you are applying Truth, you haven't got Truth at all. And so always we're stymied about this supply thing until we begin to have confidence in the Bible. It literally means what it tells us, and it gives us the most unusual way to solve the supply problem.

It's so revolutionary that when we look at it, we can't believe it. It says the way to solve supply is to take no thought about it. We do not believe that seriously the Spirit could mean such a thing, and yet it precisely says that and gives us many examples; and the Master Himself shows us that His own disciples go forth without supply. No purse, no script. But they're prepared for the journey with knowledge of Self, knowing that Identity is supply. Now let's look closely at the revolutionary teaching about taking no thought for supply in order to have supply, and perhaps it would be wise to see why, with our application of Truth and our thought about Truth, we have failed to really nail down the meaning of supply.

You know that the teaching of Jesus starts with God is Spirit. That's the foundation. "In the beginning God . . . ." And if you do not start with God, you have no place to start because God is the beginning and the end, the alpha and the omega. "In the beginning God . . . ." In the beginning Spirit. And you must begin there. God is Spirit, and quickly follows God is All. Spirit is All. The Allness of Spirit is the fact. And because Spirit can only beget Itself because like must beget like, Spirit can only beget Spirit and never become anything else. Spirit remains Spirit. The Allness of Spirit remains the Allness of Spirit, and there's nothing but Spirit. And this is the revolutionary teaching, then, of the Bible: God is Spirit. Spirit is All.

Spirit begets Itself, and there is nothing but Spirit. And you are faced with the fact that matter is unreal. And so any concept of supply that has to do with matter is an unreal concept. It is destined to failure. *You cannot find material supply.* You may call it material supply and discover to your chagrin that it isn't. And we find that matter being unreal—because Spirit can only beget Spirit, and Spirit is All—we have to identify this matter. And we find that the Bible is telling us that it is a mental concept; that all matter is imagination. And it tells us that this imagination is cosmic, a universal imagination. And that through our sense perceptions, we become aware of what is called matter, which is imagination; and therefore, we have mental matter. All matter, according to the Christ teaching, is made of the human mind.

In other words, you're seeing nothing except what is in your mind. Nothing is there outside of your mind. As far as the eye can see you're looking at your own mind, and you're calling it matter, place, person, thing, and condition; but it is your mind. You're looking at your thought everywhere, and now your thought says, "I lack. I need. I want. I desire. I must pay the rent." But God is All, and God is Spirit. Spirit begets only Spirit. That which is not Spirit is not there, is not real. What are you lacking? You're lacking Spirit, but you think you're lacking matter. And therefore, you perpetuate the illusion of lack by seeking the matter that you're not lacking. You don't even have it when you have it. You cannot have it or lack it. It doesn't exist.

And so a spiritual teaching is about Spirit as All. And finally, we see that the senses have fooled us into seeking that which has no existence in Reality. We have called it supply, but we were seeking a material identity, which is mental, which is imagination; and it could never fully satisfy us for that reason even if we secured that which we sought. And finally, it is all wrapped up with the idea that the material world is cosmic imagination, hypnosis of the senses, unreal, illusory. And the Master says seek not the things that perish.

Now, once we have established this as fact—once we have confidence in God, knowing what God is talking about through Jesus Christ—we see that we are told that the world of matter is not Reality. It is not my Father's Kingdom, and therefore, it is not here. It is one cosmic appearance in the mind. And matter being unreal, the motion of matter must be equally unreal. And now we're coming to the place where we may be ready to know what is meant by "Son, all that I have is thine." But we're not quite ready because the mind is still under the influence of concept.

Now let's go way, way back into concept. Let's just take our little earth—which is our material concept—and there it goes spinning around the sun. And while it spins, it's turning on its axis away from the sun. And now the sun hits the earth, and then behind the earth is the shadow of the earth. The sun shining on the earth, the earth spinning on its axis, behind the earth its own shadow shaped in the form of an ice cream cone. The whole width of the earth casts a conical shadow behind itself.

And you're somewhere on that earth, and you're going to pass through that shadow. You're going to enter the shadow on one side. You're going to pass through the complete shadow of the earth, and then you're going to pass out of the shadow of the earth on the other side; and all of that time is going to be called nighttime. And when you come out of the shadow of the earth, you're going to say it's dawn. It's morning. It's sunrise. And now you're in daytime.

And the whole concept of day and night is whether or not you're in the shadow of the earth.

But there is no material earth. There is only Spirit. That which isn't there is casting a shadow which cannot be there. And the concept of night and day is based upon that which is not there. From that concept of day and night, we get time. We measure the movement. We say that time takes 12 hours for the night to come and go, 12 hours for the day. And then in that time, we measure the movement of objects, which are not there. It takes an hour to run from here to there, 5 hours from New York to San Francisco.

First we measure night by the passing through the shadow of the earth, and outside of that shadow there is no night. And in the same manner, outside of our concept of matter there is no death. And there is no aging process, and there is no time. And our concept of objects moving in time builds our sense of space because time and space exist only because we fill them with shadows called objects. Now you sit down and try to figure this all out with your mind and try to form some kind of intelligent direction to take through it, and you find you cannot.

It's the same way with trying with your mind to figure out what you're going to do about supply. The hopelessness of it is that the very earth you stand on is an illusion. You're looking at your concept of the spiritual earth, and you're identifying everything you see with that which itself has no existence—with material eyes, with material ears, with a material sense of touch. And Spirit can only beget Spirit, so nonexistence identifies nonexistence.

Supply in the midst of this is very minor. But there is a law. There is a law that removes from us the necessity for taking thought about supply, or else the Master would not have revealed that the way out of the dilemma of supply is through taking no thought. The Law of Transformation when known to your consciousness enables you to confidently relax, knowing that supply is a natural action of your true Being.

So let's look at that Law of Transformation. Let's see that supply is an expression of your Self and not something you reach out to draw *into* yourself. Let's look at the orange tree, and let's remember that the orange is not producing more oranges. The orange is the result of an action in the tree. And as long as you have the orange tree, you're not too concerned about the oranges coming out of the tree. You're not worried about getting oranges. You have the tree.

And when the tree produces oranges and they fall off, you don't say, "I have no more supply." You say, "I have no more fruit." But you know the tree will continue to produce new oranges, and therefore, you identify the tree as your supply; and you identify the oranges as the fruit of your supply. You know there's a law of transformation going on. You know the tree is doing something about minerals, about water, about air, about sunlight, and combining them, transforming them into sap; and it is pushing forth the fruitage, or the oranges. Even when the tree is bare, you're not concerned. Whether you're awake or asleep, you're not concerned. As long as you have the tree, you will have the fruit of the tree. You know the law of transformation is taking place.

Now, there is such a law in our life. We call it the law of transforming life. We know that the Substance of our Being is our Supply, just as the tree and its sap is its supply. And we know that as the Substance of our Being flows as our Consciousness, It forms Itself into those things which are needed. We learned that from the Master's teaching. As the sparrow can forget where it will be fed; as the lily can forget how it will be clothed because from within itself something is forming, we learn that within the Son of God something is ever-forming, and "Son . . . all that I have is thine."

Let the law of transformation continue to flow *through* you *as* you, manifesting its perfection wherever you are. Do not interfere, just as you would not interfere with the activity of the tree; and watch how the oranges, or the added things, appear as you become conscious of the law of transformation. Now, we know this law exists; and we have failed to do one thing. We have placed a barrier between the law and our experience of it, and the barrier is unawareness. Your consciousness of the law builds the bridge which permits the law to enter through and express. When you are not conscious of the law, it could not become an expression in your life.

Now, let's say we become conscious of the law of transformation. First, we must be the Son of God. The law of transformation doesn't work in a human being. "Son . . . all that I have is thine." Not human being, not dust man, not earth man, not man made of atoms. Son, Divine Son. And we have been stressing Identity now for six weeks in this class. Identity. We have had re-Identification.

And so, if you are not the child of God—if you are still this physical, mortal being who cannot be—the law of transformation is not taking place through your mortal selfhood. Spirit cannot act outside of Spirit. Spirit cannot act in an illusion. If you have not taken the time and the effort to re-Identify, to accept your Self as Divine Substance, Divine Being, Divine Self—if you have no confidence whatsoever in the Word of God or Jesus Christ, which is expressing the Word of God, or in the Bible which is the Word of God and Jesus Christ—then the law of supply cannot function in your Being. It will not function in the man of dust.

But as you re-Identify, as you accept that God is My Father—I have no Father on the earth but God—then you are accepting that *I*, the Son, and the Father are never separate. *I*, the Substance of God, am Spirit, never less than infinite Spirit, never less than true Being, never apart from Infinity. And now you are realigning yourself. You are fulfilling the first requisite: correct Identity, Divine Self. You are taking possession.

And now, in this Self, we are in conscious union with God. And the moment you're in conscious union with the Spirit of God as your Spirit, you are in touch with *every* Divine idea. Nothing is missing in the Spirit of God. Son, every Divine idea is in the Spirit of God, which is the Life of You. If you have no confidence in the Life of God as your Life, you have discovered the barrier that you have placed between you and the experience of your natural supply. It is lying there unexpressed because of lack of recognition.

And now as you think of it, as you know your Self to be Life Divine—not matter but Life Divine—you are saying to your senses, "I am not fooled by you. I am Spirit. I embody all that God has. All that the Father has is mine. And I have confidence in the law of Life, which is that all that the Father hath, which is mine, is expressing Itself now here. And therefore, that which I have experienced is the lie." The moment you have the presence of God where you stand, realized, you have discovered more than the law of supply. You have discovered the law of eternal Life. The moment you accept the presence of God, every problem in your life is revealed as a lie.

Now let's see what you're lacking in supply right this minute. What are you lacking? You're lacking knowledge of God's presence. That's all. You can't be lacking supply. Supply is God. Where God is, supply is. That's the law. In *My* Presence is fullness of joy. And what you're really saying when you say "I lack" is that you lack the knowledge of God's presence. "In the beginning God. . . ." You haven't begun with God. You started with matter, and you try to work back to God; and you can't. There's no way. Matter has no existence. It can't go back into Spirit. You must begin with Spirit. To have Spirit, to enjoy Spirit, to live in Spirit and experience Spirit, you must begin with Spirit.

So in the beginning of your meditation, in the beginning of your contemplation: God, Spirit. If you *want* Spirit, you must *begin* with Spirit. Always, Jesus began with God. He didn't work back from matter *to* God. *I* and the Father are One. *I* am the Way. *I* now in the midst of you am greater than he that walks the earth. We have lacked confidence in God, in God's Word, in our own spiritual Identity as the one Son of God; and so in creeps the belief of a separation. Now, you could just as well have said you had dizzy spells or stomachaches as well as saying you lack supply; and you would find the knowledge of God's Presence is the answer to all three. The knowledge of God's Presence is the answer to every problem.

And while we have been trying to memorize page 26 in a book or page 39 in the Bible—or what did Joel say in 1952 at such and such a lecture?—we have forgotten the basic principle is where you realize the presence of God, Omniscience does the rest. Omnipotence does the rest. Omnipresence does the rest. And you may be sure that every important word in the Bible and in Joel's writing was put there by the Mind of God, which knows. And so we begin to let go of this calculating, planning, striving mind. We don't have to struggle. We don't have to use strategy. We don't have to plan. We have to do precisely what it tells us to do: take no thought. Why? Because once you have established that God is present here now, the work is done. There comes a surge of knowledge that God is here, and then every Word in the Bible rings with a new clarity. It is My pleasure to give you the Kingdom.

Now watch. All of the added things appear. Why? Because the law of transformation is taking place in your consciousness. Wherever you look, whatever you see, whatever you experience, it isn't what you think it is. It's your consciousness. Your consciousness is made visible and becomes your experience. Your whole universe is your consciousness. There is no outside. There is absolutely nothing outside your consciousness. If it is, you're unconscious of it. What you are conscious of is your world, and the quality of that consciousness determines the quality of your world.

Now, when we look at the wheats and the tares, we find something very fascinating. That parable shows us the difference between our thoughts about supply and the Truth about supply, our thoughts about health and the Truth about health. Always the wheat stands for Divine thought, and the tare or the weed stands for human thought or sense perception. And you have them growing right alongside each other in your consciousness, in your field; and the sense perception or the tare says, "I lack supply."

But you really don't. You lack the awareness of the supply that is there. You're entertaining a concept, and you are not suffering from lack. There is no one in this world suffering from lack. They are suffering from the acceptance of the illusion that God is not there. Unaware of the presence of God in their consciousness, their consciousness cannot manifest that quality of God which is called abundance. But they are not lacking. Their lack is lack of conscious union with the presence of God, and that manifests as lack.

You can lack health, but you're lacking conscious union with the presence of God, and that manifests as health. And so while you are trying and dedicating yourself to what you think is Truth, the tares creep into your consciousness because you still depend on sense perception. You still believe that the world around you is out there because your senses say it's out there, and it isn't out there. There is no outside out there. There is nothing external to you.

The universe that you experience is your consciousness, and you must take possession of that universe by getting rid of the tares and not going out to just pluck them indiscriminately and uprooting the wheat at the same time—but daily separating tares from the wheat—separating sense perception from acceptance of the living presence of God here. Letting everything come through your conscious awareness of the Presence. And then Divine thought, the wheat, begins to feed your consciousness; and the tares, the weeds—the human sense perceptions—begin to dissolve. And your Consciousness being only the wheat, only Divine thought, externalizes as Divine activity and shows the law of transformation of consciousness. Divine thought transforms, and the Consciousness outpictures heaven on earth.

You're out of the shadow of earth where there is no night, where there is no darkness, where there is no death, where there is no old age, where there is no condition unlike the perfection of God's Presence. Take no thought for your life is, in a sense, a paradox. It's like that paradox last week: Be still and know. And we found out that if we are still in the mind, we will know in the Soul. And here again we are told take no thought. We also know we're told to pray without ceasing. How can we pray without ceasing and take no thought at the same time? We're also told to acknowledge the Father in all our ways. How can we take no thought and acknowledge the Father?

And so we put on our high boots, and we have to wade into that one. We have to separate these thoughts because each of them is important. Each is to open us up. Each must be faced instead of merely repeated in the mind. We are to know the Truth that sets us free and yet take no thought.

We are to separate the wheat from the tares and yet take no thought. You see, everything is forcing you into a sequence in which you begin to accept only Divine thought. All that is sense perception we begin to weed out of consciousness. We take no human thought. No human thought is acceptable. No sense thought is acceptable. No belief in anything finite is acceptable. No belief in imperfection is acceptable.

Who convinceth me of sin? No sin is acceptable. No unfulfilled need is acceptable. There cannot be an unfulfilled need. Every limiting thought is released. Every ungodly thought is released. Every thought of lack and limitation and sin and disease is released, and then you're forced to the higher ground. The acceptance that when I cease being man whose breath is in his nostrils, when I cease being a person, when I cease having friends and enemies, when I begin to accept the Divinity of my Being, then I can rest in that Divinity without thought.

Taking no thought is only possible when you have accepted Divine Selfhood because then the Mind of the Father is your mind. Taking no thought forces you into the acceptance of immortality now. Ah, but now Joel comes along and tells us so many interesting ways in which, even when we think we know the Truth about supply, we still have barriers. We have not known, for example, that supply cannot come to us unless we have sent it forth. And you say, "How can I send it forth? I don't know how. I don't know where to find it." And yet, it cannot come to you until you have sent it forth. And then he says you must obey the law of secrecy, and we never connected that with supply.

Now, there are quite a number of ways in which Joel teaches us to express supply spiritually. Mind you, you're standing in the Consciousness of Divine Selfhood knowing that all that the Father hath is mine. The Tree of Life is ever sending forth its fruit. God being perfect, the expression of God in me must be perfect; and in that you have confidence, trust. You rest without question, without seeking or striving or struggling or planning. You're accepting. And now, because supply is spiritual, if you're looking for physical supply, you're missing the point. Spiritual supply manifests as invisible spiritual fruitage. That is why you cannot see Divine supply. That is why you can be fooled by physical supply. Always the fruitage of supply is as spiritual as the supply itself.

And when you have the knowledge of that spiritual manifestation, then in the visible it shows forth as your improved concept of dollar, home, financing, food, clothing, shelter. Always the visible is merely the concept or idea we entertain about the invisible. Between the supply itself and the visible manifestation, there is an invisible manifestation known only to the Child of God; and that Consciousness of it transforms into the visible. Now, you are not conscious spiritually of that manifestation if there are certain things in your outer work that you're not doing because these are the signs. If you're not praying for your enemies, it is because you're not conscious of the invisible Circle of Christ.

You may think this has nothing whatsoever to do with supply, but yet that's the very core of the chapter. It has everything to do with it. Acknowledge Me in all thy ways. You want spiritual supply, but you will not acknowledge Spirit as the Allness. And you see, when you're praying for your enemies, that is because you are aware of the spiritual nature of each individual who appears as an enemy. Forgiveness, to forgive the offender. Why? Because the

Father says, "Forgive seventy times seven," and you say, "What's that got to do with supply?" Well, that's the point. You can't deny Spirit over here and expect Spirit on the other side to shower you with fruit. You must acknowledge Me in all thy ways. If you do this unto the least of these my brethren, you do it unto Me. In other words, if you don't have a spiritual consciousness, how can you have spiritual supply?

A spiritual consciousness is forgiving all offenders, and Joel says it isn't even enough to forgive those who in some way are unfriendly to you. No, you must forgive those who offend your neighbor. You must forgive those who offend your race. You must forgive those who offend your nation and your religion. And then he says pray for those who despitefully use you and persecute you, that ye may be the children of God. Oh, we overlooked all that. We were too busy trying to get supply. Yes, yes, you want spiritual supply. Then acknowledge Spirit as the Substance of the Universe. Look past the form.

And so he teaches us, both the Master and Joel, to look past the forms of the offending, persecuting neighbor, country, religion, or whatever it might be that is offending in some way, and to forgive all on the face of the earth by the recognition of their Divine Selfhood. And if you haven't reached the level where this is a normal thing for you, then the lack of supply will continue to be a burden.

Ah, then he says there are other things too. He says one of the greatest is gratitude, and that's where the secrecy comes in. Do not your alms in public. Now that has a special meaning. In the first place, the giving is not to a person. In the second place, the giving is not from a person. It is the expression of your spiritual Selfhood, and it is the recognition of spiritual Selfhood. Always gratitude is the recognition of a spiritual source and a spiritual recipient, and until you have caught the feeling of expressing, then the spiritual Consciousness still is not there.

Now, those who give great benevolences are not giving spiritually. The widow's mite was more important. It was what her capacity was that counted. She gave all she had. Who did she give it to? Nobody. She expressed her recognition of Spirit. Joel says this is the most important barrier to overcome in the understanding of spiritual Selfhood and in the expressing of spiritual supply. And the one thing he cautions us against is the same thing Jesus cautioned us against: Whatever your alms are, wherever your charities or benevolences are—how many orphans you keep, how many sick people you support—this is all within your Self.

It is your recognition of spiritual Selfhood everywhere. Ah, but there's a secret behind that too, and the secret is that secrecy is necessary because there's nobody to tell! The moment you feel that there's somebody to tell, you have gone out of the belief in one invisible Selfhood. You're coming into multiplicities. You're coming into personalities, and the giving is no longer spiritual recognition. The giving now is for a consideration, for a pride, for a vanity; and the point of it is gone.

A million dollars given from a human standpoint is not spiritual giving. It is not based on spiritual recognition. It has nothing to do with spiritual living or spiritual Identity. Service is a great way of expressing spiritual awareness—but the way you *express* that service. If you happen to be in a business which serves the public, you may discover that you have your ups and downs. But when you understand what you do spiritually and when you are endeavoring to fulfill a spiritual rather than a human need—when you're looking through the human need to the spiritual need behind it—you will discover a great secret.

Whereas in your physical human way you had been going up and down, up and down, pleasing some and not pleasing others—the moment you find the spiritual need that you can fulfill in your work, you'll find you always hit the target; and the need for you is increased. Any business that can transform its understanding into fulfilling spiritual needs—in other words, not the supply of an individual, not the fruitage of an individual but the inner spiritual Selfhood of the individual—will find that it is always sought after. That's how an artist or a composer achieves more lasting distinction. The need that is reached is deeper. It touches something in the Soul of the individual. That's what makes Shakespeare an immortal writer.

And when we are doing this with the idea of serving others spiritually from our own spiritual resources and serving their spiritual needs, we discover that we have an increased awareness of our own inventive genius. Talents that we had thought were not there begin to emerge, and talents that we knew were there begin to show a depth we hadn't suspected. It's the same as the physical supply. Once you fall into the law of transformation so that the invisible begins to work through into the visible by your awareness of its presence, this transformation is not just in supply.

You remember the lame beggar who had asked Peter and John at the gate for money? Gold and silver have I none. They didn't give him physical supply, but he leaped jubilantly. He walked for the first time in his life. They gave him freedom. They gave him his own Substance, and that was to teach us that when you ask humanly, we know not what to ask for. He would have been content with a few pieces of silver. Instead, he walked. We would be content with increased what we call supply. That's not enough. That's the human finite mind saying, "If I have another 30 pieces of silver, everything will be all right." That's the deceiver.

That lack of supply is going to plague us until we are lifted up beyond, until we come to the place where I know my Identity as the very Substance of all supply, and then, instead of just giving the additional silver will enable me to walk in the Kingdom. It will give me my freedom. That's the supply. The real supply is spiritual Consciousness, spiritual righteousness. To know Spirit aright is Life eternal. Would you trade Life eternal for 30 pieces of silver? Every problem, whether it's supply or health or whatever, is an arrow pointing to higher Consciousness. It's saying that when you find Me in you, then your freedom begins.

Now, suppose we look at take no thought to find out if there is something in this very familiar series of verses that says something new to us. Suppose we read all the invisible ink and see that there was a revolutionary way of thinking and of living that was being presented. A way so unique that we today who are still seeking increased supply have clearly overlooked the Master's message.

And so he said to his disciples,

"Take no thought for your life, what ye shall eat; neither for the body, what ye shall put on."

If we are to accept that, then the only way you can is to change the concept of your life. This life—yes, you've got to take thought about it. But take no thought for your Life, your *real* Life. And so in the twinkling of an eye, he has revealed that our real Life is so perfect as our Father that there's nothing to take thought about. He's lifting us into the Consciousness that we are God Life.

Be ye perfect as your Father now. And you will admit that if you knew yourself to be the perfect God Life now, would you take thought? And so when you're taking thought, you are rejecting Identity. You are saying, "I am not God Life. I must take thought about it." Reverse that. I don't have to become God Life. There's nothing I must do to become the Son of God. Spirit is all there is. I accept the teaching of Jesus Christ: God is Spirit. God is All. I am Spirit. My Life is Spirit.

Now it's just a matter of controlling the sense mind, which wants to take thought as if I was something other than Spirit Life. You see how clear that is? Take no thought for your life because your Life is Divine Life now. And every time you take thought for your life, you are rejecting your own Being. You are stepping right out of Divine Self. Divine Self doesn't have to worry about the clothes it wears. Does the Light go down to the city of Paris? Does the Light go into the shops on Fifth Avenue? You don't take thought for your clothes because you are the Light.

And so here's the message of Identity. And we have been saying, "How foolish. How can I live without taking thought?" When what we have had to say and what we shall say as we open our eyes is, "They're telling me *I* am Divine Life. *I* am the Light of the world. *I* am perfect now as My Father." And then I shall reorientate this consciousness to know this. *I* am. *I* am. *I* am.

And so we dwell for a moment in the *I* am, Divine Light. And the Light that *I* am requires no human food. The Light that *I* am requires no human clothing, no human supply, no human companionship. The Light that *I* am requires no thing, for the Light that *I* am is infinite Light. In the beginning God. And the Light of God was the Life of all men, and this is My Life now. Do you see, then, that when you begin with Identity, what follows will flow in the rhythm of Identity? Well, if you start on the lower echelons of a "me" with a clothing and a food budget, you can't work back to Identity. So at the moment we're going to stand in Identity and let these words reveal to us who we are.

∞∞∞∞∞∞ END OF SIDE ONE ∞∞∞∞∞∞

"The life is more than meat, and the body is more than raiment."

Well, all right. The Life is God, and the Body is God. And it won't matter how long you study, how many years. There will come a time when this will be accepted, and then Truth will activate itself where you are. Let's accept it for the moment. My Body and My Life must be of the Substance of God, for there is no other. Now, what do I lack in supply? Nothing. So I can let that thought go. I can drop it. And if I don't drop it, I'm not accepting spiritual Substance, Divine law. You see how you cannot accept and still maintain the belief in a lack of supply? Which is it, God or mammon? You drop the false concept. I do not lack supply. The *I* that I am does not lack supply.

Oh yes, this physical concept called "me" may lack supply; but I'm just learning that isn't me at all. Now you're in Identity, Divine Sonship; and you find that the Father hasn't overlooked a thing. The Father is much more practical than you ever were. The Father is so practical that every need has been provided for. Nothing has been missing or withheld.

"Consider the ravens: for they neither sow nor reap; which neither have storehouse nor
barn; and God feedeth them: . . . ."

And now we feel kind of silly. I was worried, really, about the food bill, the food budget. Would we have enough? And here's God feeding ravens. I just didn't have confidence in that. But it means what it said. If God feeds the ravens, what about me? Will I be unfed?

How? By the Law of Transformation in Life Itself. It is automatic. The law of transformation in your Being feeds Itself. Your Substance is the fullness of everything you need. Your Substance is Self-contained. In other words, everything is bringing you into who are you. You see why this couldn't be accepted? They thought he was teaching them that a person doesn't have to worry, that a person is as good as a raven. But he wasn't. He was teaching them that they weren't persons. But even a lowly raven, which is less than a person, gets fed.

He was teaching them and us that we are living Spirit now, without any needs; for every need has been fulfilled in our own Being. And the moment we accept the presence of God is the Spirit of My Being here and now, you're in the rhythm of the universe. Then you can do what the raven does, what the lily does, what the sparrow does. It just knows everything is taken care of, but you can't do it as a person.

"How much more are ye better than the fowls? And which of you with taking thought can add to his stature one cubit?"

And you remember that's a mistranslation: "Stature" should be length of life. They took it as length in space, but it should be length in time. Stature is the length of a person in space, but it really was length of a person in time, the lifespan, meaning: Which of you with taking thought can add to his lifespan one cubit? And we can't. And therefore, if you can't do the least of this, why try for the most? Always teaching again that the human brain which tries to think Truth, know Truth, and apply Truth is not the place where the work is done.

And so we come to a principle. A woman said to me last week, "My friend called"—or some relative—"who was sick, and I wanted to double-check the procedure." And I didn't spend the time to completely explain what should be explained. Now you're taking thought about that person's health because that person said to you, "I'm sick." And suppose that person lives a certain distance from you. Suppose, for example, right now one of your close relatives, one of your children were to call and say, "I'm sick. Will you help me?" You would always begin your work with the belief that your son, your daughter is there, and you are here; and that's because you're taking thought.

Now here's a fine point and a very important one. You receive the information where you are. You received it here, and here is where you must solve it. You cannot solve that person's health *there*, and many of us have tried to do it. We have tried to throw our thought *there*. He's there, and I've got to get him well there. Well, you're not going to get him well there if you don't get him well here. It's *here* where the work is done, and here means in your consciousness, right here where you receive the call. And here is where you must solve the call. Everything is done here in your consciousness, and that's the secret of supply.

You want it out there. You want more acreage. You want a nicer home. You want a nicer car. You want a nicer this. You want a nicer that out there. You can't get it out there. It doesn't belong to you out there. You don't have spiritual title to it out there. And even when it appears out there, it still won't be out there. If it isn't in your consciousness, the out there will never manifest for you;

and if it does, it won't mean a thing. You don't get supply out there. You get it in your consciousness, and then it appears out there. You get it in your consciousness that the Substance of My Being is God. That's where supply is. That's where your Life is. That's where your clothing is. That's where your home is.

Everything out there is in your consciousness that God is the Substance of My Being here. That's why supply is such an important subject, because it brings us right smack into the Truth of all Being—the hereness of My Substance, the faith in My Substance, the faith in the law functioning in My Substance. The law of eternal perfection is functioning here.

Now, just to show you why it doesn't come into your experience unless you know about it: You may not be conscious of the air around you right now. You may not be conscious of breathing until it's mentioned. And then when it's mentioned, oh yes, you're conscious of breathing. But you weren't conscious of breathing or the air until it was mentioned. Then it came into your thought. Then it comes into your consciousness. Do you know there was a period in our lives when we all went through becoming conscious of air, and that's how breathing became part of our being? We had to reach the place where we became conscious of it every moment until it became a natural thing to do, to breathe. We had to learn how. We don't remember it now. It happened too far in the dim past of history.

We have to become conscious of the Substance of Life as our own Substance. We have to think about it, literally take thought about it. And then, you see, your thought you become conscious of. You can't be conscious of something unless you first had a thought about it, and so you become conscious of your thought. Your thought is about the Life of God is your Substance. And ultimately that thought becomes something you're conscious of, and when you're conscious of it, it manifests in all its glory. Then you're spiritually conscious. Then you take no thought because you already have put the seed into Consciousness, and it is your permanent Consciousness.

Now, actually there's no person, then, who can suffer from lack of supply. They have the wrong idea about supply. Supply is the Substance of God, and everyone is the Substance of God. So you can't suffer from lack of supply. *You* are the supply. You can suffer from your unawareness of it because you haven't taken thought about it to make it your consciousness. It isn't in your consciousness yet, but it will be. And when it becomes consciously yours—that *I* am the Substance—then you know that the supply you have been seeking is your Substance. *I* am the Substance. *I* am the supply.

It isn't outside. *I* am It, *My* Substance. Ah, that's the meaning here then.

". . . which of you with taking thought can add to his stature one cubit?

If ye then be not able to do that . . . which is least, why take ye thought for the rest?"

All of this thought—the planning, the strategy, the mapping out of program—was your unawareness that *I* am the supply now. *I* am that Tree of Life, and as long as I know it, it will shower forth the fruitage; and it will be those things that I need. For even the need and the forms that these needs shall take is taken care of right here in this passage by the Word of God:

"Consider the lilies how they grow: they toil not, they spin not; and yet I say unto you, that Solomon in all his glory was not arrayed like one of these."

Why? Because there aren't any lilies there.

That's our concept of the perfect Light, the perfect Divine idea. The perfect Light is far better arrayed than Solomon in all his glory. The perfect Light of your Being is better arrayed than Solomon in all his glory, and there's no taking thought about it. It's the fact. It is now the perfect Light of God. Now is the fact, and we finally see the Bible has no promises for us at all. The Bible has never made a promise. Everything here is a statement of fact. There's nothing to improve, for you are that Substance now; and only when you're conscious of it does the law of transformation manifest as the activity in your consciousness.

Then the same way the invisible sap becomes the appearance of an orange, so does the invisible Consciousness of you manifest with Divine intelligence as not oranges, but whatever you need, without taking thought. As you begin to feel this more deeply, you see that the Law is already established in its fullness from beginning to end. But your enlightened Consciousness, which is the acceptance of Divinity, manifests Its own omniscience, Its own omnipotence as every form that you require. But the human self is not—the orange isn't deciding how to grow. The human isn't deciding what it needs. It's the acceptance of your own Being as the only Reality.

We all have found that in some way or another, the world we know begins where I am. I'm it. I look out. I see out there. But when you accept your Self as the Substance, you can't live that way. You can't be thinking of everything in this world as beginning right here where you are. This word "here" stretches out. It covers the universe. You begin to think of yourself in a different way, as an everywhere Self. You're not like a tree rooted in the ground, giving just fruit on this tree. You're an everywhere Self. The world, which is your Consciousness, is only going to give fruitage if you are an everywhere world and everywhere spiritual Self.

That's why you're praying for your enemies and forgiving those who offend you, and that's why you're showing service to others. That's why you're expressing gratitude. You're seeing your Self as an infinite Being. You're not limiting God to a spot. You're not limiting Being to a spot. And oh, how many times we completely forget that we're not just the person in this form. That isn't us at all. We have to get outside of this person, and that is when you can forever forget the human sense of supply. Your Universe comes back to the center of Itself where the form appears to be, and your Universe sustains Itself where you are.

If you had to raise all your own fruit and vegetables in a little patch of land, you'd find you couldn't do it. If you have to live a perfect Life as the Father says, you can't do it in a little place. You have to be in the Kingdom, in the infinite Kingdom as the infinite Self. And so catch yourself from time to time if you're trying to localize your life down to a spot within a form. It isn't you. I find just a few minutes devoted to that is a tremendous release, just the knowledge that I'm not just a point here. That little blob has got to go.

When I accept Divinity, Divine Selfhood, Christhood, you accept the infinite nature of your Being; and that's how you cast out upon the waters that which comes back. That's what Joel means when he said you can't realize supply unless you cast it out on the waters. You must give it forth for it to come back, and you're giving forth is the recognition of infinite Selfhood.

Now, that call from the friend who wanted help—if you had your friend out there and you here, you had two. There's only one Christ. How could you have two? You hadn't accepted infinite Selfhood. You had a separation between you and your friend. That's why they were out there in another city and you were in this city. That isn't true. That's when you live in the blob, in the little person; and then everything you do is from the standpoint of a human being trying to help another one. But it's not spiritual. It's not accepting. It's having no confidence in God's Word.

Now *I* and the Father are one. And what about the one who called you? Isn't that one one with the Father? And if you're both one with the Father, aren't you one with each other? Is there a separation between you and your son, between you and your daughter? How can there be? The separation is in the sense perception which sees a physical world. You and I are not separated. We never were. We never will be. No one is separated from another, only in our finite sense perception mind.

You see how all of this is connected to supply? If you have an infinite garden, do you have more fruitage than if you have a little patch? If you have a spiritual garden, do you not have Perfection working that garden? Finally, the taking possession is the recognition of the one infinite Self; and so there's no outside. There's no person calling from another city. There's only the one Self there and here as one—and rest. The law of transformation will show forth the fruitage just as if it were oranges on a tree. The law is *always* working in Identity as long as you don't interrupt Identity and make it two, three, and ten.

Ten righteous men save a city by being one, and that one is always a majority with God. Now you see how all of this comes out of the little revelation that the lilies of the field are not spinning. Something is happening from the universal, imitating the perfect idea of God. Always your perfect supply in the outer will be the imitation of the Divine idea. And when your Consciousness of your spiritual Identity is established, It will then create your world in its own Divine Image and Likeness as the forms of Divinity. The image and likeness of your consciousness is the world you are now experiencing.

When that Consciousness is Divine, then you have the Divine Image and Likeness. When it is human, you have the human image and likeness. When it is wheat and tares, you have both, a division. Divine thought can never say, "I lack." Human thought says, "I lack," so you weed out that tare. That human thought is a lie: "I lack." Divine thought says, "*I* have. *I* am." And that's where you rest, accepting the presence of Divinity. That's having confidence in the authority, in the Truth, in the words of God.

I think some of you may be wondering if we're over the hour. We're using a long tape today to see if we can do the whole class without an intermission—see if we can not break the continuity.

Where you are is God. If that is not established, you are going to have a mental teaching. Where you are is God, and wherever you go is God. At any time of day or night, awake or asleep, where you are is God. This must be your living Consciousness, and where God is the law of perfection, the law of God is functioning. When you accept that, you'll find every book ever written can add very little to your Consciousness, because that's the core from which all things must begin.

Where you are is God. You wake to this. You live with it. You remind yourself of it. You go to sleep with it, and no matter what report comes to you, where you are is God. And therefore, any report that is not reporting perfection where you are is a lie because where God is, perfection is. You are always standing in perfection. It doesn't matter what shows. That which shows as imperfection is the lie because where you are is God. That's your basis of living in the Kingdom of God.

"If then God so clothe the grass, which is today in the field, and tomorrow is cast into the oven; how much more will he clothe you, O ye of little faith?"

Again, you are the Light. You need not toil or spin or take thought. Always Identity is being stressed here, until he comes to the greatest revelation, perhaps, in this:

". . . rather seek ye the Kingdom of God; and all these things shall be added unto you."

But you are the Kingdom of God. Accept it, and all these things shall be added unto
you.

Now you have a Consciousness that *I* am the Kingdom of God, and now the world wants to break that down. The conditions of the world want to tell you, "You are not." But the Truth is that you are. The question is: Will you uphold and be faithful to that truth, or will the world persuade you that you are not the Kingdom of God? That's the issue, right down to the nub. And as the Kingdom of God, where do you begin and end? From head to toe? From elbow to elbow? Here where *I* am is God. Now, does that limit God to being just where *I* am? Here where *I* am is God, but God is everywhere.

Therefore, the moment you accept that here where *I* am is God, and God is everywhere, you accept the words of the Father, "Son, thou art ever with me." Wherever God is, *I* am; and you are laying the Consciousness of Spirit over your universe, and that becomes the law of your universe. The transforming law of your universe is your acceptance that here is God, and God is everywhere. Here is My Being, and My Being is everywhere. You are laying spiritual awareness over your universe, and there is no other universe. You are bringing everything in your universe under spiritual law, and that is why the added things will come up, just as they do in a tree. Your universe is a tree, and throughout your universe the Spirit will consciously bring Itself into fruition.

And to crown it, to cap it off:

"Fear not, little flock; . . . it is your Father's good pleasure to give you the Kingdom."

You don't have to do a thing about it. The Spirit gives. The Spirit does. The Spirit provides. The Spirit comes forth "as." Your function is to be conscious of your spiritual infinite Identity as the invisible spiritual Universe. This is only the center of it, you might say. This center is the awareness center. The whole television set works because you do a little something on the knobs. The knobs—that's this form, you might call it. Where you stand is the knobs. The universe is the television set.

This is the control center. The control center is where you know the Truth, and then relax. Know the Truth of your infinite Universe and its ever-present perfection. There's no lack of supply in It. It is your Father's good pleasure to give you the Kingdom. Now, in take no thought—which you find it either in Matthew or Mark or Luke in the Sermon on the Mount—when you have given it enough consideration and contemplation and understanding so that you can accept it, then it's the law unto you; and whoever would deny that law has no power.

There's no power outside of the Kingdom of God. And if you are the Kingdom of God—if you are standing in the knowledge of it—there is no other power. There is no power to lack. There is no power to die. There is no power to grow old because to know the Kingdom of God aright is to experience that Life which is the eternal Life. It is an experience, a knowledge that you are in that eternal Life. And you find you're not in the life you thought you were in. You really step over; you step out of the concept. You're in the eternal Life that doesn't know lack. That doesn't know limitation. That doesn't know opposing powers. That doesn't know sin, disease, limitation. That doesn't know any form of physical disability. There is such a Life. It is here. It is now. It is You. This is all about that.

I'm sure that Joel lived the eternal Life while he was among us. I'm sure that Jesus lived the eternal Life while he was among us. I'm sure that you and I will live the eternal Life while on this earth knowingly, and show it forth. Because that's the purpose of the teaching, that we be perfect. And then we enter into a new circle. Now you're not just trying to get supply so that this body can be healthier or live longer. That's not it at all. You're not seeking supply anymore. *I am* supply. Now you're feeding the multitude. You're not looking for supply. You're giving supply.

Jesus wasn't looking for supply. Joel wasn't looking for supply. They were *giving* supply, expressing Life—Life expressing Itself. To look for supply is the human approach to life. To give supply is the spiritual way. And so we find that without taking thought or making effort, there is an overflowing moving through you and out into your Universe; and it appears out there as someone receiving alms. It appears out there as someone receiving a gift package. It appears out there as someone else benefiting in some way from what it would appear to be your benevolence, but it isn't. It is your spiritual Selfhood manifesting in the visible without anyone taking thought about it. It is the Infinite living Itself through you.

Now that's the level we want to live out of because the Circle of Light isn't composed of those who are seeking supply. It's composed of those who are aware of themselves *as* the Light, and supply is an automatic Grace, an inner Grace that flows from their acceptance of Identity. And then we're not only a Light unto ourselves, but to our families. A Light to our little groups. A Light to our present society, to our community. A Light to our nation. And we join the eternal Light, that Circle which stretches throughout our infinite Being.

We're making our transition from man of earth to the Light of God. Lifting the consciousness out of the false beliefs of yesterday. No longer having needs, for we have found the Kingdom of God in which all things are Self-fulfilling; and It isn't a place called Heaven in the sky or in tomorrow. We have found that Heaven is our Substance and our knowledge of that Substance. We have the knowledge that we are the Substance and the continuing Consciousness that we are that Substance, and that's confidence. That's your prayer without ceasing. That's all there is to it. And you're making a turn. It begins to flow the other way. You're not reaching out for it. You're producing it from within your Self. You're not thinking it into existence. *God* is.

There was a woman on the phone this morning with a stomachache, and she told me about something Joel said on page 36 of one book and 78 of another book, and she was going on and on. And every word she said was true, but she still had her stomachache because she was trying to make the words "do" something, forgetting who *she* was. Please don't make words *do* something. Seek ye first the Kingdom of God, and after you have found the Kingdom of God, which is your Being, your Substance—knowing that, holding that—there should be an end some day of seeking the Kingdom of God.

# CLASS 24

# CHRISTMAS EVERYDAY

*Herb:* This is the last class of *The Contemplative Life*. But actually, it's nothing more than a continuation into *The Mystical I*.

Usually we do Christmas at Christmas time, and we mentioned how every day is Christmas. This time we're doing June, Christmas in June. And one of the nice things about Christmas in June is that it reminds us that unless the Christ peace is upon us, the complete New Testament is of no value to us and has not entered into our consciousness. This should have been a day in which each of us this morning first established Identity—in which we invited the Spirit of the Father within us to live Itself without any human intervention—in which we recognized that which already has overcome the world, Christ within, as My Identity.

And then your day begins with the acknowledgment that this is a Divine day, a God-governed day, a day in which all already has been prepared for those who dwell in the Spirit of the Father. And then as we rest in that understanding, feeling the Presence, knowing Him aright, we are filled with the power and the wisdom and the glory of the Spirit. And we're ready now for a Christ day, which makes it Christmas in June. And because Christ is the infinite Spirit indwelling every man, every woman, every child, every form, we accept that Presence everywhere. And as we accept the Presence everywhere, there is a diminishing of the anxieties, the concerns, the doubtings, the plannings, the hopings, the fearings.

All of the things that might have decoyed us into human thought now become unnecessary because we have accepted omnipresent Christ, and so we are prepared, for the Spirit walks before us. Our mind is at ease. We are in that state which has accepted that God is now everywhere being God. And so should we read the headlines and discover that there's a division in the consciousness of man, that there's corruption in high places, that there is subterfuge, we recognize as of old that the world consciousness is trying to always reject the Christ. The Christ of My Being stands here to meet that rejection. But now, being enlightened to the point of knowing Christ everywhere, you no longer stand in a personal sense of Christ, denying the world consciousness where you are alone. But rather, you rise to that higher level, the level that Joel now teaches us was always his constant purpose: to meet world consciousness everywhere with Christ Consciousness everywhere.

We learn to impersonalize world error. We're not drawn into these heated arguments. We're not startled that anti-Christ shows and wears a disguise—whether it calls itself the President of the United States, the Congress of the United States, or whether it calls itself a tyrant in a foreign country. Always, this is recognized as world consciousness, and never do we personalize the error down to an individual. What's the difference what title world consciousness assumes or what form it appears in? It is always the same world consciousness hitting where the vulnerabilities are greatest.

We even become very grateful for form because without form we would never see world consciousness externalized into form, and it would be much more difficult to recognize it. But then it takes a name and a form and a condition, and we can recognize it because it makes itself known to us. It stands right up and says, "Here I am. I am world consciousness." And our function, then, becomes to pray for our enemy, to recognize this world consciousness. Not to join in the world condemnation of it, but to impersonalize it. To see it, to know it for what it is; and then within our own Self, quietly, to know this is the anti-Christ.

I won't give it a name. I won't give it a human name. I won't call it a Republican. I won't call it a Democrat. It is world consciousness made visible in high places and in low places, and I recognize not the world consciousness but the Spirit that stands where world consciousness would try to deceive me. It is denying the All-ness of God, but it is meeting my Christ Consciousness. And there it is meeting its own Higher Power, and it is dissolved. Your Consciousness of Christ refuses to acknowledge anything less than the Father even when your neighbor seems to be one who is inconsiderate of the entire human race.

You are loving your neighbor by recognizing there the invisible Spirit of God, and you have taken the error out of person; for it never was *in* person. It was always manifesting as person, but in Christ Consciousness you do not accept person as Reality. Now while we are doing this, we ourselves are not rejecting Christ. We are not rejecting the Christhood of any individual on this earth. We know that God is Conscious, that God is Consciousness, and that God is Consciousness everywhere. And therefore, has God moved aside for corruption to take God's place? Has God moved aside for sickness to take God's place, for error and problems to take God's place, or are we being challenged by the anti-Christ?

Always we find that the only thing we suffer from is the belief that God is unconscious, that God has moved aside, that God has in some way allowed these things to happen. And then you discover what you really have done is repeat an age-old error. You, too, have had no place in your inn for the Christ. Instead, your inn was crowded with fear, with emotions. With all forms of condemnation, with judgments, and sometimes with possessive love. We find that when the inn of our own consciousness is overcrowded, we forget to turn to Christ. And so, unknowingly, we turn away the gentle stranger.

We find ourselves floating with the tide of world thought until suddenly we realize what we have done. We have failed to recognize the anti-Christ ever-present, ever all powerful to those who are not dwelling in the secret place. And the moment we find our own center instead of rejecting Christ—instead of mentalizing, instead of entering into thought and defending ourselves with all kinds of affirmations—we do that one thing that overcomes the world illusion. We accept Christ, *I* am. We don't have to reach out. We don't have to hold up an argument to anything. We don't have to reason it through. We don't have to remember something. We must *be*.

Now when you turn to Christ in you, *I*, Christ, have overcome the world. The responsibility is not yours. Your function is to accept *My* Self as your Identity. And once you accept Christ as your Identity and rest in the Word, then *I* who have overcome the world, *I* show you why you can walk through a wall. *I* show you why you can be everywhere. I show you why you are not lacking. *I* show you why there is no cancer. *I* show you why every human problem is nothing but false world belief using you as a channel to externalize itself. And then *I*, being your Consciousness realized, reveal *My* Kingdom, which is the presence of God on earth as It is in Heaven. And in the revelation of *My* Kingdom on earth where you stand, that which we had considered something to fear, something to doubt, something to be concerned about—whatever its nature—becomes nothing but a shadow to disappear as the Light of Christ blazes forth in your Consciousness.

Never is the responsibility on you to remove an error. Always Christ reveals the non-reality of the error. Always the moment the inn of your Consciousness says, "I have Christ right here. I will turn to Christ."—not to reason, not to intellect, not to memory, not to mind power—just the gentle realization that Christ is present; and then whatever the error may be, whether it's on the land or in the sea or in the sky, Christ has overcome.

Christ has dominion. And the recognition of Christ in me, Christ in you, Christ in him, Christ in her; the one invisible Christ in all regardless of the name, regardless of the color, regardless of the creed, and regardless of the condition of the slavery or bondage to problem, Christ is the only answer that you will find permanently effective. And the question then is can you trust the Christ, or in distrust do we unconsciously reject the Christ?

Let's look at the anatomy of fear. We worry about something, and we say, "This concerns me gravely and deeply." And the question is, why are you worried? Always it is because you do not believe God is present, either here where you have a problem or there where someone else has a problem. And so, you feel God being absent there or here, you have to worry. And why do you reject Omnipresence that way? Because there is a condition that appears to you—and even though you know instinctively and through study that God is there and God is here—the condition is there. And so you have evidence of the condition but you have no evidence of God. And so you are willing to accept momentarily that evidence of a condition, and you give authority to the sense mind, which is reporting the condition. And at this moment, anti-Christ is uppermost in your consciousness.

So we have accepted that God is not present because the condition is, and yet we *want* God to be present, so we look for signs. We seek signs about the evidence of God while believing that the very condition itself seems to be evidence that God is not there. So we are divided. And can we, can we possibly look at these conditions, can we look at the world today and say God is there? Can we look at Vietnam and say God is there? Can we look at the tombstones of those killed in action and say God is there? Are we willing to face that we are not willing to say God is there *in our hearts* because the sense evidence for us has been too overwhelming? Now that is rejecting Christ, when you find it impossible to know God is there.

In spite of all the evidence of war and hate, all the evidence of fear, all the evidence of destruction, all the evidence of poverty and famine and emotional upsets—when in spite of these things you can turn around and say, "Even though this is reported to me, it is nothing but world consciousness made manifest. It has no cause in God. It is world hypnosis, and it is meeting in me the knowledge that only God is present."—then you are accepting the Christ teaching. Then there's room in your inn. Then you're not letting the world evidence close up your hotel and telling the Christ to go peddle Its papers.

That moment, that glimpse that this cannot be because God *Is*, is the opening of the stable when Christ steps in. And even though it's a small beginning, that glimpse is ultimately going to change the entire world consciousness. It isn't a question of when. It is already done. It's a question of when are you going to catch on to it? *I* have overcome the world. *I'm* not going to do it tomorrow. Before Abraham was, *I* overcame the world; but you are rejecting *Me*. You are not awake to the fact that *I* am you, and you are walking in the identity of one who is seeking, wanting, needing but never accepting Identity. And you discover, to your horror, that you have put identity in form. You have looked at form, and you have given it identity, when all that is there is the incorporeal Christ.

Every time you label an error and a person with an error, you are putting identity in form; and there is no identity in form. Identity does not confine Itself to form. Identity is free. Identity is limitless. Identity is before Abraham. And then you see what you've really done is you have not accepted your Self to be the Christ of God. Are you before Abraham? Have you consciously realized that you are? Are you earth-bound, space-bound, time-bound, gravity-bound? Christ isn't. How can you be the Christ and be bound by space and time and gravity? How can you be the Christ and lack and be limited? How can you be the Christ and have a problem?

And so, isn't the problem, isn't the being bound by time and space and gravity and earth rejection of the Christ? Isn't our breathing as human beings a rejection of the Christ? And then we find that we have been talking about Christ but not knowing how to live Christ. We've been in the kindergarten stage. We've known a good deal about how to meet a problem. We've known a good deal about how to increase our supply. We have found a way to make humanhood happier and smoother, and we have said, "That's living Christ." Joel calls that the kindergarten stage, when you find the lamp of Aladdin and you rub it, and the genie appears and nice things are done; and you're very proud of yourself. But we're still accepting a world. Christ has no world. Christ overcomes the bad and the good of the world.

So it dawns upon us that there are those who will remain in the kindergarten stage. There are those who will always want to have the good part of humanhood. That may be us. Then again, we may be among those who are the ransomed of the Lord who are returning, unwilling to settle for less than the fullness of Christ in every way. Unwilling to accept one error on the face of the earth as Reality, as power, as existent—because God Is. And then we will not deny Omnipotence.

What changes Omnipotence? What power pushed God aside and said, "I am going to do this wicked thing?" No power whatsoever. What power pushed aside God's creation and said, "I'm going to make it imperfect?" No power whatsoever. We may be persuaded such a power has existed, but it never has. The only sickness there is is in the belief of the world consciousness. The only error there is is in the belief of the world consciousness. But where Christ is *your* Consciousness, whatever momentarily appears as error is quickly dissolved by the Truth that makes you free. And that Truth is your living Christhood meeting all things before they ever appear.

Now when a problem arises and you reach out for some kind of solution or when you try to analyze the possibilities, you're wrong instantly because there's only one possibility, God. Every other possibility is anti-Christ or your rejection of Christ. There are no possibilities. There's only God. And we come to a revelation that is even greater than the revelation of *I* am. As this bursts upon your Consciousness, you realize what is meant by Jesus taking us from the law to Grace because it was his revelation. *I* am is not enough, however beautiful it is. God is the only Being. It doesn't matter where you're looking. God is there and no other. Not only *I* am, but *only* God Is. Wherever you look, God *Is*. There is no other.

When you take it into consciousness and dwell with it, you find, "Acknowledge me in all thy ways" is telling you just that. Only God Is. Love your neighbor because only God Is. Everywhere you turn biblically, you find you're being told that only God Is. You can't wake up in the morning in a world where there's someone besides God. That's no alcoholic out there. That's God invisible. That's no arsonist over here. That's God invisible. And there's no corruption. You're looking at God invisible. Wherever you look, God invisible is, and no other. And the sense mind will see everything *but* that. The Christ mind will see *only* that.

So when you're seeing something besides God, you're hypnotized. You have closed up the inn to the gentle stranger. You have rejected the Christ which says, "I and my Father are one," and you have populated the perfect Kingdom of God with all kinds of good and all kinds of evil by your acceptance of a world belief. On the other hand, as you rest quietly in the knowledge that God being All, only God Is, you'll find some inner strength to look past all of the evidence of the senses which says, "There is God and this condition, God and this person, God and this corruption, God and this massacre." And you will look at *everything*, recognizing always the world consciousness which rejects Christ and lives in its own false belief and presents the shadows of belief as the evils that we call our world.

What do you do about them? *I*, Christ, have already overcome that world. It has no existence, and all of the errors in it have no existence. Come unto *Me* within you—within your enemy, within all those who suffer from the error—*I* am, and touch *Me;* and you touch *I* in them. And then rest, and *I* who have overcome the world will reveal to you the secret of *My* Presence and *My* Power.

When Hawaii was made a state back in the late 1950's, we probably did one of the greatest things we could ever do for the other 49 states. We took in a new level of consciousness—not just a state—a level that's going to be an important part in overcoming world consciousness. There was a Minister there, Hawaiian, Chinese-Hawaiian. He was so elated with the statehood of Hawaii that there was a meeting in one of the old churches there. Something he wrote and said that day became very popular all over the world, and this little sheet came into my hands the other day. He explained the meaning of "aloha." Something was caught there by this Chinese-Hawaiian minister which the world is going to catch. I'd like you to listen to it. This was from Dr. Abraham Kahikina Akaka in a Thanksgiving service in his church in Hawaii. He said,

"We do not understand the meaning of aloha until we recognize and realize that its foundation is in the power of God at work in the world. Since the coming of missionaries in 1820, the name of God to the Hawaiian people has been Aloha. And one of the first sentences a child learns from its mother is this from holy scriptures: Aloha ke Akua. In other words: Aloha is God. Aloha is the power of God seeking to unite what is separated in the world. The power that unites heart with heart, Soul with Soul, life with life, culture with culture, race with race, nation with nation. It is the power that can reunite a man with himself when he has become separated from the image of God within."

We don't hear things like that too often in the church.

"Thus, when a people or person live in the spirit of aloha, they live in the Spirit of God. And among such a people whose lives so affirm their inner Being, we see the working of the scripture, that all things work together for good to them who love God. From the Aloha of God came His Son, that we might have life and that we might have it more abundantly."

And then the Minister says,

"Aloha consists of a new attitude of heart, above negativism, above legalism. It is the unconditional desire to promote the true good of other people in a friendly spirit out of a sense of kinship. Aloha seeks to do good to a person with no conditions attached. We do not do good only to those who do good to us. One of the sweetest things about love and the Aloha of God is that it welcomes the stranger and seeks his good. A person who has the spirit of Aloha loves even when the love is not returned. Such is the love of God."

That's from our $50^{th}$ state, where east and west meet.

The interesting thing about this particular sheet of paper that was given to me is that it came from a family where there was an interfaith marriage, and buffeted between the different faiths of the parents was the child. And the child went to one faith to satisfy one parent, but couldn't quite adjust because of the difference in faiths between the parents. And so both the parents and the child were in a state of confusion. But Spirit waits for no man. And so in grade school it became an assignment for the children to study what this Minister had said in Honolulu. And there, not in the faith of the mother or the faith of the father but in a higher faith, in the faith of Spirit, the child learned something above what both faiths had been unable to give her. Not a partisan love for my religion or yours, but the Aloha Spirit. Coming above the human levels, Spirit taught a child.

We have another interesting situation that developed to show how beautifully Spirit does things. Within the past three or four weeks, we here together have studied the walking on the water. How Jesus could be on a mountaintop and they were in the ocean or the lake over here, and suddenly he was walking on the water while they were in a frantic turmoil trying to be released from a tempest. And we learned that he wasn't walking on water. That was the Spirit of God being manifest to them. That was the Body of the Soul. It took no thought. It was where it had to be. And while we were doing that in this class, something was happening somewhere else quite similar as a confirmation, perhaps, of our lesson.

This just came the other day from someone who had written for some help. And oh, we forgot all about it; never heard about it again. It seemed to be over a month or two ago. And then the letter started out:

"Just received your letter yesterday."

It's from Alaska, by the way.

"The man who was collecting our mail, which was forwarded to us from Nenana, had to evacuate his house in a hurry when Galena was flooded. He just found his mail, our mail, and gave it to us on our first trip back down the river."

This is from a woman who was a cook on a barge along the Yukon. Now watch what happened. The person asked for personal help. Spirit made the person ask for personal help in anticipation of something else, and Spirit appeared there, just like Spirit walking on the water; and this is what happened.

"We were frozen in Bear Creek, 10 miles below Galena, for almost a month. Most of the villages along the Yukon were flooded when the ice jams broke, and Galena is now a disaster. The base there was okay, as it has a dike around it. My sons both flew out there once a week, so I saw one of them when we stopped on our way up the river. We were certainly in God's care while we were at Bear Creek. The ice and water, when the river flooded, broke all over the cables and pushed us miles up river; and we had no engine working and were powerless. We finally were stopped by ice jams ahead at the right stop with trees to tie up to. We were all ready to abandon ship, but didn't have to."

Now you can see the disciples rowing over there and the storm is abetted. And you can see this barge going through the ice jams and all the concern because help isn't nearby. But somebody, a cook on board, had requested help; and the Spirit was there.

Nobody *went* there, no person. Nobody knew any Truth. Nobody made any affirmations. The Spirit did Its own work there because there was someone reaching out for the Spirit. And not even knowing what to ask for because they had no way of knowing what was going to happen. For all I remember, this might have been about a stomachache.

And so you see, always the answer is Christ recognition; and the power of Christ is so amazing that we don't even have to know what the condition is. That answers your question about treatment, specific treatment. How do you give a specific treatment for something that hasn't yet happened? How do you give a specific treatment when there are so many problems in the world consciousness? Do you sit down and anticipate the things that are going to happen? Or instead, do you rest and really get down to accepting that Christ is my Being. Christ is her Being. Where do you go from there? You rest in the Word.

And that's your faith in Christ *is* the one Identity. You've taken the label off of the form of a sick person, an ailing person, a suffering person. You've re-identified. You've accepted. You've stopped rejecting Christ. Your inn has been opened. You have said, "Christ, come in." It didn't happen 2,000 years ago and then that was the end of it. It happens every day. We reject or we accept. Our consciousness is always the inn, and in it is Christ or not.

And if Christ isn't in our consciousness, we are in the world. And we're going down the river in an ice jam, and there won't be anything to stop us.

What a priceless gift we have been given to know that we can stand in Christ and look at the insanities of the world declaring God is either absent, unconscious, or indifferent; and we can know they who reject Christ will not get me to join in that rejection. Joel says that it's a sign of progress when we come out of accepting Christ because we're trying to help me and mine. But rather, when we have lost all of that personalized sense of helping me and mine and can see the broader picture of meeting the world consciousness everywhere—so that you're not concerned whether it's friend or foe—meeting the world consciousness becomes the work of Christ realized everywhere.

It's a bigger picture. It's an unpersonalized picture. And if you find you're in it, you can be sure you're moving in the higher echelons of the Spirit. All personal sense is gone. You're seeking nothing, but you are alert—alert to the fact that all around you Christ rejection is the law of the land. And your ears are pricked up. Every word you hear—it's the Christ Consciousness of you. Every opinion, every judgment, every fear, every turbulent heart that comes to you meets Christ Consciousness. Instant recognition for the ones who are unable to accept Christ within themselves. You take them over through your silent recognition. You open the inn of their consciousness without their knowing it, without telling them, without persuading them or converting them. You recognize Christ in the inn of their consciousness for them. You are meeting world mesmerism everywhere.

It was the fidelity of Joel to this which has given this world its foundation. It was the fidelity of those who have known the Word that have lifted us up to the point where we can know now that the world consciousness is being dismantled. It is falling apart. It is nothing for you to be inflamed about. It is inevitably falling apart. And as it falls apart, it must manifest as confusion, as treachery, as subterfuge because anti-Christ is now being made visible as never before.

Quickly the world consciousness is making visible to us those things which up to this point the world has not known. Man is coming face to face with his own inabilities as a human being. We are discovering that there are no human answers. The only answer is Christ. And though we may seem to be a moment ahead, it wasn't a moment too soon because you're being called upon to stand in the midst of what may appear to the world as a series of disasters.

They are *not* disasters. There is no disaster in Christ, and only Christ *is*. The Truth that God is the only Being is where you stand in the face of every apparent disaster. There cannot be God and disaster. The All-ness of God, the fullness of Christ is the basic principle; and it gets easier and easier to stand there. You simply cannot go anywhere where God is sharing that place, that time with another.

Now if we have accepted Christ and, therefore, rejected the possibility of anything unlike Christ, our Christmas becomes more of a daily event. We're in the position of being able to open Christ Consciousness in many places because the Light of your own Being accepting Christ no longer dwells in the world thought of a human mind. Every activity dwells in its own Source, its Christ Source; and it carries with it an ordination, an appointment. It's Self-contained. It's producing its own perfect Divine effect. And when you find yourself living that way—that everything you do is coming from the Source of your own Christ activity—then Omnipotence needs no sword. It is an automatic act Grace.

Would you make it a point to dwell for a short time this coming week on the fact that God is the only person you could ever meet that day. And then regardless of what stands before you in form or what condition, know that the All-ness of God is your Divine guarantee that no one is there but God. It isn't your son. It's the invisible Christ. It isn't your husband. It's the invisible Christ. It isn't your friend or your enemy. It's the invisible Christ. And no matter where you go or who you see, only the invisible Christ is there. You don't have to differentiate between the types of conditions or the behavior or the attitude or whether the person is low-born or high-born, rich or poor; whether the person is an alcoholic or a cripple.

You can look at every country in the world and know there are no Chinese in China. There are no Russians in Russia. There are no Americans in the United States. There is only God. God is the only inhabitant of this Universe. And when Spirit within confirms this in your Consciousness, you'll find a freedom you've never imagined. That's all there is. And again, standing beside

Jesus looking out, you'll discover that's all Jesus could accept. That's all there is. Who convinceth me of a condition when God is All? Who convinceth me of hunger when God is All, of insecurity when God is All, or even of death when God is All?

There's not a lot of new Truth to learn. There is the actual coming to grips with the fact that God is All, and letting It teach you how to live with that knowledge so that all fear and concern departs, so that there's nothing to seek. Everything that you could seek, Christ already has; and the seeking denies the Christhood. There's nothing to improve. Only Christ is. I found myself, for example, not really believing enough to sit with the Christ long enough to accept the important ramifications of Christhood. Christ in the 20th century isn't Christ. Christ on earth isn't Christ. Christ in San Francisco or Menlo or Burlingame isn't Christ.

Before Abraham was is Christ. There's no time when Christ wasn't. And therefore, to be Christ now, you must be that Christ which has existed before time, consciously. You must be that Christ which will ever exist; that Christ which isn't waiting for the world to end because to that Christ that world doesn't exist. You must be that Christ which isn't a reincarnating form in your consciousness. You must be that Christ which can feed 5,000 and still have 12 baskets full; that Christ which can look at anything and forgive, meaning see through it. And if we're not living up to our own Identity, we are rejecting the Christ. And that is how we lose the meaning of there was no room in the inn. That's a challenge every minute of our lives. What minute are we saying there's no room in the inn?

Now you may find you cannot break the attachment of the senses to things, to person, to form. But Christ *can* break that attachment, and so it's not necessary for *you* to break it. It's necessary for you to accept the inner Christ and then watch Christ break the hypnosis, break the attachment, break the mesmerism of form. Some of the ways in which Christ breaks the attachment in which we pave the way for this Child in the inn to grow in our consciousness, these are the things we'll discuss as we take a little rest today. Let's take a short meditation and then a five- or ten-minute rest.

Let's dwell on the All-ness of God. There's a form to your left, and there's a form to your right. When you're looking past the forms, there's a form behind you and a form in front of you; but you're looking past the forms. You're bringing everything down to the one Reality of existence, God. The Spirit of God is All that is ever-present no matter where you go. That will be the Truth tomorrow and a million tomorrows. And when you accept it in the Now, it goes before you into every tomorrow. Only God will be here tomorrow. Only God is here today.

And though the world may tempt me in many ways, especially where I'm the most vulnerable, I will remain alert to the fact that I will not reject God by accepting another as being present.

". . . to thine own self be true."

To the Divine Self that we are, which is God, be true.

"And it must follow, as the night the day,

Thou canst not then be false to any man."

How can you hurt a person on this earth if you know that invisibly God is in him? How can you do anything but lift them up? And then the blind shall see, the deaf shall hear, the cripple shall leap like a hart, for the ransomed of the Lord have returned. In the knowledge of the All-ness of God, we are truly hid in Christ. The tempter is overcome, for in the knowledge of God is All, your Soul takes dominion over the human mind. Your spiritual Consciousness takes dominion over the mental consciousness of the world. You break the continuity of the universal lie that there is God *and* someone else.

And so let's rest a moment now, and I'll see you in about five minutes.

∞∞∞∞∞∞ END OF SIDE ONE ∞∞∞∞∞∞

We find that when Jesus had appeared on the desert to feed the multitude, he was acclaimed far and wide. But a strange thing happened. The Pharisees came to him, and looking at the man who had overcome the law of lack, overcome the law of material insufficiency—the man who had in some way brought abundance out of nothing—instead of saying to him, "Apparently you have access to some supernatural power which is of value to the world"; instead of saying, "We can now abolish poverty and famine"; instead of welcoming him for the good he could do, even only for the Hebrew nation if that's where they wanted to limit it, the Pharisees said to him the very strangest thing you ever heard. It's almost incredible.

They had noticed that the 5,000 who ate this hidden manna had not obeyed a very strict Hebraic law. They hadn't washed their hands! They had actually broken a law. In a sense you might say that the world today still works on the small little picayune things, overlooking the Christ. Here the man feeds a multitude and somebody says, "But they didn't wash their hands." And so they actually had the effrontery now to come up to him and say to him and accuse him of letting his disciples eat without washing their hands. This rankled them!

Of course, they were living in a million yesterdays. They were living before Jesus. They were living in Leviticus, where the ordinance was laid down, in which it said if you didn't wash your hands, you deserved every punishment now and forever. And of course, the washing of the hands was a rite, a ceremonial rite of purification. It had much more to it than just washing the hands, but the way you went about it was very complicated.

And so in here somewhere in Matthew or in Mark, it says they washed with their fist. It seems that they had to use the right fist to wash the left hand so they wouldn't contaminate the fingers of the right hand, and then the left fist to wash the right hand so that no dirt would get in between the fingers. And then they had to lift their arms up this way so that the water would run down from the fist to the elbow instead of the other way. And after a while it became such a fetish that they had to wash a second time unless they declared that their first washing was to cover the entire day. And this was called an inventive or an elective, and this enabled them to get by with only one major washing.

And if you broke the law, woe onto you. So much so that if you didn't have water where you were, you had to walk for it; and if it was four miles that's all right. Now this was well and good, but they came to the wrong man with their complaint. They came to one who knew the Hebraic law better than they. Now the world thinks that he was attacking the Pharisees. He was not. This was meeting the world consciousness right there. Not an individual Pharisee here and a Pharisee there, but meeting world consciousness which is concerned with living in the external material formalities. And he called them "hypocrites," and he cited how they were being hypocritical in that they had taken the fifth commandment of Moses: "Honor thy father and thy mother," and they had altered it to suit their purpose. In other words, you could alter the law when you wanted to for yourself; and they had altered the law in a very strange way.

In order to help the Hebrew treasury, they had made a law which made it possible for a person who, according to Hebraic law, had to support his aged, poor parents even if he had to go out and beg. They had even changed that Talmudic law, and they said now there is a new law that if you declare that your funds have been already vowed to the temple, then you don't have to honor thy father and thy mother with those funds. And so this was their way of increasing their treasury. They broke the fifth commandment to increase their treasury, so that a man could now tell his parents, "Oh, I've already committed those funds to the temple." And if you'll remember in the Sermon on the Mount: Forswear not. Let all your vows and oaths speak for God alone. [Matthew 5:33] That was one of the reasons.

And now he called them on it, and he called them hypocrites. They had broken the fifth commandment, and they were now chastising him because his disciples hadn't washed their hands. And what he was really pointing out is that as long as our minds are stayed on basic rituals, ceremonials, and token observances without the letter, without the Spirit behind the letter, without the knowledge of the presence of God, we have no religion. There's no religion in a form.

The sin of the temple in that day is the same sin of the church in our day. Mortal mind manifests the same way today. Without the knowledge of the Christ of each individual, it doesn't matter what religion we call it. This is what a Pharisee is: one who is concerned about the material observance of the law. The book says do this, and you must do this. But these are man-made laws. God didn't make them. And so when someone is accused of breaking the law, they're not breaking God's law. They're breaking man-made laws.

And if you don't go to Mass one day, you're not breaking God's law at all. That isn't God's law. That's a man-made law. And it's shocking to look into the many laws which we are told we break, when they're not made by God. They're made by man. They're made by the Pharisee, the lawmaker who can break his own law when it suits his own pocketbook. And coming to Jesus with this cry was wasted, because then he taught us a great principle: That which cometh out of the mouth of man, that's what he suffers from.

He was telling us that when we are not still, when we are not in the Christ, that which cometh out of our mouth—that which is the action of our body and our mind—is the world consciousness that functions through a Pharisee, making him observe only the material letter of the law and missing the Life of God. You can wash your hands until the skin peels off, but if you still live in material thought, there is no God experience; and there is no religion.

Now the Pharisees had made themselves the mouthpiece of God, and they were not authorized. And there are those all over the world today who have made themselves a mouthpiece of God, and they are not authorized. The only mouthpiece of God is Christ in you. There will never be another. And when you're not hearing Christ in you, you're not hearing God's word in you.

Jesus, then, taught us not to wash our hands but to wash our minds, that the purified thought—that thought which expresses Christ in you, that thought which expresses the Word of God—when that externalizes, then your life outwardly is a perfect expression of Christ within. That is why it was so necessary to make a point of the washing of the hands and the rebuke which he gave to them who had come to rebuke him. We spend much time in the letter, or in the washing of the hands, overlooking the realization of Christ *is* the perfect answer to every appearance that faces us.

Now we know that Jesus was able to touch a leper, and the reason he could touch a leper, whereas no Pharisee would dare, is because they saw contagion there. They had the thought that contagion was there, but Christ within has no thought of contagion. Christ within enables you to live in the purity of thought which can touch the contagion because contagion is only the impure human thought. There is no contagion. Did God create it? Wash your hands, and you still won't touch contagion; but wash your mind and you will.

Pilate resorted to that washing of the hands to wash himself clean of something, but he went mad anyway. In the inner immersion, as we are washed by the Spirit—not by outward elements—there is a removal of the world consciousness, a removal of material thought. And those of us who have put this off, have postponed the meeting of material thought with the Truth of Christ presence, are still not willing to let the Christ into their inn. You in your material thought are saying to Christ, "Stay out." This is the major adversary.

We have not overcome the belief in a material world and a material self with material things, material possessions, material conditions and problems. And as long as we have a belief in the reality, the existence, the power of matter, we are rejecting Christ. And we're 2,000 years late in doing it. It isn't a new idea. It isn't something you just read in a book yesterday. It's something that the human mind keeps postponing. It's going to get around to it, you know, but not right away. It still has some good things in the material world that it must do. And, you know, every time you have good things in the material world that must be done, you are rejecting Christ just as much as when you are accepting the bad things.

Now those kindergarten days are over for most of us. And as the world around us becomes more and more of the material consciousness made evident, you will discover how fortunate you have been to have been led by the Spirit into the way of Christ. Because we now are on that third level where we are renouncing even the good of this world, for that which is bad today was the good of yesterday; and that which is bad tomorrow will be the good of today. That which never was of God can never be accepted in Christ Consciousness. To walk Here—not in the good of the world, not in the bad of the world—is not possible while you are living in the human sense of life—in the human mind, in the human form as a mortal being, a finite being, a person learning about Truth. That person is still rejecting Christ.

Now this beautiful book of Joel's comes along, *The Mystical I*, at just the right moment for you and me to take it and to let it show us how to open the door wide—not just the stable but the whole house including the penthouse—to Christ, the only inhabitant of our consciousness. One tenant in the temple not made with hands, Christ. So that the entire house, the entire consciousness, the entire inn becomes Christed. And then we will see how Christ within us lives not in time but in eternity and now, not in space but in infinity and now. How Christ in us is never limited and now shows forth all abundance to the very level of every possible requirement.

Now there is no inn. There is only Christ, the edifice of our very Being. And in Christ there is nothing outside of you, so you can touch contagion because it isn't outside. There is no external condition outside of Christ. Everything is *in* Christ for Christ is infinite, and everything in Christ is perfect as my Father, immaculate unto eternity. And your alertness to Christ as your Selfhood is your alertness to the nonexistence of every problem—the instant recognition of its nonexistence—because where the problem appears, *Christ is*. Every floor, every room, every mansion of your Consciousness is Christ; and you allow nothing to enter or defile.

You have no external world in Christ, no external condition in Christ, no material universe in Christ. You are looking behind the atom, above the atom, below the atom, and right where the atom is supposed to be. And you are walking consciously in the perfect Kingdom not seen with a human mind, but discerned by the activity of your Soul which is now your inn. It has been Christed, opened to Christ, receiving the infinite flow of Divinity always, without fear, without concern, without seeking. And the mystical *I* is your consciousness of that Christ where you are, where the corrupt official seems to be, where the alcoholic stumbles, where the arsonist lights his fires, where the revolutionary throws his bombs.

You can look at every stuffed shirt in the world and say, "There stands the invisible Christ." You can look at everyone in pain, every addict, everyone in every hospital, everyone in every mental or physical or financial condition and say, "These things do not move me. God is being God right there now." You must! Or your inn is closed to Christ. We go back to Pharisee days, talking about Christ with our mouths and bleating about not washing the hands before we do a miracle to feed the multitudes.

Now, I know *The Mystical I* is going to be a great experience. It isn't metaphysics anymore. It's Self living Self, being pure Being. And on the little sheet which announces it, I have asked each of you who come to class to consider going into the Silence at home before you even start out to get the feel of who you are, to bring It with you, so that we can all share the one Christ Consciousness. We're counting on this particular series, you see, to lift us into that Consciousness which can look at the world and dissolve world consciousness. To continue the great work of those before us who have, through their integrity, not faced individuals, not faced one condition or another but have faced the invisible world consciousness.

And we're beginning to change our way so we face it. This one here with this problem, we're not facing that one's problem. We're facing the world consciousness which is manifesting as that one. And as you do this, you're reversing that little termite which is nibbling at us all; and you, instead, are nibbling at the world consciousness, at the very foundation of the lie. Each of us, then, becomes an invisible messenger; and we welcome the opportunity to meet the world problem. To stand before it, and to let it hit Christ in me.

We welcome every opportunity to do that joyously because we become aware of our great mission to meet that world consciousness and let the *I* of My Being, which was before Abraham, which has overcome the world, stand there unmoved—and then reveal right where world consciousness was projecting pain and sorrow, lack and limitation, the very opposite—the perfection of God Itself—by your fidelity to Christ everywhere.

Now that's what *Mystical I* was put on this earth to do, and it will attain its purpose in us. If you haven't picked up your little announcement, do so please. They're on the little desk in the lobby. And then when you come to this *Mystical I* class, let your Presence in the class be a result of your living Silence before coming to class. You will benefit thereby.

The resurrection of Christ Consciousness in each of us is what the world calls the end of the world. But it isn't. It's the resurrection of Christ in us made manifest *as* the end of the world. It is taking place, and even those who we call our enemies become channels for Truth when you hold them in their Christhood in spite of what they manifest to your face. They literally are prohibited from projecting world consciousness when you know the Truth of their

Being, and they become a channel which, instead, pours forth even love where only hate had been known before.

And no matter who you take into your consciousness, be sure that if you see them as a person, you're missing it. But if you see them as world consciousness made manifest and meet it on that level just by recognizing it, you will release in them the birth of a Child in the inn of their consciousness. And you can do no one a greater favor on this whole earth than opening them to Christ by your silent awareness, meeting world consciousness invisibly.

So we have Christmas in June, Christmas tomorrow, Christmas every day in the enlightened Consciousness. If you'll join with me in a Silence, this will be our preparation for *The Mystical I*. We withdraw from humanhood, and leave Him on the field whose right it is to sit upon the Throne. A passage comes to mind in Isaiah:

> "And the work of righteousness shall be peace;
> and the effect of righteousness quietness and assurance forever.
> And my people shall dwell in a peaceable habitation,
> and in sure dwellings, and in quiet resting places; . . ."

He who understood the Christ assures us that in our peace, in our quietness, we are leavening the consciousness of the world. Not just of ourselves, but of the one Self. And this is a great privilege and responsibility that we carry with us whenever we face an individual or a group or any activity in the world. We address it silently with peace, with knowledge, with Christ vision, for only God is there.

[Silence]

Thank you very much.

*The End*

www.ingramcontent.com/pod-product-compliance
Lightning Source LLC
Chambersburg PA
CBHW021438070526
44577CB00002B/209